# GROW YOUR PRACTICE:
## Legal Marketing and Business Development Strategies

**Editor**
Carol Schiro Greenwald, Ph.D.

New York State Bar Association Continuing Legal Education publications are intended to provide current and accurate information to help attorneys maintain their professional competence. Publications are distributed with the understanding that NYSBA does not render any legal, accounting or other professional service. Attorneys using publications or orally conveyed information in dealing with a specific client's or their own legal matters should also research original sources of authority.

We consider the publication of any NYSBA practice book as the beginning of a dialogue with our readers. Periodic updates to this book will give us the opportunity to incorporate your suggestions regarding additions or corrections. Please send your comments to: CLE Publications Director, New York State Bar Association, One Elk Street, Albany, NY 12207.

Copyright 2015
New York State Bar Association
All rights reserved
ISBN: 1-57969-435-7
Product Number: 41265

# TABLE OF CONTENTS

Introduction .................................................................................. xv

## *Section 1—Marketing Basics*
Chapter 1    Strategy and Planning.................................................. 1
Chapter 2    Why Clients Demand Value and How Your Success
             Depends on Delivering It ............................................ 13

## *Section 2—Personal Marketing*
Chapter 3    Personal Basics............................................................ 29
Chapter 4    Client Relationships: Research and Communication
             Techniques .................................................................. 55
Chapter 5    Networking: Art and Science ...................................... 73
Chapter 6    Consultative Selling .................................................... 83
Chapter 7    Knowledge Sharing ..................................................... 103
Chapter 8    Social Media................................................................ 117
Chapter 9    Legal Ethics and Lawyer Business Development........ 137

## *Section 3—Firm Marketing*
Chapter 10   Firm Culture ................................................................ 157
Chapter 11   Law Firm Activities That Support Individuals'
             Business Development Efforts..................................... 171
Chapter 12   Client Feedback........................................................... 183
Chapter 13   The Pricing of Legal Services ..................................... 199
Chapter 14   Where Do Advertising and Public Relations Fit Into
             My Business Development Arsenal? ........................... 211
Chapter 15   Coaching....................................................................... 227
Chapter 16   Technology to Support Growing Your Practice........... 245
Chapter 17   Success Supports ......................................................... 261

Biographies .................................................................................. 277

# DETAILED TABLE OF CONTENTS

Introduction .................................................................................. xv

## *Section 1—Marketing Basics*

### Chapter 1   Strategy and Planning
*Wendy L. Bernero*

| | | | |
|---|---|---|---|
| [1.0] | I. | How Planning Begets Success ................................. | 3 |
| [1.1] | II. | What Is Your Firm's Mission or Purpose?................. | 3 |
| [1.2] | III. | Profile Your Clients ................................................ | 4 |
| [1.3] | IV. | What Is the Source of Your Competitive Advantage?............................................................ | 5 |
| [1.4] | V. | Where Are You Now?............................................. | 6 |
| [1.5] | VI. | Your Vision: Where Do You Want to Go? ................ | 8 |
| [1.6] | VII. | Write Your Goals And Objectives ........................... | 8 |
| [1.7] | VIII. | Assess Your Resources ........................................... | 9 |
| [1.8] | IX. | Take Action ........................................................... | 9 |
| [1.9] | X. | Keep Score ............................................................ | 10 |
| [1.10] | XI. | Make Planning a Habit ........................................... | 10 |
| [1.11] | XII. | Planning Tips and Advice ....................................... | 10 |

### Chapter 2   Why Clients Demand Value and How Your Success Depends on Delivering It
*Susan Saltonstall Duncan*

| | | | |
|---|---|---|---|
| [2.0] | I. | Clients Are in the Driver's Seat ................................ | 15 |
| [2.1] | II. | Some Legal Services Have Diminished in Value ....... | 15 |
| [2.2] | III. | Putting Clients at the Center.................................... | 16 |
| [2.3] | IV. | Value is in the Eye of the Beholder.......................... | 17 |
| [2.4] | V. | How You Should Communicate Value: The Value Proposition ............................................................. | 18 |
| [2.5] | VI. | The Value Proposition and Your Elevator Speech...... | 21 |
| [2.6] | VII. | How Bios/Profiles, Practice and Firm Descriptions Convey Value......................................................... | 22 |
| [2.7] | VIII. | 25 Tips to Deliver Value and Develop Highly Satisfied Clients Who Become Loyal (and Raving) Fans ...................................................................... | 23 |

*Section 2—Personal Marketing*

**Chapter 3  Personal Basics**
*Steven Skyles-Mulligan*

| | | | |
|---|---|---|---|
| [3.0] | I. | Understanding Why the Personal Matters............... | 31 |
| [3.1] | | A. Overview ............ | 31 |
| [3.2] | | B. How People Make Buying Decisions.................. | 31 |
| [3.3] | |     1. What You're Really Selling ........................ | 32 |
| [3.4] | |     2. The Importance of Know, Like and Trust...... | 32 |
| [3.5] | | C. Why There Should Be Another "P" in Marketing ............... | 33 |
| [3.6] | II. | Coming to Grips With Personal Branding ................ | 34 |
| [3.7] | | A  Practical Discussion of Brand ........................... | 35 |
| [3.8] | |     1. How a Professional Brand Differs From a Product Brand............... | 35 |
| [3.9] | |     2. Truthfulness and Accuracy............... | 35 |
| [3.10] | |     3. A Critical Intersection ............... | 36 |
| [3.11] | | B. Elements of Personal Brand ............... | 38 |
| [3.12] | |     1. Personality Type............... | 38 |
| [3.13] | |     2. Values............... | 38 |
| [3.14] | |     3. Style............... | 38 |
| [3.15] | |     4. Goals and Interests ............... | 39 |
| [3.16] | |     5. Approach to Work ............... | 39 |
| [3.17] | |     6. Kind of Practice............... | 39 |
| [3.18] | | C. Creating Your Own Brand ............... | 40 |
| [3.19] | |     1. Start With What's So............... | 40 |
| [3.20] | |         a. Golds (46% of the population) ............... | 40 |
| [3.21] | |         b. Blues (10% of the population)............... | 40 |
| [3.22] | |         c. Reds (27% of the population)............... | 41 |
| [3.23] | |         d. Greens (17% of the population)............... | 41 |
| [3.24] | |     2. Draw Conclusions ............... | 41 |
| [3.25] | |     3. Stay True to Your Values............... | 42 |
| [3.26] | |     4. Leverage Your Style............... | 43 |
| [3.27] | |     5. Focus on Your Goals............... | 43 |
| [3.28] | |     6. Acknowledge Your Interests............... | 44 |
| [3.29] | |     7. Understand Your Approach ............... | 44 |
| [3.30] | |     8. Type of Practice ............... | 45 |
| [3.31] | III. | Practice Presentation ............... | 46 |
| [3.32] | | A. Verbal Brand ............... | 46 |
| [3.33] | | B. Visual Brand............... | 47 |
| [3.34] | | C. Evaluate............... | 48 |
| Appendix A | | ............... | 49 |

Appendix B ................................................................................. 51
Appendix C ................................................................................. 53

**Chapter 4  Client Relationships: Research and Communication Techniques**
*Carol Schiro Greenwald, Ph.D.*

| | | | |
|---|---|---|---|
| [4.0] | I. | Introduction ................................................................ | 57 |
| [4.1] | II. | Clients Are in Charge ................................................ | 57 |
| [4.2] | III. | Client Service ............................................................. | 58 |
| [4.3] | IV. | 360-Degree Understanding of Clients ....................... | 59 |
| [4.4] | V. | Research: What, How ................................................ | 59 |
| [4.5] | VI. | How to Use the Data .................................................. | 61 |
| [4.6] | VII. | Client-Centric Communication ................................. | 61 |
| [4.7] | VIII. | Establishing Communication Protocols .................... | 63 |
| [4.8] | IX. | Research-Informed Communication ......................... | 65 |

Appendix ................................................................................... 67

**Chapter 5  Networking: Art and Science**
*Nancy B. Schess*

| | | | |
|---|---|---|---|
| [5.0] | I. | Introduction ................................................................ | 75 |
| [5.1] | II. | What Is Networking and How Do We Do It? .......... | 75 |
| [5.2] | III. | Choosing Your Networking Venue ........................... | 76 |
| [5.3] | IV. | Preparation Is Key ..................................................... | 78 |
| [5.4] | V. | The All Important Follow-Up and Follow-Through ... | 80 |
| [5.5] | VI. | Conclusion .................................................................. | 82 |

**Chapter 6  Consultative Selling**
*Dee A. Schiavelli*

| | | | |
|---|---|---|---|
| [6.0] | I. | When Is Selling Not Sales? When It is Consultative .. | 85 |
| [6.1] | | A. What Is Consultative Selling? ............................. | 85 |
| [6.2] | | B. How It Differs From Marketing ......................... | 85 |
| [6.3] | | C. Process and Techniques ...................................... | 87 |
| [6.4] | II. | How to Sell ................................................................. | 87 |
| [6.5] | | A. Stop Pitching ....................................................... | 87 |
| [6.6] | | B. Understanding What Clients Want ..................... | 88 |
| [6.7] | | C. Meeting Expectations (ACC) .............................. | 89 |
| [6.8] | III. | Next Steps .................................................................. | 89 |
| [6.9] | | A. Self-Evaluation .................................................... | 89 |
| [6.10] | | B. What to Incorporate Into Your Practice .............. | 90 |
| [6.11] | | C. Building Legal Services Sales Process ............... | 90 |
| [6.12] | | D. Lead Generation .................................................. | 91 |
| [6.13] | | E. Sales Conversion Process .................................... | 91 |

| | | | |
|---|---|---|---|
| [6.14] | | F. Difficulty Converting Leads Into New Business | 91 |
| [6.15] | | G. Solution Selling | 92 |
| [6.16] | IV. | Proposal | 92 |
| [6.17] | | A. Inquiries | 92 |
| [6.18] | | B. Proposal Selling | 93 |
| [6.19] | | C. Dealing With Objections | 94 |
| [6.20] | | D. Mistakes Lawyers Make | 94 |
| [6.21] | | E. Asking for the Business | 96 |
| [6.22] | | F. How to Move Up the Value Pyramid | 96 |
| [6.23] | | G. Understanding Today's Prospects | 98 |
| [6.24] | | H. Gaining Future Work | 99 |
| [6.25] | V. | Going Forward | 100 |
| | | Appendix | 101 |

**Chapter 7    Knowledge Sharing**
*Alan Levine*

| | | | |
|---|---|---|---|
| [7.0] | I. | What Is Knowledge Sharing? | 105 |
| [7.1] | II. | Potential Pitfalls of Knowledge Sharing | 106 |
| [7.2] | III. | New Technologies and Knowledge Sharing | 107 |
| [7.3] | IV. | Methodologies | 107 |
| [7.4] | | A. Bylined Articles | 107 |
| [7.5] | | 1. Advantages of Bylined Articles | 108 |
| [7.6] | | 2. Disadvantages of Bylined Articles | 109 |
| [7.7] | | B. Newsletters and E-Newsletters | 109 |
| [7.8] | | 1. Advantages of Newsletters and E-Newsletters | 109 |
| [7.9] | | 2. Disadvantages of Newsletters and E-Newsletters | 110 |
| [7.10] | | C. E-Alerts | 110 |
| [7.11] | | 1. Advantages of E-Alerts | 110 |
| [7.12] | | 2. Disadvantages of E-Alerts | 111 |
| [7.13] | | D. Blogs | 111 |
| [7.14] | | 1. Advantages of Blogs | 111 |
| [7.15] | | 2. Disadvantages of Blogs | 112 |
| [7.16] | | E. Speeches | 112 |
| [7.17] | | 1. Advantages of Speeches | 113 |
| [7.18] | | 2. Disadvantages of Speeches | 113 |
| [7.19] | | F. Seminars | 113 |
| [7.20] | | 1. Advantages of Seminars | 113 |
| [7.21] | | 2. Disadvantages of Seminars | 114 |
| [7.22] | | G. Webinars | 114 |
| [7.23] | | 1. Advantages of Webinars | 115 |

| | | | |
|---|---|---|---|
| [7.24] | | 2. Disadvantages of Webinars | 115 |
| [7.25] | | H. Videos and Podcasts | 115 |
| [7.26] | | 1. Advantages of Videos and Podcasts | 116 |
| [7.27] | | 2. Disadvantages of Videos and Podcasts | 116 |

**Chapter 8 Social Media**
*Nancy Myrland*

| | | | |
|---|---|---|---|
| [8.0] | I. | Social Media Use Among Lawyers | 119 |
| [8.1] | II. | Who's Using It? | 120 |
| [8.2] | | A. Two Goals of Social Media | 122 |
| [8.3] | | B. Two Very Important Points | 122 |
| [8.4] | | 1. They Must Be Integrated | 122 |
| [8.5] | | 2. Their Effects Are Cumulative | 123 |
| [8.6] | | C. Three Important Characteristics | 124 |
| [8.7] | III. | Pay Attention to These Three Sites First | 125 |
| [8.8] | | A. LinkedIn | 126 |
| [8.9] | | B. Twitter | 127 |
| [8.10] | | C. Facebook | 128 |
| [8.11] | IV. | How to Get Started | 130 |
| [8.12] | | A. Preparation | 131 |
| [8.13] | | B. Build a Good Profile | 131 |
| [8.14] | | C. Communication 1.0 | 131 |
| [8.15] | | D. Connection | 132 |
| [8.16] | | E. Observation | 132 |
| [8.17] | | F. Communication 2.0 | 132 |
| [8.18] | | G. Education | 133 |
| [8.19] | | H. Collaboration | 133 |
| [8.20] | V. | Best Practices | 133 |
| [8.21] | VI. | A Bit About Ethics | 134 |
| [8.22] | VII. | Final Thoughts | 135 |

**Chapter 9 Legal Ethics and Lawyer Business Development**
*Michael Downey*

| | | | |
|---|---|---|---|
| [9.0] | I. | Introduction | 139 |
| [9.1] | II. | Supreme Court Precedent Shapes the Framework for Regulation of Lawyer Business Development | 139 |
| [9.2] | III. | ABA Model Rules Governing Lawyer Marketing | 143 |
| [9.3] | IV. | New York Rules Governing Lawyer Business Development Activities | 145 |
| [9.4] | | A. Regulation of Firm and Personal Activities | 145 |
| [9.5] | | B. Content Regulation of Business Development Communications | 146 |

| [9.6] | C. Methods of Delivering Business Development Communications | 152 |
| [9.7] | D. Retention Requirements | 153 |
| [9.8] | E. Paying for Business Development Activities | 153 |
| [9.9] | F. Activities Outside States of Licensure | 154 |
| [9.10] V. | Helpful Guidance for the Marketing Lawyer | 155 |

## Section 3—Firm Marketing

### Chapter 10  Firm Culture
*Donna Drumm, Esq.*

| [10.0] I. | Introduction | 159 |
| [10.1] | A. What Is a Law Firm's Culture? | 159 |
| [10.2] | B. Internal Culture | 161 |
| [10.3] | C. Culture of Management | 161 |
| [10.4] | D. Dangers of Overlooking Culture | 162 |
| [10.5] | E. Law Firm Culture Is Not Transparent | 163 |
| [10.6] | F. Assessing Your Firm's Internal Culture | 163 |
| [10.7] | G. External Culture | 164 |
| [10.8] II. | Compensation | 164 |
| [10.9] | A. The Client-Centric Law Firm and Cross-Selling | 166 |
| [10.10] | B. Rainmaker to Umbrella | 167 |
| [10.11] | C. Listening | 167 |
| [10.12] | D. Warm Opportunities | 167 |
| [10.13] | E. Hot Opportunities | 168 |
| [10.14] | F. Be the Undesignated General Counsel for Your Client | 169 |

### Chapter 11  Law Firm Activities That Support Individuals' Business Development Efforts
*Carol Schiro Greenwald, Ph.D*

| [11.0] I. | Introduction | 173 |
| [11.1] II. | Finance | 173 |
| [11.2] III. | Management | 176 |
| [11.3] IV. | Marketing | 177 |
| [11.4] | A. Client Teams | 178 |
| [11.5] | B. Cross-Selling | 178 |
| [11.6] | C. Customized Service Packages | 180 |
| [11.7] V. | Technology | 181 |

**Chapter 12  Client Feedback**
*Laura Meherg*

| | | | |
|---|---|---|---|
| [12.0] | I. | Introduction | 185 |
| [12.1] | II. | Benefits of Client Feedback | 185 |
| [12.2] | III. | Client Feedback Tools | 186 |
| [12.3] | IV. | Before the Interview | 187 |
| [12.4] | | A. Client Selection and Prioritization | 187 |
| [12.5] | | B. Research | 187 |
| [12.6] | V. | Conducting the Interview | 188 |
| [12.7] | | A. Approach and Demeanor | 188 |
| [12.8] | | B. The Questions | 189 |
| [12.9] | | C. Dealing With Difficult or Delicate Feedback | 190 |
| [12.10] | | D. Capturing the Information | 191 |
| [12.11] | VI. | After the Interview | 191 |
| [12.12] | | A. Creating a Report | 191 |
| [12.13] | | B. Disseminating the Information | 192 |
| [12.14] | | C. Addressing Difficult or Delicate Feedback Internally | 192 |
| [12.15] | VII. | Common Themes and Key Trends in Client Feedback | 193 |
| [12.16] | VIII. | Case Study | 193 |
| [12.17] | | A. Assumptions | 193 |
| [12.18] | | B. Facts | 194 |
| [12.19] | | C. Follow-up Strategies | 194 |

**Chapter 13  The Pricing of Legal Services**
*Christine S. Filip, Esq.*

| | | | |
|---|---|---|---|
| [13.0] | I. | Introduction | 201 |
| [13.1] | II. | What's in a Price? | 202 |
| [13.2] | III. | Price Structure | 202 |
| [13.3] | IV. | The Effect of Discounting | 206 |
| [13.4] | V. | Preventative Measures: Economic Value Analysis (EVA) | 207 |
| [13.5] | VI. | Speed Bumps | 208 |
| [13.6] | VII. | Management Considerations | 210 |
| [13.7] | VIII. | Every Successful Sale May Produce a Loyal Client | 210 |

**Chapter 14  Where Do Advertising and Public Relations Fit Into My Business Development Arsenal?**
*Marcia Golden*

| | | | |
|---|---|---|---|
| [14.0] | I. | Why Do Lawyers Market? | 213 |
| [14.1] | II. | Who Markets? | 213 |

| | | | |
|---|---|---|---|
| [14.2] | III. | Advertising Versus Public Relations or Advertising + Public Relations? | 213 |
| [14.3] | | A. What About Me? | 214 |
| [14.4] | | B. What Does That Look Like? | 214 |
| [14.5] | | C. What Is Real News? You Know It Because You've Seen It | 214 |
| [14.6] | | D. What Does That Mean? | 215 |
| [14.7] | | E. News They Can Use | 215 |
| [14.8] | | F. What Does That Look Like? | 215 |
| [14.9] | | G. So What About You and Your Firm? | 216 |
| [14.10] | | H. Now What? | 217 |
| [14.11] | | I. A Note About Press Releases—What Are They Really Good For? | 218 |
| [14.12] | | J. What About Advertising? | 219 |
| [14.13] | | K. So Who Advertises? | 220 |
| [14.14] | | L. Who's Your Prospect/Market? | 220 |
| [14.15] | | M. What Do You Say? | 220 |
| [14.16] | |     1. Where Do I Best the Competition? | 221 |
| [14.17] | |     2. When Does Size Matter? | 222 |
| [14.18] | IV. | When Does Advertising Make Sense? | 222 |
| [14.19] | | A. What About Ads of Obligation? | 223 |
| [14.20] | | B. Original Ad | 224 |
| [14.21] | | C. What About Me? Should I Advertise? | 224 |
| [14.22] | | D. Does That Include Public Relations? | 224 |
| Appendix | | | 225 |

## Chapter 15 Coaching
*John Rumely*

| | | | |
|---|---|---|---|
| [15.0] | I. | Introduction | 229 |
| [15.1] | II. | The Value of Coaching | 230 |
| [15.2] | | A. Coaching Formalizes the Career Development Process | 230 |
| [15.3] | | B. Coaching Is the Answer to "Career Drift" | 230 |
| [15.4] | | C. Coaching Encourages a Healthy Self-Evaluation | 231 |
| [15.5] | | D. Coaching Focuses on the Business Plan | 231 |
| [15.6] | III. | Rationale for Coaching | 232 |
| [15.7] | | A. Coaching Builds on Successes | 232 |
| [15.8] | | B. Turnaround in a Career That Has Stalled | 232 |
| [15.9] | | C. Mid-Career Adjustment | 233 |

| | | | |
|---|---|---|---|
| [15.10] | | D. Preparation of Senior Associates for Partnership | 233 |
| [15.11] | | E. Integration of Lateral Hires | 233 |
| [15.12] | IV. | What Coaching is Not | 233 |
| [15.13] | | A. Coaching Is Not Mentoring | 233 |
| [15.14] | | B. Coaching Is Not Training | 234 |
| [15.15] | | C. Coaching Is Not Part of the Formal Evaluation Process | 234 |
| [15.16] | | D. Coaching Is Not Marriage Counseling | 234 |
| [15.17] | | E. Coaching Does Not Address Personal Problems | 235 |
| [15.18] | | F. Coaching Is Not Easy—It's Going to Be Hard | 235 |
| [15.19] | V. | The Size of the Firm Does Not Matter | 235 |
| [15.20] | | A. Coaching in a Large Firm | 235 |
| [15.21] | | B. Coaching in a Small-Firm Setting | 236 |
| [15.22] | | C. Coaching Can Be Done by Peers | 237 |
| [15.23] | VI. | How to Commence the Process—Getting Started | 237 |
| [15.24] | | A. The Coach Must Be Trained and Qualified | 237 |
| [15.25] | | B. Choice of the Coach | 237 |
| [15.26] | | C. Agreed-Upon Principles | 237 |
| [15.27] | | D. Assess the Attorney's Position in the Firm | 238 |
| [15.28] | | E. Set the Schedule | 238 |
| [15.29] | | F. Location, Location, Location | 239 |
| [15.30] | | G. Agree on Goals and Objectives | 240 |
| [15.31] | | H. Ground Rules | 240 |
| [15.32] | | I. Make It Fun | 241 |
| [15.33] | VII. | How to Keep the Process Going | 242 |
| [15.34] | | A. Working the Business Plan | 242 |
| [15.35] | | B. Follow Up | 243 |
| [15.36] | | C. Monitor and Reflect on the Progress | 243 |
| [15.37] | | D. Stay in Touch | 243 |
| [15.38] | | E. No Excuses | 243 |

**Chapter 16 Technology to Support Growing Your Practice**
*David J. Rosenbaum*

| | | | |
|---|---|---|---|
| [16.0] | I. | Introduction | 247 |
| [16.1] | II. | The Importance of Registering a Domain Name | 247 |
| [16.2] | III. | Creating an Optimal Infrastructure | 248 |
| [16.3] | IV. | Protecting Data—Yours and Your Clients' | 251 |
| [16.4] | | A. Password Protection | 252 |
| [16.5] | | B. Network Firewall | 252 |
| [16.6] | | C. Backup System | 252 |

| | | | |
|---|---|---|---|
| [16.7] | | D. Software Updates | 253 |
| [16.8] | | E. Antivirus Software | 253 |
| [16.9] | V. | Software to Operate and Grow Your Practice | 254 |
| [16.10] | VI. | Putting It All Together | 258 |
| [16.11] | | A. Determine Your Needs | 258 |
| [16.12] | | B. Select the Software | 259 |
| [16.13] | | C. Finalize the Platform | 259 |
| [16.14] | | D. Iterate, Review and Reflect | 260 |
| [16.15] | | E. Procure It, Implement It and Use It | 260 |

**Chapter 17 Success Supports**
*Terri Pepper Gavulic*

| | | | |
|---|---|---|---|
| [17.0] | I. | Introduction | 263 |
| [17.1] | II. | Overcoming Obstacles | 263 |
| [17.2] | III. | Leveraging Resources | 264 |
| [17.3] | IV. | Other Resources to Leverage | 267 |
| [17.4] | V. | Match Marketing with Career Development | 268 |
| [17.5] | VI. | Factors Critical for Marketing and Business Development Success | 272 |
| [17.6] | | A. Focus | 272 |
| [17.7] | | B. Interest | 273 |
| [17.8] | | C. Stretch and Learn | 273 |
| [17.9] | | D. Planning and Organization | 273 |
| [17.10] | | E. Relationships | 273 |
| [17.11] | | F. Loyalty | 274 |
| [17.12] | | G. Success Breeds Success | 274 |
| [17.13] | | H. Expertise | 274 |
| [17.14] | | I. Generosity | 274 |
| [17.15] | | J. Succession Planning | 275 |
| [17.16] | VII. | Wrap-Up | 275 |

Biographies .................................................................................. 277

# INTRODUCTION

"The sky is falling," cried Chicken Little. "A piece of it hit me on the head."[1] And so too lawyers often feel that something has hit them on the head. The legal industry is in the middle of an upheaval, the pace of change is accelerating and change itself is becoming mainstream.[2] It's a world where clients are in charge. New business models, technology innovations, and non-lawyer competition have combined to make traditional practice a thing of the past. Similarly, the Internet and new ways of sharing expertise and knowledge have transformed lawyer marketing.

In addition, newly empowered clients are flexing their muscles:

- Only 31.4% of clients are truly satisfied.[3]

- Since 2013, 60% of corporate counsel replaced at least one core litigation firm.[4]

- Three-quarters of chief legal officers said they would be inclined to use a "less pedigreed firm" if there were a 30% overall cost differential.[5]

This book is designed to help you navigate this tsunami by introducing you to marketing and management resources that can help you create a modern law practice—focused on clients, providing services that take advantage of technology products, and competing on value rather than price. As Jordan Furlong says:

> Now is the time to create "image campaigns" that tell clients . . . why a lawyer's ethics, professionalism, expertise, reliability and integrity are worth the premium that we [lawyers] inevitably will cost. These are marketing campaigns that communicate the extraordinary value that a

---

1　Chicken Little, retold and illustrated by Steven Kellogg (Harper Collins Publishers 1985).

2　*See* Jordan Furlong, *You Say You Want a Revolution?*, Dec. 20, 2013, www.law21.ca/2013/12/say-want-revolution.

3　*13 Striking Opportunities for 2014*, The Mad Clientist, Dec. 16, 2013, www.btibuzz.com/buzz/2013/12/16/13-striking-opportunities-for-2014.html.

4　*60% of Clients Replaced a Core Litigation Firm—The Law Firm Purge Has Begun*, The Mad Clientist, Sept. 29, 2014, www.btibuzz.com/buzz/2014/9/29/60-of-clients-replaced-a-core-litigation-firmthe-law-firm-pu.html.

5　*2013 Chief Legal Officer Survey: An Altman Weil Flash Survey*, Altman Weil, Nov. 2013, p. 10, www.altmanweil.com.

lawyer brings—while recognizing and readily conceding that not every situation requires a lawyer's services.[6]

The book is divided into three sections.

- *Section 1—Marketing Basics* includes chapters on strategy and planning and a chapter on value, including what clients want and how to communicate your value to them.

- *Section 2—Personal Marketing* includes chapters on personal branding, research-based client relationships, consultative selling, knowledge-sharing techniques, online activities and ethics.

- *Section 3—Firm Marketing* includes a firm's culture, business development supports that organize and enhance individual marketing efforts, client interviews, pricing strategies, public relations and advertising, training and coaching, technology supports for marketing and resources to enhance individuals' successes.

The chapters are designed to be standalone, which means you decide how much knowledge you need at the moment. You can dip into whatever chapter is relevant to your current plans, or you can read several chapters together in order to create something new. Whatever you do, we hope you find the book both useful and enjoyable.

All of the chapters are written by topic experts. Some are lawyers, some are marketing professionals who work with lawyers, and some are lawyers turned marketing professionals. They all donated their expertise and time to enable the New York State Bar Association to provide a book that will help their constituency grow.

Carol Schiro Greenwald, Ph.D.
*Editor*

---

6   *See* Jordan Furlong, *You Say You Want a Revolution?*, Dec. 20, 2013, www.law21.ca/2013/12/say-want-revolution.

# CHAPTER ONE

# STRATEGY AND PLANNING

## Wendy L. Bernero

# [1.0] I. HOW PLANNING BEGETS SUCCESS

Whether you're an individual lawyer or the leader of a firm or practice group, your success depends upon establishing goals, developing a strategy, and following a plan to achieve them. Business planning is much like vacation planning. Most of us would never consider leaving on a trip without a destination, budget and a list of activities we seek to experience. Without this information, how would you know what to pack?

Your business plan is the opportunity to define what success looks like for you. It also outlines the steps you will take to achieve it, including:

- your firm's business purpose (mission statement);
- where you are now (current situation assessment);
- where you want to be in the next one to five years (the opportunity); and
- how you will get there (the strategy and implementation plan).

Developing a business plan doesn't have to be a long and onerous exercise. In fact, you can develop a very useful business plan in just a few days if you follow these steps.

# [1.1] II. WHAT IS YOUR FIRM'S MISSION OR PURPOSE?

The first step in planning is to envision what you want your practice to become. The goal is to balance your hopes and desires for your practice (the types of clients you want to represent, the types of work you do/do not want to do) with what is possible given your capabilities, experience, geographic reach, budget, etc.

Your mission statement outlines your firm's purpose or reason for existing. It serves as a guide for day-to-day decision-making, most often by helping you to reject opportunities that are not in sync with your firm's mission.

Some of the questions that your mission statement should answer are:

- What are you trying to accomplish?
- What type(s) of work do you want to do?

- What type(s) of clients do you want to serve?

- In what type of environment do you aspire to work?

Here is a sample mission plan for a Personal Planning practice:

> **At Thomson and Giordano, we pride ourselves on providing high-net-worth families, retirees and small-business owners in New York's Finger Lakes-Wine Country region with highly personal and sophisticated trust and estate planning services. We are dedicated to maintaining a positive and supportive work environment for our team of lawyers and staff, as well as giving back to our community and improving the lives of its residents through our volunteerism and charitable giving.**

## [1.2] III. PROFILE YOUR CLIENTS

If you want to take your practice to the next level, you need to understand your clients' needs and expectations. Put yourself in your clients' shoes and ask yourself:

- What are our clients' needs, motivations and preferences?

- What do they appreciate most about our service offerings? Where can we improve?

- Why do they select us as their law firm?

- What future legal needs do they have?

- How do we uniquely provide value to our clients?

- How can we improve our services to ensure that we delight our clients and attract new clients?

The best way to answer these questions is to ask your clients! They will be flattered that you cared enough to ask and consider their opinion.

## [1.3] IV. WHAT IS THE SOURCE OF YOUR COMPETITIVE ADVANTAGE?

All businesses need to have a clearly stated point of differentiation from their competitors. Your competitive advantage statement is the articulation of what your firm does better than its competitors. It answers the question every prospect will ask: "Why should I hire you instead of someone else?" The client profile you created in Step Two will make this step easier for you.

In today's highly competitive legal market, your competitive advantage statement may be the most critical section of your plan. While many lawyers and law firms successfully compete based solely on relationships and reputation, differentiating your practice will give prospects an objective rationale for selecting you over others with whom they might have strong (or stronger) personal relationships.

It is important to note that when goods or services are undifferentiated, commoditization occurs. The lack of differentiation among law firms is a principal cause of the pricing pressures facing the legal profession. If all service offerings have the same attributes, and are therefore indistinguishable, the only basis of selection for a client is price. By the same token, differentiating your services can provide you with an opportunity to clarify the unique value you provide and garner higher fees.

In order to test your competitive advantage, it is important to fully understand the identity of your principal competitors, their service offerings and the means by which they compete. Completing this chart can be a useful means of keeping an eye on your competition. Update it regularly by tracking your competitors using Google Alerts or another online resource.

| Competitor (Indicate Type of Service Provider) | Number of Practitioners | Competitor's Advantages/ Strengths | Competitor's Disadvantages/ Weaknesses |
| --- | --- | --- | --- |
| _____ | _____ | _____ | _____ |
| _____ | _____ | _____ | _____ |

Here is a sample competitive advantage statement for a corporate practice focused on serving small businesses:

> At Long & Silverstone, our small business clients receive 24/7 assistance with all of their critical legal needs. L&S lawyers have backgrounds in business and finance, and most have earned both MBA and JD degrees. They are fully focused on the business implications of legal issues as opposed to just the technical legal rules—enabling them to serve as valued advisors to clients. Our small-business services offering includes a retainer-based monthly advisory service that provides you with an unlimited on-call legal resource to help you identify and mitigate risks and maximize opportunities during the course of your business decision-making. As part of this service, we also hold quarterly brainstorming and future-planning sessions with your leadership team, designed to help you maximize the growth potential of your business.

Remember, your goal is to identify new ways of serving clients that leverage your unique capabilities and resources in a way that will give you an advantage over your competitors.

## [1.4] V. WHERE ARE YOU NOW?

The Current Situation Assessment is an essential part of your planning process. After all, you cannot determine how to get where you want to go if you don't know where you are now! This assessment includes both an internal analysis, which provides an in-depth look at your capabilities and financial performance, as well as an external market analysis.

The SWOT (Strengths, Weaknesses, Opportunities and Threats) analysis can be a useful tool for critically analyzing your current situation. Assess your strengths and weaknesses by answering these questions:

- What do we do best?

- Where could we improve?

- What are our firm's capabilities and how do they measure up?

- How does our infrastructure and service delivery system measure up?

Assess your opportunities and threats by answering these questions:

- What is happening externally that will affect our firm?
- What is happening in the world that might affect our business (technology, regulatory/legal changes, market changes, and economic cycles)?
- What is the firm's current market position?
- What are clients' buying preferences?
- Why do clients use the firm and for what types of work?
- What are clients' perceptions of the firm's capabilities?
- What is the current economic environment?
- What are the future market and regulatory trends?
- What are some economic scenario projections?
- Who are potential new competitors?

Below is an example of a SWOT analysis for a litigation practice:

| **STRENGTHS** | **WEAKNESSES** |
|---|---|
| Extensive trial experience. | Limited depth of subject matter expertise in intellectual property and ERISA litigation. |
| Strong track record. | |
| Excellent legal project management and e-discovery capabilities. | Most senior litigator and biggest rainmaker will retire in two years. |
| **OPPORTUNITIES** | **THREATS** |
| Expand commercial litigation work for major client to other regions. | National litigation boutique opening an office in region. |

New state employment laws will generate increased employee lawsuits.

Major client considering move to lower tax state. Will others follow?

## [1.5] VI. YOUR VISION: WHERE DO YOU WANT TO GO?

Creating a strategic vision of your firm can be the most enjoyable part of the planning process. This is your chance to imagine the future of your firm. Be bold and imaginative—the higher your aspirations, the greater your achievements will be.

A strategic vision is the image of your firm's future—the direction in which it is headed, the client focus it will have, the market position it aspires to occupy, the business activities to be pursued, and the capabilities it plans to develop.

Your strategic vision should (1) delineate what your firm aspires to become and (2) infuse the organization with a sense of purposeful action. To write a vision statement, answer this question: What do we want our firm to look like in five years?

Sample Vision Statement for a general practice law firm focused on start-up businesses:

> **At Taylor & Stevens, our passion is helping start-up companies succeed. We are dedicated to continuous innovation, providing businesses in Rochester and its environs with affordable suites of legal services and solutions that enable their growth and success by leveraging opportunities and minimizing risks. We fully utilize technology and knowledge management, and partner with other business service providers, to ensure that we offer a state-of-the art, efficient and streamlined service delivery model.**

## [1.6] VII. WRITE YOUR GOALS AND OBJECTIVES

Goals and objectives are the guideposts to help you achieve your mission and vision. Business goals are high-level and strategic, encompassing the entire team and every department in your business. Objectives are the measurable targets that you will pursue to achieve your business goals.

Goals set the agenda, are broad, and global in nature. You should set two to five goals that will help you achieve your mission/vision and will take three to five years to achieve. Then, develop objectives to achieve each goal. Objectives should be measurable, quantifiable, and support your goals. You should be able to achieve them in a one-year time frame. Objectives should state what will be done, by when, and by whom. Both your goals and your objectives should build on your strengths, reduce your weaknesses, capitalize on your opportunities and address your threats.

## [1.7] VIII. ASSESS YOUR RESOURCES

Now that you have completed your goals and objectives, it is time to conduct a resource assessment. Time and money can be the biggest obstacles to even the best plans. No budget is ever sufficient to do everything you want to do. Prioritize your goals by asking: Do the goals I set forth make sense from a resource perspective? Do I have the money and the time/people to achieve my plan?

## [1.8] IX. TAKE ACTION

Your next step is to determine the specific actions and tactics you will utilize to help you achieve your goals and objectives—basically a to-do list for each objective. Ask yourself:

- What do I need to do to achieve this objective?

- What obstacles need to be removed?

Use the answers to these questions to develop action items for each objective. Assign responsibilities and deadlines to ensure implementation.

Goal: Enhance partnership with/value offered to top five clients

Objective #1: Expand educational resources available to clients

| Actions | Costs | Start/End Date | Assigned to: |
|---|---|---|---|
| Expand CLE marathon to other offices. | | | |
| Assess client interest in creation of high-level, small-group CLE | | | |

sessions for senior executives. Create in each office.

Become certified to provide CPE credits for accountants and finance executives. Research requirements and apply.

Consider having partners participate in existing corporate board- member training institutes. (See Beecher-Carlson Top Boards program, www.beechercarlson.com). Leverage Board Room Bound for this purpose.

## [1.9] X. KEEP SCORE

In step six, you set measurable objectives. Put these measurements and targets on a scorecard (in Excel), which will serve as a dashboard to measure your progress toward achieving your vision. Check the dashboard regularly to keep tabs on your progress.

## [1.10] XI. MAKE PLANNING A HABIT

Use your plan as a means of celebrating your successes and focusing your efforts, resources and team. Share the plan with your partners and associates, and as appropriate, with clients. Hold regular strategy meetings to report on progress and amend the plan.

## [1.11] XII. PLANNING TIPS AND ADVICE

1. Your plan is a living document that will need to change as circumstances change and new opportunities present themselves. So don't consign it to the back of your file drawer. Review your plan periodically. It will be a valuable tool for benchmarking your progress.

2. Some people resist planning because they don't want to feel "restricted" by rules. Keep in mind that a big piece of your plan is eliminating those things that you will not do. This is a big timesaver

as it stops you from having to think through every situation or opportunity that presents itself.

3. The perfect is the enemy of the good and complete. You don't need to answer every question. Further research and discovery can be an action item. Avoid analysis paralysis – planning is not an exact science.

4. Look outside for inspiration. Aspire to continuous learning and exploration. It's important to make time to look up from your work and get a 10,000-foot view. This can be difficult to do.

5. Don't try to be all things to all people. No one will believe that you are good at all aspects of law. Invest your energy and resources on niche markets in which you can become well recognized. You can then choose to do whatever work you want.

6. Celebrate your successes!

CHAPTER TWO

# WHY CLIENTS DEMAND VALUE AND HOW YOUR SUCCESS DEPENDS ON DELIVERING IT

Susan Saltonstall Duncan

## [2.0] I. CLIENTS ARE IN THE DRIVER'S SEAT

For at least a decade, clients have been getting both more selective and more sophisticated in how they consider and hire lawyers. Several recent market forces have put clients more firmly and permanently in the driver's seat as clients today have many more choices for getting the legal help and information they need. The supply of licensed lawyers greatly exceeds demand, and there are many alternative legal service providers available in the form of legal process outsourcers, virtual and contract lawyers, and many paraprofessionals who can do much of what is required. In addition to professionals providing services, many clients can access tools and content to complete legal documentation and processes online and inexpensively.

The surplus and disruption in the profession has resulted in three major challenges for lawyers in private practice. First, lawyers now compete much more regularly and aggressively with each other for new business or even to hold on to clients. Second, when supply exceeds demand, clients can and now do force lawyers to compete on price. And third, with so much available on the Internet and through software programs, and with many lower cost providers available, it can be difficult to convince clients why they should spend significantly more money to have a lawyer do what they perceive others can do faster and/or cheaper.

## [2.1] II. SOME LEGAL SERVICES HAVE DIMINISHED IN VALUE

As evidenced by what clients are and are not willing to pay ever-higher rates for, much of the work traditionally done by lawyers has diminished in value. Clients themselves have a good idea whether their legal matters require high-end, highly customized attention and expertise, or whether they fall where 60 percent or more of legal needs typically are, which is in the category of routine, standardized or commoditized services.

Alternative service providers have burgeoned to provide many of the content, routine and commoditized services. These alternative service providers offer many services that traditional firms had considered their bread and butter, e.g., pre-litigation work, research and discovery, contracts and agreements, and even trademark filings and patent prosecution.

## [2.2] III. PUTTING CLIENTS AT THE CENTER

Lawyers who best understand and deliver value to their clients are those who put clients' satisfaction and loyalty at the center of their practice and their firms—ahead of their own profits, ahead of their own agendas, and ahead of their drive for intellectual pursuits. Essentially, achieving clients' goals are the lawyer's or firm's top priority. Being client-centric is a mindset, and in a few firms a core tenet of their culture and their mission; however, most talk about it but do not completely execute on it.

What are some of the qualities that client-centric lawyers or law firms embody?

- Like Jeff Bezos of Amazon, they symbolically leave an empty chair at the table for every discussion about the client and about firm policies, management matters and approaches in order always to ask, "What is in the best interest of the client? How will this decision, policy or approach benefit or disadvantage our clients?"

- They ask great questions and are avid listeners.

- They learn everything they can about the client's expectations, needs, worries, communication style, and working preferences.

- They worry about and think ahead about issues or problems that will affect the client and creatively think about new approaches and solutions.

- They treat their client's money as if it were their own.

- They make every client feel as though he or she is that lawyer's only client.

- They measure, promote and reward everyone in the firm on the basis of how well they serve and satisfy clients over the long term.

- They provide some insights, advice and information without charging for it.

Lawyers with a client-centric mindset are in a much better position to be aware of and to create value for their clients.

## [2.3] IV. VALUE IS IN THE EYE OF THE BEHOLDER

Discussions about value often revolve around the pricing and cost side of value, but it is much more complicated than that. It's true that clients are demanding, and getting, better prices. Law firms are learning how to become more efficient and creative, while still maintaining profitability. But value is about much more than just the price of something. Value is subjective—what one client believes is worth the cost, another might not. Usually clients describe the lawyers or law firms they get value from as

- getting results;
- achieving the objectives we establish;
- being trustworthy and reliable;
- being readily available and accessible whenever I need them;
- being creative and innovative;
- being among a very few with a specific skill or expertise;
- thinking outside the box;
- having institutional knowledge about my business or organization;
- going above and beyond;
- treating me as if I were their only client; and
- having all staff know me and being helpful and respectful.

In order for you to deliver value, you need to establish up front how individual clients define value and how they will measure whether or not they receive it from you. At the outset of each engagement, define the clients' objectives and the approaches and parameters they'd like you to apply in order to achieve the outcomes they hope for. Ask them to articulate what it is specifically that will make this a successful engagement. This requires a customized approach for each client.

The fact that value is in the eye of each beholder is good news. First, clients still appreciate and look for value that means more than just price—they know that cheapest isn't always better or even good enough.

Second, relationships still matter. For many lawyers, 80 percent of new business comes from referrals, the majority of which are current or former clients. If you can build loyal clients who are very satisfied with your service, results and value, you will receive referrals of new clients from them. Third, there still are many aspects of legal advice and representation that can be provided effectively only by lawyers. The secret is to figure out how you truly deliver value and differentiate yourself and your services from all the other options clients have available to them.

## [2.4] V. HOW YOU SHOULD COMMUNICATE VALUE: THE VALUE PROPOSITION

Since it has become increasingly more competitive for lawyers trying to attract new clients or even retain them, value will continue to be something you not only need to deliver but also communicate. This communication will take many forms and will occur at various times along the marketing spectrum, from an initial introduction in an elevator speech to the way you describe your services in a proposal or a meeting with a prospect to the discussions you have with existing clients on whether they are receiving the value they want and need.

A value proposition reflects the concrete results and benefits a client receives by selecting and working with you or your law firm. It is what helps a law firm stand out from others by conveying what is distinct about its services, culture and infrastructure that make it the better choice over its competitors.

Traditionally, lawyers and their firms have promoted their services from a features-oriented basis. Whether in a self-introduction or a description of a practice area, their focus has tended to be on capabilities and services offered, credentials, location, history of the firm, size of the team or firm, etc. This approach is firm- or lawyer-centric, and does not make the case for why a client should hire you over someone else and, in many cases, does not even give clients a clear idea of how you will help them. When you focus only on features, the client or prospect is left wondering "How does this help me?" or "How is this any different from the firm I already use?"

Some real examples of self-focused descriptions or those that focus on features:

- We take pride in providing our clients with exceptional guidance and practical solutions to a vast array of legal matters.

# WHY CLIENTS DEMAND VALUE § 2.4

- [Law firm] takes pride in providing our clients with the utmost level of care, respect, attention, and understanding.

- That's why we take pride in our team's knowledge, experience and intelligence to best represent our clients' interests.

- Our practices are based on the tradition and principle of providing legal excellence with integrity to our clients.

- The firm was founded on the commitment to providing the highest quality professional legal service available.

Selling your services and the value clients derive from retaining your firm must be focused on benefits, not features. Your value proposition should speak to the tangible results and solutions you bring to their pressing challenges—how your services will make their lives easier. You need to articulate tangible, perhaps quantifiable, examples of specific advantages and results you bring them.

Your value proposition should focus on specific ways in which you help clients; for example, how you

- save them money;

- help them access capital or financing or find acquisitions or acquirers;

- grow their revenues, grow their market share, and protect and grow their assets;

- help them recover expenses and compensation following a personal injury;

- help them through a difficult divorce and achieve the financial stability or protection they need;

- help them get out of trouble and stay out of trouble;

- minimize legal and business risk or exposure;

- navigate complex regulations to stay compliant and out of investigations or enforcement actions;

- minimize their negative public relations exposure;

- help them hire and retain employees;

- help them find and retain customers;

- make important business or political connections or alliance partner introductions for them; and

- help them sleep better at night!

A strong value proposition

- is compelling and interesting, creating the desire of the prospect to ask and learn more about you;

- focuses on the client, client needs and how your solutions help the client;

- differentiates you from your competitors;

- includes concrete, tangible examples that have metrics/measurable outcomes; and

- could not be substituted as your competitors' value proposition.

One of the best ways to identify and test out your tangible benefits and distinctive qualities is to ask your clients how they define your value and what makes you distinctive, especially compared to other lawyers they have known or with whom they have worked. This will prevent you from promoting qualities that are too general or generic and not perceived as valuable, distinguishable or helpful to those who may retain you.

Your value proposition should speak to the tangible results and solutions you bring to their pressing challenges. When possible, every feature should correlate with a benefit. For example:

*Feature:* **We have 80 lawyers in five offices throughout the state.**

*Client or Prospect:* **So what? How does this help me?**

*Benefit:* **This enables us to help you resolve disputes and navigate local laws and regulations as you expand into new cities, get access to and have a voice in the state capitol, and identify potential companies to acquire in other major markets across the state.**

*Feature:* We have eight trial lawyers who have participated in over 300 appellate matters in the state.

*Client or Prospect:* So what? How does this help me?

*Benefit:* Our appellate team, which includes a former Chief Judge, a former solicitor general and four certified appellate specialists, has secured reversals of $5 million to $20 million jury verdicts, including the largest punitive damages award obtained by an individual plaintiff in our state's history.

## [2.5] VI. THE VALUE PROPOSITION AND YOUR ELEVATOR SPEECH

An elevator speech is an opportunity to tell people you meet in a business or social setting what you do or are currently doing in a way that is meaningful to them and conveys benefit. The term is derived from the concept of stepping onto an elevator with a prospect or referral source and having 15 to 30 seconds during the elevator ride to explain what you do in a concise way that makes them want to know more about you and your services.

An effective elevator speech will tell people what you do, not just who or what you are, and provide an interesting but short and focused description of the work you do and solutions you provide, as well as the types of clients you serve and the general geographic market. You should be able to articulate value and solutions so other people can understand easily, especially if you are speaking with a non-lawyer. Try to relate what you do to current events and reflect passion for what you do.

*Poor introduction:* **My name is Jane Downing. I am a corporate associate at Brown & Todd.**

*Better introduction:* **My name is Jane Downing. I am a business lawyer at Brown & Todd where I help small biotech companies form business partnerships with universities and research labs in the Research Triangle in North Carolina.**

*Poor introduction:* **My name is John Martinez. I am an IP litigator.**

*Better introduction:* **My name is John Martinez and I am a trial lawyer at Pearl & Stone, an intellectual property law firm based in Austin. I work with international computer software companies that are** sued for infringing on others' patents or when they believe their own technology inventions have been stolen.

*Poor introduction:* My name is Jordan Smith. I am a plaintiff's attorney and I handle personal injury cases.

*Better introduction:* My name is Jordan Smith and I am a trial lawyer with the plaintiff's firm of Cassidy, Letkin and Pandry in Cincinnati. I help my clients evaluate whether they have a valid case against a doctor or hospital that may have made a mistake in treating them or a family member.

Your elevator speech will vary depending upon the other person and the venue. If you truly meet someone in a neutral place, your introduction will be like those above. If you are meeting someone at a more targeted event, e.g., a specific conference on a legal or business issue, an industry program or a bar association event, you will modify your introduction to make it more likely to resonate with those attending the event.

## [2.6] VII. HOW BIOS/PROFILES, PRACTICE AND FIRM DESCRIPTIONS CONVEY VALUE

With this approach in mind, look at the current versions of your bio, firm and practice descriptions. Make sure that each sentence or description reflects the benefits and value you deliver to clients. Revise them to include specific examples of the outcomes relating to services, issues and industries; examples of representative cases in which you include specific examples of size of transactions or jury awards, types of individuals, companies or industries; and the geographic reach of your client representations. Include only information that you honestly think matters to clients, e.g., sometimes bar activities may be less relevant to clients and prospects than business, industry or community and charitable activities. These web pieces should be updated regularly to reflect new successes, insights on new trends and hot issues, and recent speeches or articles on topics that are timely.

## [2.7] VIII. 25 TIPS TO DELIVER VALUE AND DEVELOP HIGHLY SATISFIED CLIENTS WHO BECOME LOYAL (AND RAVING) FANS

1. Become an active and avid listener. Don't try to convince clients of all you know or your point of view. Instead, start focusing on the client—his or her needs, interests, and questions. Be genuine in your interest and listen without interrupting.

2. Define value for each client. Ask each client what criteria they use to determine the value of legal services in general and then, specifically, the level of value you deliver to them and how or why. Be clear on how they will measure your success.

3. Get to know your clients. Take time to get to know them professionally and personally, their hobbies and passions, what drives them, and what their life goals are. Do some searching on the Internet to see what you can find on LinkedIn, Facebook or on their company/organization website.

4. Establish firm service standards and protocols. This is a set of commitments you make to clients about the quality of your services and usually includes how quickly you respond to voice and email messages, how you staff matters, how well you will get to know each client, and how you try to meet clients' goals effectively and cost-efficiently.

5. Develop client-specific service plans. When beginning work with new clients, discuss their preferences for how, with whom and how often to communicate, how they prefer their billing, whether they want to be included in strategy discussions, whether they want status reports and, if so, how often and in what format (by email, phone or formal reports).

6. Use approaches, technology and tools that lead to efficiency. Continually evaluate how effectively you manage client projects by using technology, project management protocols and early case assessment.

7. Don't reinvent the wheel. Do some research internally and externally to find prior projects and precedents similar to the one you are doing for clients, including reaching out to colleagues who may have done similar cases or projects.

8. Scope and budget matters carefully. Break down matters in stages and components and, if available, look at previous similar matters for a delineation of time and level of skill needed. Prepare budgets for clients that are detailed and that have certain milestones by which you and the client can evaluate progress and status against the budget.

9. Manage expectations. Once you begin working with a client on a new matter, keep the client apprised of the status of the project, discuss any roadblocks or expanding scope of work requested or required especially if it affects the budget, and let the client know when you have added any new professionals to help staff the matter and why.

10. Be sure your bills are clear, accurate, frequent and transparent. Some lawyers think billing is an accounting function and that getting them paid is a collections activity. This couldn't be more wrong. Clients pay bills when they believe the value you are delivering is in line with what you both agreed upon. They hate surprises, e.g., budget overruns or additional people they've never met billing to the file. Even worse are bills with errors or time billed that is over a month old. Call clients in advance if a bill is likely to be more than you estimated or they are expecting. Billing is a chance to see how you are doing relative to the client's perception of value and to nurture the relationship.

11. Look at alternatives to the billable hour. If a client is willing, proactively explore retainers, flat or project fees, pricing by stage of work, or holdbacks with a potential bonus. Remember that most clients prefer predictability so they can budget for legal expenses in advance.

12. Consider all staffing options. There may be a number of ways in which you could get a project completed on a client's behalf. Be sure to delegate what can be done by lower cost personnel—a lawyer, paralegal or project manager—in your firm or, if necessary, by hiring contract staff. Alternatively, ask the client if he or she has anyone available to help with part of the case.

13. Get to know people who are important to the client. If a business, become familiar with other key members of the client's organization, including secretaries. If an individual client, get to know who is in the immediate circle of influence and importance. Add all relevant contacts to your contact data base and categorize them by client.

14. Stay in touch regularly. Be in contact with every active client at least once a quarter, preferably every month. Make a call proactively just

# WHY CLIENTS DEMAND VALUE § 2.7

to check in even if you are not working on an active matter with them at the moment.

15. Always be helpful. There are many ways you can help clients, in addition to the legal services you are providing. Keep your ears open for other needs clients have—a referral to a doctor or school, an introduction to a banker for a loan, a good real estate agent, a college recommendation for a son or daughter, or a recommendation for a good vacation spot.

16. Be available and accessible. Try to answer your own phone personally. At a time when, technically, you could be available 24/7, determine with the client what is reasonable. Provide your cell phone number but establish boundaries for when clients should or should not use it. Whatever you do, don't ask your secretary to place a call to a client for you, then have the client hold for you. This makes clients feel that your time is much more important than their time. Set an out-of-office response when you will be away from the office for a day or more. Your message should indicate when you plan to return to the office and whom clients should contact in your place.

17. Be responsive. Respond to all emails within four hours of receiving them. If you are not available, ask your secretary to respond for you and indicate when you will respond personally. Make sure that your voicemail message is client-friendly and helpful. Voice messages should be updated regularly to let clients know where and how to reach you or who else they can call. Doing so shows clients and other callers that you check voicemail often and that their calls are important. Be sure you use a tool that converts any phone messages into emails so you get those in your inbox instantaneously.

18. Produce excellent work and avoid errors. Keep others informed of the status of matters by sending emails, reminders and copies of correspondence. Avoid last minute demands of clients. Don't wait to send clients a draft of a document they see for the first time only 24 hours before it needs to be filed. Share calendars and remind team members in advance of commitments and deadlines. Maintain a tickler system of all ongoing projects and matters for this client and meet deadlines. Make sure all work that goes out is proofread and checked again for typos, grammar and citation accuracy.

19. Use email effectively and properly. Try to keep messages as concise as possible, including only relevant text. Avoid using common email

abbreviations, email slang, smiley faces and all lowercase letters. Address your messages as you would a letter to the recipient (i.e., Dear Ms. Smith or Dear Jane). When you are unsure, stick to the more formal salutation. Use your email subject line accurately and strategically, especially if you are confirming a deadline or asking a specific question. It will help the recipient focus on the critical aspect of your message.

20. Give away some free time. Provide some free counseling time and note it on the bill as "General Advice, No Charge." Indicate the amount of time given so that the client can attach value to this free advice.

21. Seek feedback regularly and formally. Regularly ask your clients if they are satisfied with your services and those of others whom you supervise. Ask them if there are areas in which they are dissatisfied or the firm could improve. Conduct client satisfaction surveys (by email, telephone or in person) annually with all clients to get feedback on service. At the completion of each matter, send an end-of-matter questionnaire.

22. Stay ahead of the curve on trends. Find out and stay informed about what municipal and state issues clients are faced with. Look for the next big need or trend in your practice niche, market or clients' industries. Read daily news feeds on local and state issues as well as business and industry issues that may affect clients. Set up a Google alert to send you news daily on key issues, clients, practice trends or industries. Let clients know you are keeping your finger on the pulse to bring them new ideas or updates about how other clients may be tackling similar problems.

23. Add value beyond your representation. If you represent a company and it employs in-house lawyers or senior management, offer to do a tailored, free seminar on a timely issue. Take business clients to your business/industry seminars and to important political, civic or business events. Inform your client about a good business deal. Try to put clients together who could share business information and opportunities. Offer to "lend" lawyers and support staff to clients when clients are in a crunch, for a week, a month, or even a year.

24. Think about client problems proactively. Conduct "preventative" audits to help identify potential regulatory compliance violations, risks and issues before they become legal problems. Develop a man-

# WHY CLIENTS DEMAND VALUE § 2.7

ual or prevention checklist for your clients. Point them to free online resources and information.

25. Constantly look for ways to help clients. Whether it is about their legal needs or, as important, their personal agendas and objectives, keep clients on your radar at all times. Help them as they maneuver internal politics, try to find a new job, advance their own career and expertise, need school and medical referrals, or introduce them to a civic or charitable leadership opportunity. Clients are people who struggle with many of the same challenges you do. If you are helpful, reliable, resourceful and produce the results they seek, you will engender loyalty and develop client fans who can become your best sales force.

In conclusion, the value you deliver must be defined and perceived as genuine by your clients. Your value proposition must reflect your distinctive expertise and experience that result in client solutions. Value is something that your clients will measure, evaluate and either make referrals of new clients as a result of or become a detractor who may share negative perceptions about you with others. If your value proposition and value delivery are working effectively your practice will reap the benefits because you will

- stand apart from your competitors;

- make it easier for clients to understand how what you do actually helps them and solved problems;

- develop loyal and long-standing clients; and

- grow your revenue more easily with loyal clients who send you repeat work and who serve as your best spokespeople for sending you new referrals.

# CHAPTER THREE

# PERSONAL BASICS

Steven Skyles-Mulligan

# [3.0] I. UNDERSTANDING WHY THE PERSONAL MATTERS

## [3.1] A. Overview

Attorneys often look at marketing with distaste, viewing it as, at best, a necessary evil and, at worst, an exercise in hyperbole that bears little relationship to the work they do, consumes valuable resources and produces uncertain results. For these reasons, in many smaller firms the marketing function, such as it is, gets consigned to a staff member as a part-time assignment or to an outside consultant with legal industry expertise. The former approach will keep the essential transactions—such as maintaining the firm website or sending out periodic newsletters—flowing, while the latter might ensure directed efforts in strategic client acquisition or building up a consistent, valuable firm brand. Both of these approaches miss a critical point: the decision to retain an attorney, even when the matter relates to business, is intensely personal.

This means that, in order for the marketing of legal services to be effective in attracting the clients the attorney is best suited—and most wants—to serve, it should have a strong yet considered bias toward the personal. This chapter will survey the fundamentals of personal elements in marketing a legal practice.

## [3.2] B. How People Make Buying Decisions

To genuinely grasp why the personal is so important in marketing a legal practice, it is essential to understand how people fundamentally make buying decisions. And make no mistake, the decision to retain an attorney—regardless of the apparent urgency or inconsequentiality of the matter—is a choice to make a purchase. Given that the law is generally an intensely rational, and certainly highly intellectual, endeavor and that clients hire attorneys in large measure for their ability to think strategically, one might expect that the decision to retain a particular attorney or firm is solely a logical one. Does the attorney have the skills needed to increase the likelihood that the matter will be resolved favorably? Is the projected fee within the range that the client is willing to spend? Is the matter likely to be resolved in a time frame that is acceptable to the client? But the truth, borne out by numerous research studies,[1] is that *people consistently make buying decisions on emotional grounds and then inductively gener-*

---

[1] *See, e.g.*, David Court, Dave Elzinga, Susan Mulder and Ole Jørgen Vetvik, *The Consumer Decision Journey*, McKinsey Quarterly, June 2009, 3.

ate the rational argument to support the choice. This would indicate quite strongly that a marketing approach based solely on the rational is not going to get you very far. But how can you begin to appeal to clients' emotional instincts in your marketing without leaving behind your own sense of professionalism and propriety?

## [3.3]  1. What You're Really Selling

The key is to understand what it is your clients are really buying from you. Other chapters in this book will show that it is not the features of your practice—however excellent they may be—and certainly not your billable hours. Clients are also not, deep down, buying from you either something as difficult to quantify as a legal strategy or as comparatively straightforward as the legal documents that support it. What they are, in fact, buying from you at that emotional level just discussed is *the feeling they get when sitting across from you with either a potential crisis weighing on them or a likely opportunity opening before them.*

Obviously, each client has a slightly different experience of you—as you do of each client. However, if you consider the occasions when you felt the most personal and professional satisfaction in the work, and the client's satisfaction seemed to match your own, you may begin to find a pattern. It could be that you are particularly good at easing client anxiety from the beginning of a matter through its conclusion. Perhaps you have command of all the details while the client tends to be scattered or prefers to take a more removed stance. Maybe you tend to help your clients moderate their innate tendencies and act strategically, rather than impulsively. Or possibly you protect client interests with a thoughtful aggressiveness they could never muster on their own behalf.

Regardless of which pattern seems most familiar to you, in your most successful client relationships you typically provide something—beyond legal knowledge—that your clients cannot readily provide on their own. That generates a feeling or experience which is what your best clients actually buy from you again and again.

## [3.4]  2. The Importance of Know, Like and Trust

That feeling or experience that your best clients feel—and that perhaps you feel in return when working with them—is often summed up as, "*we prefer to do business with those we know, like and trust.*" While it's certainly not impossible to work with people outside of this construct, it can be less satisfying to both attorney and client, less profitable for the attorney and less likely to result in repeat business.

### Table 1: Know, Like and Trust

| Know | • Attorney understands client's objectives, risk tolerance, fee/time sensitivity.<br><br>• Client recognizes (and values) attorney's style and approach. |
|---|---|
| Like | • Attorney and client enjoy each other as people. |
| Trust | • Client relies upon attorney to act in certain ways that will protect his/her best interest.<br><br>• Attorney relies upon client to work in good faith, make requests instead of demands and pay bills in a timely manner. |

This probably makes some sense in the context of the way you practice law, but what does it have to do with marketing that practice? *The best marketing seeks to anticipate—and even begin to cultivate—ideal client relationships.* It presents the attorney or firm in a way that is knowable, likable and trustworthy to people who are likely to appreciate that particular attorney's or firm's qualities.

## [3.5] C. Why There Should Be Another "P" in Marketing

For the past several decades, marketers have spoken about the *"four Ps" of marketing:*

1. Product: what is being sold

2. Place: where it is being offered/distributed

3. Price: what the purchaser is charged

4. Promotion: how potential purchasers are informed

As more attention has been given to the differences between marketing products and marketing services, some experts have added three more Ps to the service marketing mix:

5. Physical evidence: what shows that the purchaser received something of value

6. People: those who are providing the service, their skills and manner

7. Process: how the service is delivered

Both the original "four P" model and the "seven P" adaptation for services provide a useful overview. However, both leave out a critical element to capture the emotional and interpersonal aspects that form the backbone of the successful attorney-client relationship:

8. Personality: what intangible elements make a good attorney/client "fit"[2]

Unlike the other Ps, personality can be very difficult to capture, quantify and project, but there is an established marketing tool that can be very helpful if it is employed correctly.

## [3.6] II. COMING TO GRIPS WITH PERSONAL BRANDING

Depending on whom you talk to, branding is generally surrounded with mystery, hype or some mixture of the two. It's actually neither as insubstantial nor as enigmatic as it seems. There are three main purposes of branding:

- It gives form to the invisible (which is true even for products).

- It helps prospective clients and customers remember.

- It provides focus and clarity for promoter and purchaser alike.

Basically, then, a brand is *a symbolic summary of a collection of ideas and emotions.* Having a strong, well-defined personal brand is one of the most important steps in capturing and projecting that "what clients feel when working with you" essence that they are really buying—that powerful "personality" element of the marketing mix.

---

2   The Wikipedia article *Marketing Mix* gives a thumbnail overview of both the "four Ps" and the "seven Ps," along with history and citations: en.wikipedia.org/wiki/Marketing_mix. The article also deals with another marketing framework, the "four Cs," which is not incorporated into this discussion.

## [3.7] A. Practical Discussion of Brand

## [3.8] 1. How a Professional Brand Differs From a Product Brand

We are all familiar on some level with brands and what they stand for: razors that promise to shave closer than the competition; automobiles that project affluence or romance; clothing that provides enduring quality and timeless style. But these—and many brands you can readily think of—represent products, not services or the people who deliver them. Because products are not people, the emotional connections they create en route to a sale are often based far more in the consumer's head than in the reality of the situation. This gives product brands *tremendous freedom to be "aspirational,"* to take would-be purchasers on a journey that leads to greater sex appeal, apparent prosperity and other aspects of an idealized "good life." The risk for the product manufacturer and distributor in this is relatively small; people are willing to take the risk that the purchase of a particular product will make them feel what the manufacturer promises. If it turns out, as it often does, that the product falls short of the mark without doing actual harm, purchasers may turn to a competing product or may just shrug it off because they didn't rationally believe the induced emotion anyhow.

Professional brands generally do not have this luxury. Because they promise work that will be based at some level on direct interpersonal interaction, they cannot typically afford to be "aspirational"; they have to deliver on the promised outcomes and even on the projected emotional connection. Failure to do so can result, particularly in this age of instant online reviews, in immediate damage to reputation and potential loss of income. There are, of course, notable exceptions, such as the famous—and so far demonstrably true—old saw that "nobody ever got fired for hiring McKinsey" when considering a management consulting firm.[3] **Most law firms are not so gamely forgiven if they make a connection—even if only through their brands—and fall short in the delivery.**

## [3.9] 2. Truthfulness and Accuracy

While product brands can be—and often are—inventive constructs, *professional brands should be created from what is actually so.* This is

---

[3] Duff McDonald's *The Firm: The Story of McKinsey and Its Secret Influence on American Business* (2013) details a number of instances in which the firm's delivery did not quite measure up to its reputation, with no apparent downside for the firm.

because the brand presents a context within which attorney-client relationships can be initiated. Any discordance between what is presented as the brand—the stand-in for a likely emotional connection—and what clients experience can result in an unhappy client because people simply do not like it when they are led to expect one thing and instead receive something else. How bad can having a few unhappy clients be? According to a study released by the White House Office of Consumer Affairs, each dissatisfied customer will tell 9 to15 people about his or her experience; 13% will tell more than 20. That produces a pretty strong headwind for a small law practice to struggle against. It gets even worse if you have built up experience working with certain industries because an unhappy past client is very likely to know many of your potential future clients and poison the well before you even get to it.

There is no point in trying to create or maintain a professional brand that is not based on truthfulness and accuracy because you will soon be found out and exposed as, if not a fraud, at least as someone who does not deliver on promises. This will greatly reduce your scope of opportunity. Also, consider this: while clients will be impacted if they come to you expecting one thing and getting another, you will also be impacted. *If you put the wrong thing out as your brand, you will probably attract the wrong clients and they won't be the only ones who end up unhappy.*

### [3.10]  3. A Critical Intersection

It simply does not make sense to ignore the concept of brand as it relates to your practice. While it may seem that you neither have nor need a brand, the reality is that *all professionals have one, whether or not they have actively and strategically shaped it.*

Professional brands begin to take form at the point where image and reputation intersect.

Your brand is being *generated and refined every day as a direct result of your day-to-day practice activities*, regardless of whether you spend a moment thinking about it.

## Table 2: Image Shapers and Reputation Shapers

| Image Shapers | Reputation Shapers |
|---|---|
| How you speak | Your legal track record (especially for litigators) |
| How you dress | Your billing rates |
| The state of your workspace | Your ability to relate well to colleagues, both from your own firm and other firms |
| Market-facing material without legal content:<br>• Business cards<br>• Stationery<br>• Brochure<br>• Website<br>• Professional bios (LinkedIn, etc.) | Peer reviews (Martindale, Chambers, Best Lawyers, etc.) |
| | Reported client experiences, both verbal and written (word of mouth, AVVO, Yelp, etc.) |
| | Market-facing material with legal content (e.g., articles in professional journals) |

Clearly you have more direct control over your image than over your reputation, but you are far from powerless to shape either. Also, keep in mind that a carefully shaped and maintained image will spill over into those aspects of your reputation that have to do with how others experience you.

## [3.11] B. Elements of Personal Brand

In order to take a more active hand in shaping your own brand, you will want to examine some of the underlying elements that influence and form both your image and your reputation. These include the following.

### [3.12] 1. Personality Type

The essential "raw material" of your professional brand is *who you are as a person*. The best insights into this come from outside observation. Assessments can be particularly helpful in "codifying" the various elements that comprise a complex personality and can provide insights into why you might like one type of work or client and be unengaged by or uncomfortable with another.[4]

### [3.13] 2. Values

The things that *drive you in your work and inform every professional interaction* you have are loosely termed values. Note that this is different from the concept of value discussed elsewhere in this book, which is always defined by the client. Here, the term refers to a combination of ideals and principles that are at the heart of why you became—and why you remain—an attorney. Clients should experience your values loudly and clearly when they work with you, but you get to define them.

### [3.14] 3. Style

Brand is about creating an emotional connection, and an emotional connection in the practice of law is about experience, so aesthetics are an important component of the professional brand. Style encompasses *things that can be picked up by the senses.* How you, your space and your materials look, how you sound, how you smell and how you physically interact with others all fit this category.

---

[4] There have been a number of studies that purport to debunk personality type assessments as bad science. Admittedly, no such assessment is going to provide information that is either perfectly accurate or immutable. What they can do, though, is provide focal points and present possibilities in a highly structured manner. It is always up to those who use the assessment to ask fundamental questions, such as "Is this so?" and "If this is so, what does it mean?"

## Table 3: Elements of Personal Brands

| Personality type | Who you are | Profile |
|---|---|---|
| Values | Why you practice law | Principles |
| Style | What the senses can perceive about you | Presentation |
| Goals and Interests | Where you are trying to go | Purpose |
| Approach | How you like to do things | Process |
| Kind of Practice | What type of law you practice—and where you practice it | Preference |

### [3.15] 4. Goals and Interests

Values are your drivers; *goals and interests are what you are driving toward, whether in a purposeful manner or simply whenever you have the time.* They include both professional and personal objectives and can relate to professional milestones you wish to attain, lifestyle aspirations, intellectual pursuits and leisure activities. They are important to your brand—and to your professional identity as a whole—because they are always lurking somewhere in the back of your mind and will inform choices you make every day. They may also provide avenues for you to create deeper relationships with clients who share them.

### [3.16] 5. Approach to Work

Brand is an effort to project an experience, so *how you do your work can be as important to branding as what you do.* You could consider this an extension of style that goes beyond aesthetics and looks at process and procedure.

### [3.17] 6. Kind of Practice

This one is self-evident, but then again, all good marketing efforts start with a firm grasp on the obvious! The purely descriptive is an essential part of a brand and should not be overlooked.

## [3.18] C. Creating Your Own Brand

### [3.19] 1. Start With What's So

A personality assessment, such as the Meyers-Briggs Type Indicator, can tell you a great deal about who you are as a person and "codify" it for you in ways you cannot readily do for yourself. Skill assessments—such as DISC or one of the numerous "strengths" systems—may also provide insights, but are not quite as useful for the purpose of building a personal brand. The ColorQ is a streamlined version of Meyers-Briggs developed specifically with business applications in mind.[5] Under this very elegant system, everyone belongs to a primary group, has a secondary tendency and an extrovert/introvert component. An overview of the primary types appears below.

### [3.20] a. Golds (46% of the population)

Grounded, realistic and accountable, Golds are the backbone of institutions of all kinds—corporate and public. They are society's protectors and administrators who value procedures, respect the chain of command and have finely tuned systems for everything, from raising children to running large divisions. Golds get involved in details and are known for following through and mobilizing others to achieve concrete goals. They are the most effective in making lists, planning in advance and working with what has previously worked in the past.

The best work environment for a Gold is stable and predictable and provides a clear hierarchy and progressively higher levels of management responsibility.

### [3.21] b. Blues (10% of the population)

Theoretical, competitive and always driven to acquire more knowledge and competence, Blues are unequaled when it comes to dealing with complex, theoretical issues and designing new systems. As natural skeptics, their first reaction is to criticize and set their benchmarks against which they measure everyone and everything. They are highly precise in thought and language and future oriented, trusting only logic, not the rules or procedures of the past. Blues are visionary and do best in positions requiring strategic thinking. Then they move on with little interest in maintenance.

---

5   You can take an abbreviated version of the ColorQ assessment for free at www.colorqpersonalities.com/colorq. There is also a link to pay for the full assessment and related coaching.

The best work environment for Blues provides complex problems, continuous learning and the opportunity to create new systems and designs.

### [3.22]   c. Reds (27% of the population)

Action-oriented, spontaneous and focused on "now," Reds need freedom to follow their impulses, which they trust over the judgment of others. Cool headed and ever courageous, they get things done and handle a crisis better than most. Found in careers that provide freedom, action, variety and the unexpected, they bring excitement and a sense of expediency. Work must be fun and the environment collegiate. Reds resist schedules and hierarchies. Long-term planning is a low priority.

The best work environment for Reds provides variety and change with little bureaucracy and few rules and procedures.

### [3.23]   d. Greens (17% of the population)

Empathetic, humanistic and creative, Greens need an environment that is supportive and egalitarian, and that provides the chance to impact the lives of others. Gifted in their understanding of people's motivation, they have an unusual ability to influence and draw the best out of others. They also excel in verbal and written communications and in the ability to position ideas. Greens are enthusiastic spokespersons for the organization or cause of their choice, creating a unique, charismatic quality that sweeps others into their cause

The best work environment for Greens provides them the opportunity to impact society in a meaningful and creative way without too much interpersonal tension.[6]

### [3.24]   2. Draw Conclusions

Review the assessment results carefully to see if you agree with them. If you don't, spend some time mapping your disagreement, point by point. The important thing is to have an organized personality profile that can remind you of what others are likely to experience with you and what is most likely to motivate and repel you.

Once you have that down, the next step is to draw some simple conclusions about how your personality type contributes positively to your work

---

[6]   © Shoya Zichy. Reprinted with permission.

and produces benefits for your clients. In the list below are some possibilities using the ColorQ system.

**Table 4: Personality Type Contribution to Legal Work**

| Gold | • You help your clients avoid costly mistakes.<br>• You create tightly constructed legal strategies and documents. |
|---|---|
| Blue | • You develop legal strategies for complex circumstances.<br>• You protect your clients from the perils that are hidden in the details. |
| Red | • You will pull out all the stops to gain a legal victory for your clients.<br>• You can both readily create and effectively respond to unexpected legal arguments. |
| Green | • You take care of your clients in difficult or trying situations.<br>• You understand the human implications of legal matters. |

Of course, each of these examples reflects what most attorneys think they do most of the time. The key is that you are likely to provide first and foremost those benefits that map to your personality type; the others will follow (in the ColorQ system, the benefits that come with your secondary tendency would come next).

## [3.25] 3. Stay True to Your Values

You could spend a great deal of time thinking about your values; you are, after all, likely a relatively complex human being. One way to gain insight into them for branding purposes is to play a fast word game. Use Appendix A at the end of this chapter to describe:

• Who you are in your work.

• What clients experience when they work with you.

- What you do.

- How you do it.

In a full-scale branding exercise, you might then create a short contextual statement around the words that appeal to you most strongly. Remember, branding is an effort to create an emotional connection; for your brand to be effective, it should appeal to your emotions, too.

### [3.26]  4. Leverage Your Style

Like values, style can be tough to nail down. Another word game using continuums of paired words can provide insights quickly. Use Appendix B to map your style in terms of

- persona;

- attitude;

- commitment;

- distance;

- language; and

- visuals.

If you took a personality inventory, this may feel somewhat similar, but it has different and more direct applications.

### [3.27]  5. Focus on Your Goals

A great deal has been published on setting and accomplishing goals. For branding, you need only capture the big picture. This can be streamlined to two components.

- *Mission:* Why you're in business (aside from making money).

- *Vision:* What happens in the world (or at least your clients' world) if you are successful in your mission.

Use Appendix C to develop mission and vision statements that fit you and your practice. Note that these are not intended to be shared with clients and prospects; they are the marketing equivalent of "let me tell you my philosophy" (snooze). But they are intended to help you focus any market-facing conversation you have, orally or in writing.

Another consideration is how you want your practice—and your life—to shape up over the next five years or so.[7] You can ask yourself such questions as

- What will your personal work life look like five years from now?
- Who will your colleagues be?
- Who will support you in your work?
- What will your firm be known for five years from now?
- Who will your clients be?
- What is your exit strategy?
- What are the biggest obstacles you face in making all of this happen?

Again, this is not intended to be market-facing; it's simply a fairly powerful tool to help you keep focused.

### [3.28]  6. Acknowledge Your Interests

Your personal and professional interests are also integral components of your brand. Professional interests can help direct you towards the type of client engagements you should take and away from those you might do well to avoid. Personal interests—including leisure and family activities, as well as civic and charitable organizations—can add texture to conversations with clients and prospects; shared interests tend to lead to deeper emotional connections and stronger relationships. It is good practice to keep a list of your top five interests in both categories and revisit it on an annual or semi-annual basis.

### [3.29]  7. Understand Your Approach

Approach is paradoxical: on the one hand, it can be difficult to capture coherently how a professional goes about doing something, while on the other it can appear perfectly obvious that Step B follows Step A. To gain

---

7   This approach is adapted from Dan Schaefer, PhD and is explored in greater depth and from a somewhat different angle, in his book *Click! The Competitive Edge for Sports, Entertainment, and Business* (2012).

some insight into *how* you approach your work, go back to your style continuum and convert the adjectives to adverbs and also look again at the adverbs column of your values exercise. This will shed some light on strengths and potential weaknesses, but you may already have a clear understanding of where you consistently measure up and where you tend to fall down.

The other side of this process is inventorying things that may seem instinctive or evident to you. Chart your approach, step by step, to various types of matters that you typically handle. Include rough time frames (e.g., 45–55 days after the retainer is received). These can become guides for helping you manage client expectations, which is essential to a brand that works.

If you are comfortable with it, you might even explain to clients what you do well and what you don't. Most people understand foibles and shortcomings as long as they are not surprised. Being direct about this may also help you create deeper personal and emotional connections with clients and prospects.

## [3.30]  8. Type of Practice

In considering how to incorporate your type of practice into your branding, there are a few things to bear in mind:

- If you say you do everything, you might as well say you do nothing. Be specific about what you do.

- Even generalists have preferences and areas in which they excel—and areas in which they do not.

- When listing services, either verbally or in writing, lead with those that you do best and enjoy most. Consider omitting those that are a drain or of low value.

- Resist the temptation to include things that you *could* do, but don't really do. For example, most trusts and estates lawyers should not claim to do elder law, as it involves some very specific skills and activities and often a very different temperament.

The type of practice you have and the services you offer are best viewed as features; while you need to know what they are, your brand and the conversations that surround it will be more powerful if you can address benefits or, better yet, the value clients receive.

## [3.31] III. PRACTICE PRESENTATION

In the previous sections, you have assembled a number of elements that, taken together, comprise your brand—your core effort to capture and project what it is really like for your best clients to work with you. Now it's time to pull it all together and use it.

### [3.32] A. Verbal Brand

Your verbal brand is reflected in every communication you make, oral and written, to clients, prospects, colleagues and potential referral sources, in marketing materials and in matter-related communications. So each communication should, to the extent appropriate for that communication,

- reflect who you are as a person and as an attorney;

- amplify your mission, vision and values statements;

- reveal your interests and passions; and

- manage expectations about how you work.

You may want to take the various pieces you have created in this chapter and reassemble them in a somewhat different order:

**Firm name/logo**

**Headshot**

**Mission statement**

**Vision statement**

**Values & context**

**Personality type & applications**

**Style notes**

Have it formatted attractively and put it somewhere visible and accessible to you. Put your firm name and logo (if you have one) or distinctive typeface at the top of the sheet. Add your headshot. This will serve as a sort of crib sheet and, if you make a habit of looking at it every day, will reinforce your branding in your daily communications. For further subconscious reinforcement, you can also turn this document into a word cloud, which pulls out key words and emphasizes the ones that are most important. Visit www.wordle.net and paste in the text. As with everything in this chapter, pick what appeals to you and disregard the rest.

## [3.33] B. Visual Brand

Your visual brand consists of a number of elements that communicate non-verbally, including how your written communications look, how you look and how your office looks. Here are eight tips for building and maintaining a strong visual brand as a small or solo law firm:

1. Make sure that written communications look consistent. Pick no more than two typefaces (one sans serif for headings and one serif for text) and use them consistently, even in email.

2. Select a palette of at least two, but not more than three, colors for your firm. Use them where appropriate in your written communications, on your stationery and on your business cards.[8]

3. Decorate your office attractively and in a way that projects the feelings you would like to encourage in your clients.

4. Develop one distinction in your dress (can be a color, particular item of clothing or type of accessory) and stick to it.

5. Obtain a headshot that you like and use it on LinkedIn and wherever appropriate.

6. Pay attention to small things like stationery and business cards; make sure they are memorable, distinctive and reflect your brand.

7. Search the Internet for some of the words from your value exercise and see what images come up. You can use them or similar images later in your website or brochure to create a more emotional connection. You can even use them as a guide in selecting artwork for your office.

---

[8] Search "color psychology" on the Internet for articles related to how we perceive color and how it can influence our actions. Gregory Ciotti's article *The Psychology of Color in Marketing and Branding* (www.helpscout.net/blog/psychology-of-color) provides a nice overview.

8. Decide what marketing materials you need and have them professionally developed to support your brand. It is better to have no website than a poor or generic one that can reflect badly on you.

## [3.34] C. Evaluate

Take a clear, hard look at yourself and the brand you have created. If there are areas where you feel uncertain or are unhappy with your response, consider getting some assistance. It is relatively easy these days to find a personal style consultant, etiquette advisor, coach or marketing consultant who can help you achieve the results you want efficiently and cost effectively.

# APPENDIX A
## VALUES CAPTURE

*Instructions:* Find words that reflect who you are and what you do. Some tips:

- Work quickly, using a timer if you need it. Three to five minutes per column should do it.

- Take the first words that come to mind; they are usually the truest.

- Adjectives are generally easiest for most people.

- Adverbs and adjectives can be interchangeable, but try not to repeat an idea.

- If you find that one column isn't working for you, go on to the next.

### Table 5: Five Words

| Five Nouns<br>Who You Are in Your Work | Five Adjectives<br>What Clients Experience | Five Verbs<br>What You Do | Five Adverbs<br>How You Do Your Work |
|---|---|---|---|
| Explainer | Meticulous | Counsel | Analytically |
| Strategist | Polished | Advocate | Conservatively |
| Fighter | Practical | Comfort | Creatively |
| Colleague | Dynamic | Resolve | Expansively |
| Protector | Clear | Expedite | Dependably |

**Optional**:

In a full-scale branding exercise, a values word is typically expanded upon to provide more context. You may want to put five of the words that most strongly appeal to you into this kind of framework:

> Practical: The legal solutions we develop are adapted or designed for actual use. Whether compliance-focused or transactional-focused advice, we understand that the client needs a solution that can be used readily on a daily basis to make their businesses more effective.

# APPENDIX B
## STYLE CONTINUUM

*Instructions:* Below are several pairs of words that are generally considered to be at opposite ends of a spectrum.

- Being very honest with yourself, mark where you feel you fit on each scale.

- If you have trouble, imagine what your best client might say and what your worst client might say.

- If the word pairs don't resonate for you, enter your own.

### persona
| | | | | | | |
|---|---|---|---|---|---|---|
| actuality | o | o | o | o | o | potential |
| could | o | o | o | o | o | should |
| offbeat | o | o | o | o | o | staid |
| enthusiastic | o | o | o | o | o | competent |
| _____ | o | o | o | o | o | _____ |
| _____ | o | o | o | o | o | _____ |

### attitude/stance
| | | | | | | |
|---|---|---|---|---|---|---|
| approachable | o | o | o | o | o | arrogant |
| assertive | o | o | o | o | o | defensive |
| fun-loving | o | o | o | o | o | serious |
| earnest | o | o | o | o | o | glib |
| _____ | o | o | o | o | o | _____ |
| _____ | o | o | o | o | o | _____ |

### commitment
| | | | | | | |
|---|---|---|---|---|---|---|
| assured | o | o | o | o | o | acquiescent |
| dedicated | o | o | o | o | o | complacent |
| passionate | o | o | o | o | o | passive |
| expressive | o | o | o | o | o | reserved |
| _____ | o | o | o | o | o | _____ |
| _____ | o | o | o | o | o | _____ |

### distance
| | | | | | | |
|---|---|---|---|---|---|---|
| warm | o | o | o | o | o | cool |
| inviting | o | o | o | o | o | instructive |
| exploratory | o | o | o | o | o | declarative |
| casual | o | o | o | o | o | formal |
| _____ | o | o | o | o | o | _____ |
| _____ | o | o | o | o | o | _____ |

| language | | | | | | |
|---|---|---|---|---|---|---|
| revealing | ○ | ○ | ○ | ○ | ○ | concealing |
| spontaneous | ○ | ○ | ○ | ○ | ○ | formulated |
| powerful | ○ | ○ | ○ | ○ | ○ | pop |
| straightforward | ○ | ○ | ○ | ○ | ○ | sophisticated |
| _____ | ○ | ○ | ○ | ○ | ○ | _____ |
| _____ | ○ | ○ | ○ | ○ | ○ | _____ |

| visuals | | | | | | |
|---|---|---|---|---|---|---|
| sporty | ○ | ○ | ○ | ○ | ○ | starched |
| off-the-rack | ○ | ○ | ○ | ○ | ○ | bespoke |
| contemporary | ○ | ○ | ○ | ○ | ○ | classic |
| quirky | ○ | ○ | ○ | ○ | ○ | consistent |
| blue | ○ | ○ | ○ | ○ | ○ | red |
| roman | ○ | ○ | ○ | ○ | ○ | italics |
| _____ | ○ | ○ | ○ | ○ | ○ | _____ |
| _____ | ○ | ○ | ○ | ○ | ○ | _____ |

# APPENDIX C
# MISSION AND VISION

*Instructions:* Read the explanations and examples below and develop mission and vision statements that feel right for your practice and who you are as an attorney. You may find it helpful to refer to the values words, style continuum and applied personality inventory for guidance.

**Mission Statement**

The mission statement helps you stay focused on the real reason you are in business, aside from making money.

*Examples:*

- We help health care providers, not-for-profits and other organizations manage their legal risk and take advantage of business opportunities while achieving balance between their operational needs and compliance demands.

- We position our clients for long-term success as defined by them. We do this by helping them delineate their goals, protect their interests, seize opportunities and anticipate questions and events. Financially, it is always our objective to return to the client more value than the amounts it invests in our professional fees.

*Your mission statement:*

I/We

[**do what**]

[**for whom**]

by

[**doing what in what way**]

**Vision Statement**

The vision statement is a commitment to making a change in your clients' worlds.

*Examples:*

- Our work helps our clients effectively operate their businesses as quality, compliant organizations so they can achieve lasting financial success.

- Working with us, our clients find that they are smarter, more confident, function more efficiently and possess a better grasp of the whole picture than they would otherwise have. Our clients typically find that they are better and more efficient at what they do directly as a result of having worked with us.

*Your vision statement:*

Working with us/Our

work/Through our collaboration

our clients

**[do/experience]**

**[what]**

**[with what impact]**

**CHAPTER FOUR**

# CLIENT RELATIONSHIPS: RESEARCH AND COMMUNICATION TECHNIQUES

Carol Schiro Greenwald, Ph.D.

# CLIENT RELATIONSHIPS § 4.0

## [4.0] I. INTRODUCTION

Clients keep attorneys in business. Good clients with interesting issues can enhance an attorney's feelings of professional satisfaction. Active clients with multiple needs add to a firm's bottom line. So it would seem that to be successful and satisfied, attorneys need burnished client service skills.

Often attorneys assume they are good deliverers of client service because clients stay with them. They fail to identify and use the basic service enhancements that can make the difference between working with satisfied clients who stay until something better comes along, and the more preferable loyal clients who want to give you more business.

In this chapter we will discuss ways to create extraordinary client service. Topics include client service concepts, client-focused research, personal communication styles and specific client service initiatives.

## [4.1] II. CLIENTS ARE IN CHARGE

Everyone tunes in to their own "radio station:" WIIFM—What's In It For Me. Clients are no exception. Today clients are loud and clear about their interest in

- focusing on results;

- working with proactive lawyers; and

- getting more value for less money.

Meeting these demands is grounded in the relationship between individual attorneys and individual clients.

Building strong client relationships should be an attorney's most basic business development activity. Contacts move from prospect to client as a sense of personal connection and trust grows—a chemistry that begins during the buying cycle. A strong client service ethic and an awareness of how each client wants to be treated create rapport. Communication with clients sets their expectations and delineates the boundaries as to who does what during the matter resolution process.

Attorneys' suggestions concerning ways to anticipate and manage risk or take advantage of opportunities deepen and expand the attorney-client trust connection. Exceeding clients' service standards leads to more work, creating a depth and breadth of service that can protect an attorney from the "poaching" efforts of others. And of course, practice growth should go to increase the financial bottom line.

## [4.2] III. CLIENT SERVICE

Google provides 19.6 million responses to a query for "definition of client service." That said, most share some common themes:

- Keep clients happy.

- Provide value over and above expected routine service levels.

- Communicate effectively so that there are no surprises—including the cost for service.

- Manage the relationship to help clients understand, keep track of and buy into the plan to resolve the problem at hand.

- Treat clients with respect and, whenever possible, speak with them as equals as you work together to resolve their problem.

- Anticipate as well as meet client needs.

- Define needs broadly to include referrals to other service providers or pro-active advice on issues unrelated to the matter at hand.

- Understand clients' definitions of time both in terms of personal response-time and moving the process along on time.

Notice that on this list there is no mention of legal acumen or competency; usually this is assumed. On one hand it is a hard concept for non-lawyers to measure. On the other hand, service itself can be evaluated against the client's own service ethic, and easily compared to other service providers from car mechanics to Amazon or Zappos' online services. And clients do compare. Let's discuss the most effective ways to meet this challenge.

# [4.3] IV. 360-DEGREE UNDERSTANDING OF CLIENTS

Asked what the most important factors influencing selection of outside counsel are, chief legal officers rated "demonstrated understanding of your business/industry" as most important.[1] Attorneys often assume this means knowledge related to the matter at hand or derived from an accumulation of matters for one client. In the 21st century, it means much more than that. It means: know me as I am in my world with my issues, my concerns, my predilections and my peccadillos.

"Actors and factors determine the choices of your customers."[2] This pithy sentence sums up the basic requirement underlying superior client service: an understanding of each client as an actor in his or her own world. This understanding begins with acceptance of the truism that clients—businesses or individuals—operate in a context that influences all their actions. They have competitors, partners, products, services, markets, customers, organizational culture or family dynamics. To really know a client is to understand this confluence of internal and external forces that impact their choices on a regular basis.

Attorneys need to be familiar with those relationship webs that influence clients' motivations and their definitions of need, appropriate processes and results. Understanding all this allows an attorney to create personalized service initiatives that meet each client's needs and expectations.

This endeavor can be time-consuming. To keep it effective and manageable the effort should focus on "best" clients. Typically best clients are easy to work with, have a similar approach to life and work, need help with interesting issues and pay their bills on time. Best clients are a personal choice that reflects an attorney's personality, goals and skill sets as well as an assessment as to how these clients will help the practice grow.

# [4.4] V. RESEARCH: WHAT, HOW

The goal of client-centric research is to create a picture of the total client including:

---

1 Altman Weil Flash Survey, "Special Excerpt: Why Clients Choose Law Firms," Chief Legal Officer Survey, 2012.

2 http://liveworkstudio.com/topics/know-the-actors-and-factors-in-your-customers-world.

- Client structure: family tree for individuals, organizational structure for businesses.

- Client relationships: within the family and with important outside influencers or for businesses, the interpersonal relationships of the people who work for and with the client.

- Trends: economic, political, social and legal trends that relate to clients' products, services, competition, rules and regulations for businesses, or an individual's sources of income, geographic reach, applicable laws.

- Service initiatives: The problems and opportunities the client encounters or might encounter that call for legal advice or action.

Armed with this intelligence, attorneys can offer the kind of forward-thinking counsel that shows clients their depth of understanding about them and their world. Looking at clients' worlds with an attorney's eye unearths latent customer needs which, in turn, lead to new business opportunities.

One way to control the scope of research is to think about content in terms of the 5 Cs:

- *Company*—the client entity, either business or family.

- *Clients*—the customers of your business client or the people and entities impacted by the individual's situation.

- *Collaborators*—business clients' partners including influencers, suppliers, media channels, etc. or extended family relationships for individuals.

- *Competitors*—business clients' competitors, individuals' opposition [e.g., other spouse, insurance company, employer], your own competitors vis-à-vis the client.

- *Context*—The trends, laws, rules and regulations that will impact the future of your client.

There are many online resources which you can use to obtain this kind of information, such as

- Google Alerts and other online tools that push information to you as it appears online;

- trade and professional association publications, newsletters, blogs;

- online affinity groups, especially within LinkedIn; and

- issue-oriented white papers.

You can also use paid research databases either through the firm or the public library. You should plan on updating the information and culling out old data on a regular basis. Establish a routine and then calendar it. See the Client Characteristics Worksheet in the Appendix for more suggestions.

## [4.5] VI. HOW TO USE THE DATA

Now that you have accumulated piles of data, how do you use it to improve client service and develop deeper relationships with these clients? The strategic next step involves laying this data out against your firm's capabilities. Using a SWOT (Strengths/Weaknesses/Opportunities/Threats) analysis, identify the client's strengths, weaknesses, opportunities and threats, and then add on the same information about your firm vis-à-vis this client. The resulting matrix should highlight areas of strength to pursue immediately, opportunities to build on, weaknesses to remediate and threats to avoid. This information becomes the basis for your action plan vis-à-vis the client.

## [4.6] VII. CLIENT-CENTRIC COMMUNICATION

Communication is the primary means for creating and maintaining a personal trust bond with a client. In the legal profession, the primary product is this intangible relationship between client and attorney. It is created through the interactions of all parties. Attorneys use client communications to educate clients as to the available options, explain processes and set time lines. This content helps to set client expectations as to expected outcomes. As attorney and client work together, the way in which you treat your client and your ability to explain legal options in language the client understands will either construct a strong relationship or destroy one.

Communication involves speech or writing, but also in one-on-one situations it includes vocabulary, tone, attitude and body language. Clients parse these behaviors looking for cues as to their standing with their attorney, the importance of their matter, and a sense of how the case is moving along.

*Vocabulary:* For example, vocabulary includes both commonly used words and jargon words (words specific to an industry, trade or profession). For example:

### Table 1: Attorney Jargon

| Attorney Jargon | Attorney Means This | Client Thinks It Means |
|---|---|---|
| Matter | A case, lawsuit, legal proceeding—a way to identify the project they are working on | A situation of consequence (i.e., "Something is the matter.") |
| Tort | A wrong, an injury, a wrongful act | A cake |
| Motion | An application made to a court or judge for an order or ruling | Movement; a bodily movement or change or posture, gesture |

Whenever people hear words that are unfamiliar they tend to lose their focus on the conversational thread. Jargon creates a psychological separation between client and attorney which may negatively impact the client's perception of the attorney's service. Clients want conversation filled with everyday action words focused on practical ways to reach a solution to their problem.

*Tone:* Often attorneys seem arrogant to non-attorneys. This perception, like jargon, can erode the essential trust that makes the relationship work. Clients use tone as a way to gauge attitude. Tone becomes a way to show respect for the client's situation and empathy for those involved. By validating the client's feelings of unease, the attorney allies himself psychologically with the client's situation. Emotion is a key lubricant in the attorney-client relationship, paving the way to commitment, trust, loyalty, and continued business.

Clients are usually vulnerable when they hire attorneys. Even the most seasoned general counsel can be disconcerted when asking another lawyer to accomplish something of major importance. It means relinquishing control. Non-lawyers are even more off guard because they don't understand the rules and mores of the judicial system.

Clients want their attorney to smooth over their worries, absorb the hassles and teach them not to be afraid. The communicator-attorney will show empathy, concern and an awareness of the sensitivities, emotions and politics that complicate the client's situation—whether it be a general counsel enmeshed in a bankruptcy or a parent fighting for custody in a divorce.

*Attitude:* Sometimes it's just a matter of attitude. If clients' calls are viewed as an opportunity to cement a relationship, then the attorney who smiles as he says "hello" projects friendliness and accessibility across the phone line and the client feels welcomed. In a similar vein, a controlled and positive response to client complaints and misunderstandings can defuse a potentially destructive situation and guide the client toward an amicable resolution. This requires use of active listening skills which involves summarizing the client's comments, thereby assuring that both of you are talking about the same thing. Active listening is also a validation technique. It says, "I hear you," even if the conversational tone is argumentative.

*Body language:* People lie, bodies don't. An attorney leaning back with legs crossed and hands fiddling idly with a pen suggests a disconnect from the client. Contrast that with an attorney who walks out from behind her desk and sits in a casual setting across from the client. As with tone, clients looking for relationship cues unconsciously register these signals. Similarly, people see messy offices and paper piles as signs that the attorney is disorganized and sloppy. Meeting rooms with leftover papers from the previous meeting mock the notion of client confidentiality.

Effective communication is the sum of small actions and attitudes. Clients sniff out fake behavior, so each attorney has to find a personal blend that comfortably fits his or her style.

## [4.7] VIII. ESTABLISHING COMMUNICATION PROTOCOLS

Trust builds through the small daily activities and office procedures that demonstrate each attorney's unique approach to client service. It can also be eroded by the simplest form of miscommunication—responsiveness. How long should it take to return a phone call? Answer an email? Review a document? Complete a court proceeding? Clients' perceptions of acceptable time spans are usually much shorter than attorneys'. Remember clients are vulnerable, nervous, worried and looking for reassurance. When an attorney, stuck in court all day, fails to return a call within the client's anticipated time frame an entire relationship can fall apart if the client interprets "the delay" as a sign of disinterest or bad news.

One way to immediately set up the connection as one of equals is to discuss and document communication preferences. Does your client want you to use the office number or the mobile phone? Does he or she prefer in-person meetings to emails? Does the client want continuous involvement in decisions about the case, or does he or she allow the attorney to resolve the matter within broad guidelines that they set together? A good time to have this discussion is during the initial client meeting when you discuss the case, set out your office procedures and generally establish the working framework.

Ask:

- How would you like to be contacted: via office number, direct line, home phone, mobile phone, email, fax, mail?

- Do you prefer to talk or text?

- What is your preferred time of day to receive communications?

- How important is it that we be in regular contact even if nothing new has happened?

- For meetings, do you prefer in-person meetings, video conferences, Skype, or phone conference calls?

Just as validating a client's feelings doesn't mean you agree with them, so, too, asking about communication preferences doesn't mean that you always will be able to abide by their preferences. Obviously, if you are in court you can't make or take a call. However, by asking these questions you are communicating your interest in a collegial relationship of equals in which each person plays his or her assigned role—the attorney as the legal expert in charge of execution of the client's wishes; the client as the final decision-maker regarding an acceptable resolution of the case.

Deal with the issue of promptness. Clients know that their attorney works on multiple matters simultaneously, so a failure to respond within their definition of promptness is often seen as a sign that their matter is less important to the attorney. To others, slow responses suggest that the attorney has forgotten it is the client's time and money at stake. When you deal with this issue, begin by asking the clients how they handle response time in their own business. Then explain how you integrate call-backs into your work schedule. Memorialize your decisions about communication patterns in an agreement that sets out their preferences and your pattern for returning calls and responding to emails.

Attorneys should also introduce clients to their whole team from office receptionist to all those working on their matters and give them a call list directory with everyone's direct dial number and email address and identifying whom to call depending on the nature of the request. Make sure they meet whomever will take their calls in your absence so that they immediately associate a face with the name. This reinforces the communal feeling and encourages the client to feel part of the team, which in turn, is a precondition for extending your own trust relationship to those who work with you.

Initiating a communications ground rules discussion and setting communication guidelines positions an attorney as a reliable communicator who wants to accommodate his service posture to meet the work habits and preferences of his client.

Communication rule-setting should extend beyond clients to colleagues and others in your business network. Attorneys who work together regularly can set common communication ground rules. Solo practitioners who use an answering service can tell them to let callers know when they will be available. Solos can also put a message on their phones that explains when they will pick up these messages and when they will return the calls. The purpose in all these situations is the same: to use rules to smooth the edges of interpersonal relationships by eliminating uncertainties.

## [4.8]  IX.  RESEARCH-INFORMED COMMUNICATION

This brings us full circle to the role of research in communication. A key part of effective communication involves anticipating and communicating pro-active counsel. This is a mindset, an intellectual exercise and a timing issue. Awareness is a mindset; knowledge of their goals and the context in which they operate is an intellectual exercise and when to combine the two is a timing issue. Understanding the client's objectives and world view allows you to anticipate obstacles. Suggesting alternatives while there is still time to respond positions you as a valued advisor working for and with your client.

Use your 360-degree knowledge of the client to introduce him or her to colleagues you anticipate will be useful at a future date. This takes the "sale" feeling out of introductions because the client has a chance to know and evaluate them on personal terms before they need to work together. It builds on the truism that trust precedes buying decisions.

All the aspects of 360-degree research-informed, client-centric communication reinforce each other. As you use this expanded concept of communication with your clients, you will create deeper and broader relationships that morph from individual matters to sustaining relationships.

# APPENDIX
## CLIENT CHARACTERISTICS WORKSHEET

| Corporate Client Characteristics | NAME OF CLIENT | Individual Client Characteristics | NAME OF CLIENT |
|---|---|---|---|
| **The Basics** | | **The Basics** | |
| Their website | | Their website | |
| Legal form | | Gender | |
| Geographic reach | | Geographic reach | |
| Headquarters location | | Where They Live | |
| Number of years in biz | | Age | |
| Primary product(s)[a] | | Religion or race (if relevant) | |
| NAIC / SIC official industry classification codes | | NAIC / SIC official industry classification codes | |
| Primary service(s) | | Occupation / client's title | |
| Major markets for products/services: and geographic reach | | Major markets for employers' products/services and demographics | |
| Revenues for last fiscal year | | Financial status | |
| Ownership arrangements | | Marital status | |
| Number of employees | | Children: gender/ages Exes | |
| Growth cycle stage | | Socio-economic level | |
| **Industry [SIC/NAIC]** | | **Demographic cohort** | |
| Industry trends | | Demographic trends | |
| Most important trends for client | | Most important trends for client | |
| Major trade & professional associations/groups to follow | | Major trade & professional associations/groups to follow | |

| | | | |
|---|---|---|---|
| Relevant federal/state/local laws | | Relevant federal/state/local laws | |
| Relevant government actions | | Relevant government actions | |
| New legislation to track | | New legislation to track | |
| **Relationship information** | | **Relationship information** | |
| Key characteristics of the culture | | Family dynamics and/or family business dynamics | |
| Referral source of the client | | Referral source of the client | |
| Key decision-makers you know | | Key decision-makers you know | |
| Key decision-makers you need to meet | | Key decision-makers you need to meet | |
| Who else in the firm knows whom? | | Who else in the firm knows the family/family business? | |
| How strong is your relationship with the client? | | How strong is your relationship with the client? | |
| Current rumors or hearsay about them that can affect working relationships | | Current rumors or hearsay about them that can affect working relationships | |
| **Client's sources of information about the business** | | **Client's sources of information about the problem** | |
| Online | | Online | |
| Print | | Print | |
| Associations / groups | | Associations / groups | |

a. Use the general product line name and then the NAIC/SIC classification, which is more precise. Use this website to translate product names into NAICS/SICS: www.naics.com/search.htm.

# SAMPLE CLIENT-FOCUSED SERVICE POSTURE IMPLEMENTATION AGREEMENT

**Client-Focused Communication Implementation Steps for an Individual Attorney in a Matrimonial Practice**

**Assumptions**

- Clients are in control: they hire you, can fire you and are required by the Model Rules to be involved in all major decisions affecting the matter.

- Clients should be treated as colleagues and encouraged to participate in the execution of their matter.

- Clients are "always right," even when from a logical, legal viewpoint they are wrong.

- Client participation and buy-in is managed most effectively by setting and reinforcing expectations.

**Beginning of Relationship Communications: Initial Matter Meeting**

(Come out from behind desk and sit across from client in armchairs, offer something to drink, make them comfortable.)

- Learn about client's needs and the players in their drama. Counsel them to understand the habits that led to the situation they are in, so that going forward history doesn't automatically repeat itself.

- Lay out their options—explain how the legal system works in terms of constraints and opportunities.

- Explain the concept of time in the legal process and why delays occur.

- Explain your belief in divorce as a stepping stone, not an ending, your rationale for a pragmatic, minimal emotion strategy.

- Explain how you work—set expectations, re: availability, responsiveness, etc.

  Go through communication preferences checklist.

  Be clear that you want and expect their participation in all decisions.

Explain how process transparency will work.

Understand the level of their need for hand-holding.

- Send initial meeting summary with representation agreement.

    De-legalize documents such as representation agreement.

    Redraft them to put the client situation first followed by client obligations.

**Thank-yous**

- Send an email "thank you" to the client once you receive the retainer check.

- Send a handwritten thank-you note to the person who referred the client to you.

**During engagement**

- Set agree-upon call times.

    If client needs hand-holding, check in once a week even if no new activity has occurred to assess their "emotional temperature."

    It is easier to preempt than to pacify emotional responses.

- To continue expectation management: Schedule a short call with client each time a document arrives in order to explain the document and its impact on their divorce process.

    By managing their expectations you set the stage to lower their emotional responses.

    The call also ensures that their expectations remain in sync with yours.

**At the end of the engagement**

- In the final bill include a client satisfaction survey.

- Follow-up: "How are you doing?" calls to see how you can continue to assist them.

- Offer to introduce them to other professionals they now want to meet.

- Schedule these calls for six weeks and three months after client gets divorce decree.

- Send anniversary card on first anniversary of the decree date asking how they are doing and if there is anything you can do to help them.

# CHAPTER FIVE

# NETWORKING: ART AND SCIENCE

Nancy B. Schess

## [5.0] I. INTRODUCTION

Think about those people in your world who are true connectors. We all know them. They are the first in the room to go through their contacts, and even more important, when they offer to help, they actually do. With good reason, people are attracted to "connectors." Did you ever consider what characteristics "connectors" have in common?

Connectors have mastered the skill of what has come to be called "networking." Networking is undoubtedly both art and science. The art is around building relationships. Like so many things both in and out of the professional world, networking success stems from the strength of our relationships. Said another way, the secret to good networking is knowing how to start and build relationships in a way that expands your resources and referral sources. But, with that admittedly amorphous statement, there is actually a formula for the building blocks of this process. That formula comprises the science of networking and specifically, the nuts and bolts of processes that nurture relationships.

This chapter will focus on the science of networking and unpack some of the critical "nuts and bolts" which are the cornerstone of in-person networking success.[1] That said, this chapter is intended to offer some observations of successful connectors. Networking is a personal process that everyone approaches with their own style. While there are steps to the process, they can and should be adapted to fit your personal approach.

## [5.1] II. WHAT IS NETWORKING AND HOW DO WE DO IT?

There was a time that "networking" had something to do with connecting computers together. While in some circles it still does, when talking about growing your practice networking has a different definition. Merriam Webster's dictionary defines networking as "the exchange of information or services among individuals, groups, or institutions; specifically: the cultivation of productive relationships for employment or business."[2] Sometimes simple really is best.

---

[1] In addition to in-person networking, online opportunities to connect with other professionals and service providers abound. While this chapter focuses on in-person networking, consider how to complement your in-person activities with your online ones.

[2] Networking, Merriam-Webster Online Dictionary, www.merriam-webster.com/dictionary/networking.

Starting from the premise that people do business with others that they like, trust and respect, building strong relationships is critical for growing your practice on every level. Those relationships become resources for help in so many areas—practice management advice, resources to help clients, sources of new business and more.

Think of it this way: as service providers, the more value you can bring to your clients, the more important you become to them. As a trusted advisor, you strive to become the professional your clients turn to as their problem solver. This scenario can only be good for growing your practice. The broader and deeper your network, the more help you can offer. Similarly, the broader and deeper your network, the stronger your sources for new business.

Against this background, networking is *not* attending as many events as you can, gathering a record number of business cards and throwing them all in a file in your office. Networking is not even compiling all of those business cards in an organized fashion to keep track of the many people you have met along the way. Networking *is* taking the handful of business cards from the event you attended last night, thinking about you how might help those people and following up promptly to try to connect. Now we are talking about a process that builds a relationship.

The best connectors start with the question "How can I help you?" and not "What can you do for me?" This is true regardless of whether you ever ask either question out loud. In short, the strongest networks are grounded in relationships built on helping other people. The rest follows because "what goes around comes around."

Make sure, however, to have reasonable expectations of the process. Networking is an investment that starts with planting seeds and is not about immediate gratification. When you attend an event, expect to meet new people who, once you get to know them, might be helpful to you and your practice. Do not expect to meet someone who will introduce you to your biggest client the very next morning. Otherwise, you will most likely be disappointed.

## [5.2] III. CHOOSING YOUR NETWORKING VENUE

Deciding where to spend your networking time can be overwhelming. There are likely as many networking opportunities and venues available as there are stars in the sky. On any given day, you could attend all sorts of different types of networking events and even multiple venues. Consequently, it is important to choose your networking activities carefully or they could take over and leave little time for the actual practice of law.

Think about the type of venue you are interested in. Do you want to attend a cocktail event? A business seminar? A charity dinner? Are you ready to commit to joining an industry group? These are all networking events in one form or another. In actuality, anything that puts you in an environment to meet new people is a networking event. It may be playing on a sports team or talking to the other parents at the middle school concert. When your networking radar is honed, you truly never know where you may meet someone with whom your practice has synergy.

Think about your own personality and where your comfort zone lies. If you dread walking into a cocktail party, then you might shy away from joining a group that has only these types of meetings. Similarly, if you have a particular focus in your practice, you may consider volunteering time for a non-profit in that space. Volunteering creates an avenue to meet new people, so consider this type of venue.

Consider the size of the event, the time of day and the culture. Are you more comfortable in a large or small setting; breakfast or dinner? Of course, make sure the culture of any group you may consider joining is consistent with your own approach. As discussed above, the best networking is about giving, not taking, and so, by definition, the best networking environments will foster that attitude. Be comfortable that the culture of the venue you are considering is respectful of your needs and expectations as a legal professional.

Pay attention to the time commitment you will need to make. Networking opportunities are diverse and the range of commitment required is equally diverse. For example, you may be attending a one-time cocktail event sponsored by your local chamber of commerce or you may be considering joining the board of that chamber of commerce. If you cannot make the time commitment for the type of venue you are considering, then be honest and move on to the next opportunity.

Include both wide and deep opportunities in your networking agenda. In order to build a strong network, you will need to meet a lot of people. Therefore, constantly expanding your opportunities to shake hands with someone new is important to your networking success. Hence, the wide opportunities. That said, make sure to also look for the opportunities to deepen your relationships since they are the building blocks of networking success.

Overall, don't ignore the "feel good" factor. Wherever you decide to spend your networking time, you are about to make a commitment. Invariably, if you do not enjoy the time you spend, you will likely not continue. By definition, networking fails if you can't devote your time and attention to it. Nonetheless, while finding venues for networking that are comfortable and consistent with your own personality is important, sometimes networking requires pushing outside your "comfort zone." Consider whether it is time to push those limits.

## [5.3]  IV. PREPARATION IS KEY

Would you walk into court unprepared? Would you attend a settlement conference without having thought about the potential parameters of the deal your client is looking for? Of course not. Preparation is critical to the practice of law. It is no less critical to the networking aspect of your practice.

Good preparation is important for three reasons. First, expanding your network productively means meeting people you want to meet. Second, as discussed above, unless you plan your networking time well, the process has the potential to take over your day and leave little time for practicing law. With so many interesting networking opportunities available, the temptation to overdo is real. Good preparation controls that temptation and helps you keep a healthy balance. Third, preparing in advance takes the edge off of that uncomfortable moment when you walk into a room of strangers. While there are certainly some people who enjoy walking into a room of strangers, most people do not. It is amongst the more difficult things that we do in the business world. As explained below, advance preparation helps to give you more control of the situation and a mission to follow.

As lawyers, we are trained in the skill of research. Put that skill set to work for you in your networking efforts. Find out where the people you want to meet spend their time. If you have decided that small business owners in the technology space can help grow your practice, research the industry and figure out where they meet. If you have decided that volunteering for a non-profit will be part of your networking plan, consider which ones are sufficiently aligned with your practice and can expose you to people you want to meet. If you are attending a cocktail event, call ahead and ask if you can see a list of attendees. Apply your research proficiencies and identify a handful of attendees that you might want to meet. Even better in the context of building relationships, have a conversation with the event organizer to find out more about the host organization and see if there is any way for you to help. Establishing the start of a relationship before even walking in the door increases the chance that your new contact is going to be interested in introducing you to others in the room.

Consider your "ice breakers." Some people refer to the art of small talk, but there is nothing small about this process. The art of conversation is critical for networking success. Think about how you can start and maintain a conversation while both learning about this new person you have just met and sharing some information about yourself. That may sound like a tall order, but an ice breaker can help to get that process started.

Your ice breaker may be as simple as a handshake together with, "Hi, my name is _____." You might ask, "How do you know the host?" or "What brings you to this event?" In fact, to test the process, the next time you are at an event walk right over to someone standing alone and try it. You will likely be surprised at how receptive people will be to meeting you.

Ask questions of and about the other person. For example, "How did you get started in your business?" or "Do you live in the city?" Be careful about the question, "What do you do?" It is a perfectly logical ice breaker in many networking environments but runs the risk of turning the entirety of the conversation into a figurative exchange of business cards, which is the opposite of starting a new relationship. If you use this ice breaker make sure to ask follow-up questions so that you really do learn something about the business rather than turning the conversation back to your own practice. In short, think about ice breakers that give your new contact a chance to talk about himself or herself, whether personal or professional.

Good conversation is equally about listening. Always ask open-ended questions and follow-up questions, but don't forget to listen carefully to the answers. First, those answers are clues to how to effectively continue the conversation. Second, and particularly if the questions worked well, you will be learning something about these people, their business, how you can help them and ultimately, how they might help you someday.

Toward that end, always ask, "What can I do to help you?" This might be an introduction to someone who has synergy with your new contact or a restaurant recommendation, but finding ways to help others is the essence of networking. Of course, be cautious about what you might offer and think carefully about whether you can deliver. Being able to deliver is important to your credibility as a strong networker.

Perfect your "elevator speech." When the point in the conversation turns so that you can offer something about your practice, you should be ready to explain with precision.[3] Remember though that your "elevator speech" should always be tailored to the networking environment you are in. A canned response comes off just like a canned response.

Never underestimate the importance of your handshake. It is a significant component of the first impression you will make. Think about the handshake you want to have and practice it. Get comfortable with how you extend your hand when meeting new people.

Think about how you will gather information during the event so that it will be accessible to you afterward with whatever details you may want to remember. As noted above, gathering bundles of business cards is not the objective. Gathering information so that you can have concrete follow-up is most definitely the objective. When you collect business cards, think about where you will keep them and consider writing down anything notable you may have learned. You can take notes directly on the card, on your phone, or in any other way that works. For this purpose, notable means personal and distinguishing information about this new contact which will assist in your follow-up (i.e., her favorite charity; she has three children; she lives in a small town; wants to meet physicians).

Plan your calendar for, at a minimum, the next month. This is an important step for managing your networking efforts so that they are balanced and do not consume either too much, or not enough, of your time. Neither is effective. While you must give critical thought to the types of networking activities you decide to include in your calendar, every so often reach outside the usual suspects. Trying something new keeps networking interesting and you may find great contacts in the most unexpected places. Last, always leave time in your calendar for follow-up.

## [5.4] V. THE ALL IMPORTANT FOLLOW-UP AND FOLLOW-THROUGH

The cocktail party or networking meeting is over. You thoroughly enjoyed the experience and left excited about some of the new people you met. You go back to your office the next day, however, to the call of the big case you are working on. It is so easy to get distracted from the fruit of the previous evening with today's work. At all costs, resist that temptation. Without strong and focused follow-up after meeting someone new,

---

3   See Chapter 2 regarding how to craft your "elevator speech."

the networking opportunities you cultivated will be no more effective than a pleasant memory.

After the networking event is over, strategically plan your follow-up. As a rule of thumb, follow-up should take place quickly, ideally within one business day. In most cases, you will know when you leave the event which contacts you were most excited about having met. Make sure those are at the top of your list for following up. Think about the type of follow-up that makes sense in each situation. For those you estimate to be the best contacts, you might reach out and schedule a cup of coffee or a lunch. For others, you might send a short email saying that you enjoyed meeting them and look forward to continuing the conversation. If there is an article or event of interest following something you spoke about (whether personal or professional), send it along.

Unless there is a clear reason to do so (such as having been specifically asked), refrain from following up with unsolicited information about your practice. This makes your new contact feel like he or she is being "sold." Blanket emails introducing yourself to the entire attendance list are similarly ineffective since they are, by definition, impersonal.

Following through is as important as following up. When you offer to make an introduction, make it and do so quickly. When you offer to circulate your new contact's son's resume, do it. When you suggest that you can help with travel tips for your new contact's next vacation, send them the next day. Following through tells your contact that you take the process seriously and can be relied upon.

Always be respectful of your contacts' time. You know how precious your own time is during the day and your contacts will appreciate that you are conscious of the same for them. For example, clear an introduction with both parties before making it. An email introduction to two of your contacts suggesting that one call the other and have a meeting may sound good at the time. However, if you misjudged the synergy, you may have just created an obligation rather than a good introduction.

Sometimes, even with the best of intentions, it turns out that you cannot deliver what you thought you could. Own that quickly. Explain that you tried but could not deliver and explain why, if you can. This still counts as follow-up and follow-through. While you may not be able to make the connection you thought, your new contact will respect your effort.

Perhaps of most importance, if someone is generous with you and makes an introduction or suggestion, don't forget to express your gratitude. Follow-up and follow-through includes feedback and thank you.

## [5.5] VI. CONCLUSION

In today's environment, networking is a key tool for expanding your practice. Honing your networking formula creates opportunities for productive experiences through which you will undoubtedly meet many interesting people and they will meet you. From those connections, good things will follow.

**CHAPTER SIX**

# CONSULTATIVE SELLING

**Dee A. Schiavelli**

## [6.0] I. WHEN IS SELLING NOT SALES? WHEN IT IS CONSULTATIVE

### [6.1] A. What Is Consultative Selling?

"The consultative sales process is primarily focused on the experience that [your prospect] feels and sees during . . . interactions with you. It's about how you find ways to provide your [prospects] with value and make it all about them. Not your product, your business, your numbers. The consultative sales process is most especially not about you," points out Mark Kilens.[1] Your goal in this process is to advance your relationships and to find prospects with needs that you can solve.

### [6.2] B. How It Differs From Marketing

Marketing is creating demand and recognition through communicating to the public—the many people who may need your services. Consultative selling is selling directly to the individual that currently needs your services. This person has likely heard of or maybe met you through your marketing activities, but it is through the in-person meeting that he or she may decide to retain you.

Marketing tools are used to establish awareness of your capabilities. Non-contact in nature, these tools are designed to promote your practice, establish confidence in your knowledge and experience and give you exposure. Prospects look for lawyers that have the experience they need and your promotion using these tools can achieve that and help build your reputation. Through writing and publishing you demonstrate your knowledge. Through websites you offer your biography, which spells out your experience. Through branding you create the image you want others to see and know.

Traditional (non-contact) marketing tools include:

- advertising;
- articles;
- branding/image;
- brochures;

---

[1] Mark Kilens, *The Consultative Sales Process (6 Principles)*, HubSpot Academy, blog. hubspot.com/customers/bid/172099/The-Consultative-Sales-Process-6-Principles.

- CRM/database;

- directories;

- newsletter/blog;

- public relations;

- website; and

- writing/publishing.

Business development is different from marketing in that it builds relationships and results through in-person contact. It takes time, patience, and persistence. Business development is where networking and socializing come into play, along with social media. Key tenets are that people do business with people they know, like and trust. You can do this through networking at social and business events, participating on boards and contributing to organizations through your knowledge and experience, and building your network and sharing information through social media.

Traditional (in-person) marketing activities include

- events (sporting, conferences, awards, celebrations);

- memberships/organizations (boards, committees);

- meetings (proposals, lunches);

- networking;

- social media; and

- speeches.

Business development helps identify and target prospective clients and establishes awareness of you or your firm's capabilities to decision makers. Social media is an extension of networking. It helps lawyers build on existing relationships, communicate often, share information, develop new relationships and establish themselves as knowledgeable and expert in their field. Using these tools leads to consultative selling opportunities.

## [6.3] C. Process and Techniques

Consultative selling in professional services such as law is not a quick sell. It begins with a relationship built on knowledge, experience and, ultimately, trust. Some lawyers eager to bring in new clients try to close sales almost immediately upon meeting someone new. That is because they have had little to no training in being a consultant, but often have read books about sales that don't necessarily apply to selling legal services. "With consultative selling the [prospect's] needs come first," says Linda Richardson, Founder and Executive Chair of Richardson Sales Training.[2] Lawyers have to identify those needs through probing questions and thorough research that lead to understanding. Richardson defines the consultative selling process as different from sales. Consultants

- ask more questions;

- provide customized vs. generic solutions;

- are more interactive; and

- provide insights to their prospects' businesses.

## [6.4] II. HOW TO SELL

### [6.5] A. Stop Pitching

To begin to learn how to sell, stop "pitching" your services until you know the prospect's personal or business needs. Lawyers tend to focus on their services, not on the needs of the prospect. An intellectual property lawyer might say, *"We are intellectual property lawyers and work with start-up clients as well as established businesses."* This does not tell the prospect how the lawyer can help him in his business. Often this is because lawyers clearly understand their practice and what they do, but have not thought through how they serve the needs of the prospect from the prospect's perspective. Lawyers need to communicate a benefit. What they might say to a small software startup is, *"We recently worked with a small startup software company, helping them to patent and trademark their intellectual property and helped the company grow through licensing to become a major force within two years."* This speaks directly to the prospect's needs. A family lawyer might say, *"I recommend my clients rewrite their will once a child is born. Too many people wait and then for-*

---

[2] *Defining Consultative Selling*, Richardson Company, www.richardson.com/Who-We-Are/Thought-Leader.

*get to do it.*" A young family expecting their first child has a lot on their mind and is not likely thinking about this type of protection for the new baby.

As soon as possible, demonstrate that you can meet prospects' expectation by understanding their issues. To do this, lawyers should ask questions about the prospects' business or current issues affecting them. If you have just met, your conversation needs to be a learning experience about them (focus your questions on them and their business, listen and confirm understanding). Your goal at this moment is to start a relationship that you can build on.

If you planned the meeting in advance, you want to learn all you can about their business, their industry and their competition before you meet. Read their website, LinkedIn profile and annual reports; search for news items on both the company and the industry. Based on your advanced knowledge you will be able to ask tailored questions and communicate that you understand something about their business. Once you have done your research, you will already know how you can most likely help them with their legal needs and be able to express this. This positions you as a consultant with a law degree.

## [6.6] B. Understanding What Clients Want

Not until recently did lawyers need to "ask for the business." The dreaded "sales" word, initially ignored by lawyers as unprofessional, finally reached legal services. This led to collaborating with clients to understand their needs. In addition to obvious business needs and concerns, communication and behavior needs outlined in the Association of Corporate Counsel (ACC) Index, there are underlying needs which may not be verbalized but can be summed up. Clients want to

- make money;

- save money;

- look good to their boss; and

- sleep well at night.

If your practice fits their legal needs, be sure to include through your language how you will help meet these underlying needs.

## [6.7] C. Meeting Expectations (ACC)

Lawyers and clients saw service from different perspectives for many years. Lawyers focused more on the features of their practice—what they did, not how they did it. What clients valued was not clear to lawyers until the Association of Corporate Counsel (ACC) came out with their Value Index in 2009. This spelled out what corporate counsel wanted from their lawyers, and it has become the standard. Prior to the ACC Index, most lawyers felt their legal education and experience to be the most valuable need of prospects. Although quite important, the ACC Index identifies other things considered valuable, such as understanding objectives, communication, predictable costs, etc. A well-educated lawyer with appropriate experience is expected—it is what gets you in the door. Meeting the ACC Index challenge will help you get the business.

The American Corporate Counsel (ACC) Value Index judges lawyers on

- understanding objectives/expectations;
- legal expertise;
- efficiency/process management;
- responsiveness/communication;
- predictable cost/budgeting skills; and
- results delivered/execution.

It is considered an instrument to help shape the thinking and dialog between firms and in-house counsel about what constitutes "good value" in legal services. ACC members can search the Value Index by firm name, matter type or office location.

## [6.8] III. NEXT STEPS

### [6.9] A. Self-Evaluation

To evaluate how you approach a prospective client, conduct the self-assessment found in the Appendix to this chapter. Determine where your strengths are in the consultative selling assessment and what you need to do to gain experience in areas where you are inexperienced or lack confidence. In any areas where you feel you need to learn more or to gain more visibility, identify how to go about it. This may be something your firm offers associates, your Bar Association offers in CLE, or your marketing department can help you with. In addition, there are many seminars, workshops, webinars, blogs and books dedicated to legal marketing. Seeking an experienced marketing consultant who understands the legal industry is another option. Because they are familiar with the legal industry and its ethics rules, they can coach you in an appropriate manner for lawyers and personally focus on building your skills.

### [6.10]  B.  What to Incorporate Into Your Practice

Once you assess your skills, decide what to incorporate into your practice. If your practice focuses on large companies or specific industries, what you will need to learn will be different than if you work with small businesses. For large companies you will want to become involved with your prospects' industry, understand the key players, economic issues, laws that apply to them, and risks companies face.

If your clients are individuals, you will need an understanding of personal needs. For someone seeking a family lawyer, your approach will be different than if you have a personal injury practice. Since most individuals seek personal legal advice, you need to be where they are going to look for a lawyer. Ask yourself, where do people go to find a family lawyer (e.g., business associations, religious organizations, children interests, community activities, etc.)? Are you connected to appropriate referral sources (e.g., bankers, accountants, doctors, local Chamber of Commerce)? What needs do families have and what risks can you resolve? How can you communicate with the broader audience? Plan your marketing campaign based on these questions.

As a personal injury lawyer you also want a strong referral base. Questions you may be asked include: Do you do contingent work? What types of injuries have you helped people with? Catastrophic? Slip and fall? Automobile? DUI? There are many personal injury lawyers; what makes you different? (This is a good brainstorming exercise on establishing your brand/image.)

### [6.11]  C.  Building Legal Services Sales Process

Today's lawyer who is providing consultative selling should think about what he or she can learn from the sales process. Too many lawyers approach marketing by doing what every other lawyer does, without much thought to what would work best for them. It results in an inconsistent approach, wasted time, and wasted resources. It's time to focus on how to get leads and convert them into business.

## [6.12]  D.  Lead Generation

Lead generation is about qualifying people who need your services. Most lawyers use marketing and business development tools to position themselves, enabling them to be found by those seeking the legal advice they provide. But positioning does not necessarily qualify the prospect for you. Terms like marketing and business development are not the same as lead generation—they are the preamble.

Marketing and business development activities should result in identifying leads. It is through leads that you will find consultative selling opportunities.

## [6.13]  E.  Sales Conversion Process

Sales conversion is demonstrated by what is called the "sales pipeline" which looks like a funnel. Leads go into the funnel and while in the funnel, you qualify them. Qualifying each contact helps you see them clearly. Are they a suspect (known by name only), a prospect (a suspect that has been in contact with you in a casual way), or a lead (a prospect when a current or near future need has been established)? Understanding where contacts fall in this process enables you to put the right resources of the firm into play.

Qualifying leads includes asking yourself questions such as: Do they have an immediate need for my legal services? Will they have a need in the future? Can they afford my services? Could they be a referral source? Not everyone met at a networking event is a lead although he or she might become a good contact leading to referrals or new business in the future. The time and resources you should put into action depends on whether or not they are a lead.

## [6.14]  F.  Difficulty Converting Leads Into New Business

Lawyers haven't been invested in lead conversion because it hasn't been a process commonly used by the legal industry in the past, and lawyers don't necessarily understand it. It is important to appreciate the process, though, in order to plan the best use of your time, efforts, and resources.

Some lawyers rely on referrals almost exclusively, but we no longer live in a world where one can wait for the phone to ring with new business. Referral sources are important, but they aren't a guarantee of new business or the type of business you want. Take the time to qualify referral sources and adjust your time, efforts, and resources based on the results you have received. It is as important as qualifying prospects.

### [6.15]  G.  Solution Selling

Sometimes consultative selling is referred to as solution-based selling. Wikipedia[3] describes Solution Selling as a sales methodology. "Rather than just promoting an existing service, you focus on your prospect's pain(s) and address the issues with your service solutions." Clients seek you out because they have a problem and you likely have a solution. **Instead of thinking in terms of what legal service you provide, think in terms of what solutions you provide that would help this person.** This will help you understand your prospect's needs more clearly. Understanding the solution prospects want helps you to position yourself based on their needs and enables you to use their language.

## [6.16]  IV.  PROPOSAL

### [6.17]  A.  Inquiries

Not all business inquiries are formal. If you are part of a smaller firm or a solo practitioner, you may find yourself with an opportunity because someone has met you, been referred to you or found you in other ways due to your marketing activities. The prospect might invite you to their office to meet with their people (decision makers/influencers) and ask you to make a presentation or, if an individual, he or she may come to your office. If it is a meeting in the prospect's office they are giving you an opportunity to meet their team, discuss your experience, and answer questions that are specific to their current needs. The meeting will likely result in their deciding about you (pro or con). It is important that you find out as much as you can in advance about what they are looking for and their specific legal issue. In this situation, do your homework upfront and learn as much as you can about their business and how you can address any current problems. This does not necessarily require a prepared document but many lawyers bring one. The document may be a PowerPoint presentation or some other professionally prepared material tailored to the pros-

---

[3]   en.wikipedia.org/wiki/Solution_selling.

pect that provides information about the law firm's lawyers, their experience in this legal matter, process, budget, and fees.

Although you might have prepared material, it is better to go ready to establish a relationship, introduce your team (if you have one) and your team's experience, focus on the prospect's questions and your understanding of what they are looking for. If you don't have time to review your document, you can leave your material behind as long as it supports the discussion and contains information that the prospect would find useful to review at their convenience (don't include information that is irrelevant to the prospect's business or legal issue). Always understand that it is about the relationship, your knowledge and experience that will build trust in the meeting, rather than a document.

## [6.18] B. Proposal Selling

Depending on the size of your firm and the type of law you practice, you may receive proposal requests or requests for qualifications. (These can be time consuming and expensive to produce. Respond to the ones that are the best fit for your firm and your practice goals.)

In medium to large firms, proposals often come formally from prospects or current clients. When it comes from a current client, the client usually wants to contain the cost of expensive matters. Your personal relationship can influence this over your competition.

These proposals are known as Requests for Proposal (RFPs). Government entities are often very specific in what they want to know and may also limit what you can say in the RFP. There are usually core steps for preparing your answer as well as laying out the scope of work. RFPs from large corporations are also specific, but often leave you leeway to promote your services by allowing you to provide more depth of information about you, your experience, your firm, fees, your approach, budget, etc.

One of the key things in an RFP is to answer all the questions thoroughly. Occasionally lawyers may be inclined to skip questions in the RFP because they feel they aren't important or that they have already answered them in an earlier section. It is vital to realize that different people in the organization asking for the RFP may only read sections important to them or their department. If you think you included requested information in one section, but it asks for it again or for something similar in another section, repeat your answer or restate it. Do not leave it blank.

## [6.19] C. Dealing With Objections

Be prepared to handle objections that the prospect may have during the interview. Objections are often an opportunity to better understand your prospect. Here are some insights on how to overcome objections. John Doerr, co-president of The Rain Group, says to remember your goal is to "[o]vercome the objection and make advances towards gaining commitment from the prospect."[4]

- *Address the objection.* If you plow through the objection without addressing it, the underlying reason for the objection will usually come back to haunt you.

- *Understand the objection.* Your goal is to fully understand the objection, isolate it, and respond to it appropriately.

- *This might be a process vs. a quick answer.* Build a case for overcoming an objection instead of answering quickly.

- Listen fully.

- Ask permission to completely understand the issue.

- Ask questions, restate or clarify the objection.

- Choose your response carefully and keep it short.

- Propose your resolution to overcome the objection.

- Ask whether your answer/proposed solution will satisfy the objection.

## [6.20] D. Mistakes Lawyers Make

The following are common mistakes lawyers make:

- *Asking for business when you first meet rather than focusing on building a relationship.* Regardless of how much experience you have, a stranger is not likely to retain you without knowing you better. You need to build their trust.

- *Just because you know someone, that doesn't mean you have a relationship.* You may have met before, been introduced by a colleague or met

---

[4] John Doerr, "Your Fees Are Too High": Objections That Will Get You Closer to the Sale, RAIN Selling Blog, 2014.

in some other place, but if the prospect doesn't realize your experience, doesn't have confidence in you yet, you need to build the relationship.

- *Expecting your presentation to a prospect to do the selling for you.* Your presentation may be perfect, but it doesn't build the relationship—that depends on you personally.

- *Forgetting that the client or prospect wants to*

    make money;

    save money;

    look good to their boss; and

    sleep well at night.

These are four motives people often have but may not say. You have to demonstrate that you can fulfill these subliminal needs.

- *Not researching the prospect's business, industry, competition, work environment, economic issues, or personal interests of their leaders prior to meeting them.* It is up to you to do the necessary advance work to demonstrate your knowledge of their business, their goals, and their interests. People want an ally, someone who cares about them. Advance knowledge demonstrates that.

- *Forgetting what the prospect wants and only focusing on what legal services you provide.* Lawyers understand their practice, but your prospect may not understand how that solves the problem if you focus only on the features. You want to demonstrate that you understand his or her needs by giving examples where you have solved similar matters for others. A mini case-history of a similar client matter (without names) can do this.

- *Not identifying your unique selling proposition (USP).* What makes you different from other lawyers? How do you treat your clients? What do others say about you? What makes you unique should be included in your presentation. People often think that all lawyers are alike. Tell them why you are different.

- *Not qualifying and/or quantifying the value you add.* How do you manage matters? Do you budget appropriately for the matter? What is your fee structure? Do you use technology to provide faster and better service? What else do they receive because they are a client? Everyone wants value-added service.

These mistakes are easy to overcome through preparation and self-assessment.

### [6.21] E. Asking for the Business

Now that you have established a relationship with your prospect, studied his or her business and the issues faced, and have a clear understanding of what your prospect needs, you can begin to plan on asking for business. If you are invited to present to executives or in-house counsel, you have a clear opportunity to win their business assuming you have done all of your homework, understand their business and personal needs, focused your presentation on what their issues are and the solutions you could provide. (This also applies to any type of RFP.)

If you haven't been invited to present on a matter but can see that there are issues or risks the prospect might not be aware of (but should be concerned about), you can bring it to their attention. Assuming you already know them, you could do this by making an appointment to meet in their office, or meet for lunch or at some other venue. If you don't already know them, you want to try to find a referral source or establish the beginning of a relationship through some other organization or social media. (Writing about a topic and sharing it with interested parties or through newsletters or social media enables you to be the thought-leader on the issue.)

Depending upon the seriousness of the issue, you may not want to discuss it in public. Bring up the overall points that make it something your prospect should know more about and ask to schedule a private meeting so you can discuss the risks and possible solutions. After you have piqued their interest and made the appointment, plan out your strategy for the meeting. Who will be there? What are the company/business risks? Provide information on the issues and explain how and why you could help them. What do you bring to the table that is unique? Why they should hire you versus someone else? See IV.C, "Dealing With Objections," above.

### [6.22] F. How to Move Up the Value Pyramid

*Commodity Work.* The type or level of work you acquire depends on your experience and expertise. If you are recently out of law school you will likely find only commodity work until you can prove yourself otherwise qualified. If you work in mid-large law firms, you may gain that experience more quickly, working with skilled lawyers who can teach you. New associates in larger firms initially do routine work—tasks such as document review, cite-checking, multi-jurisdictional research, repetitive, process or predictable work—with the more interesting work going to more qualified lawyers.

In today's cost-conscious world, even with new associates, routine work may no longer be profitable for large law firms because there are alternatives for prospects other than using more expensive lawyers for commodity work.

In *Tomorrow's Lawyers*, Richard Susskind says, "[B]ecause a lot of work is routine and repetitive, it can be outsourced, off-shored, done by computers and standardized."[5] As Susskind points out, competition is coming from outside the legal field. For example, some work can be outsourced to tech businesses that can do the work faster and better because of their technology expertise and specially designed programs, even though they are not practicing lawyers.

When the fees of a large firm are too high for the firm to continue to do commodity work with new associates, it may hire contract lawyers. If you are a young solo lawyer just starting out, there are opportunities for you to acquire this routine work from larger firms that may be profitable for you in your early career. It is a good stepping stone. Without having the high overhead costs, young lawyers are able to learn, gain experience, and demonstrate their knowledge and work product. In addition they learn the legal process and build good relationships with other lawyers and those that refer this business. From there young lawyers can begin to build their reputation and eventually gain more important work.

Smaller businesses also want lawyers who can do this work at a lower cost. This means technology can be used by you to move your practice forward faster and easier when doing routine work. Adapt to these drivers of change and you will be able to fill in where traditional legal businesses will fail.

*Important Work.* How to move from selling commodity work to selling important work depends upon your experience, expertise, and the prospect's or client's needs. Commodity work, though, might be about 30 percent of a company's business. If you are a solo practitioner or a small law

---

5   Richard Susskind, Tomorrow's Lawyers: An Introduction to Your Future (2013).

firm, commodity work could be your bread and butter. But in order to focus your practice on bringing in business that is not commodity work you must gain experience in your legal area and build your reputation for knowledge and quality. Work which is considered important (requiring advanced knowledge and content) can be about 50 percent of a client's work depending upon their size and business. This is not the kind of work that can be outsourced and is likely to be your goal by providing steady clients and meaningful work.

*High-Level Advice.* The next level of the value pyramid is high-level advice. Prospects will spend more for expertise and trust. Ten percent of a client's work might be considered high-level advice. This level requires you to be considered one of the best in the field and trusted as an adviser to the company or client. Lawyers able to provide this advice usually have been practicing in their field or with a particular client for a long time and have the legal experience, industry knowledge, and personal relationship with the client.

*Bet-the-Company.* The very top of the value pyramid is considered "bet-the-company" matters. This may mean staying out of jail or threats to the company's or business's survival. This top category would likely demand the highest fees from very experienced lawyers with a proven track record.

All of this is called Value Pricing. People are willing to pay more when they have a need for greater skills and knowledge.

*What Work Can Be Done Using New Technology.* "The evolution of legal services begins with standardization," says Richard Susskind. "With the advent of information technology, a further step can be taken—that of systemization." This will impact workflow systems by producing efficiency and may result in packaging legal services. Whenever they can, lawyers should learn about and use new technology that improves their practice and meets client demands. Because this may be more efficient, a lawyer can reduce the time spent on or even eliminate commodity work, and then focus on the important work.

## [6.23]  G.  Understanding Today's Prospects

Today's prospective clients don't operate as they once did. They actively seek out information for themselves, find lawyers through Internet searches, and arrive at decisions about their legal needs often before they retain a lawyer. By the time a lawyer is contacted, the prospect has already vetted choices. Not all lawyers, though, will be found through this process. Lawyers need to be more actively involved in the process and shouldn't wait to be found. They should take control of finding and qualifying leads that are most likely to need the lawyer's services.

## [6.24] H. Gaining Future Work

All lawyers can learn to build their experience and reputation. To ensure this happens, a lawyer should create a written plan by identifying what he or she needs to know and where to find appropriate experience. They can do this by writing about key issues on changes in the law and seeking to get them published in industry periodicals or legal publications. Speaking engagements on major topics in front of industry groups or organizations that would find this information valuable is another way to demonstrate legal knowledge. This will help build a lawyer's reputation. In consultative selling, this demonstrates to prospects that you understand the law that affects them and how it can be applied to their business.

Lawyers can also maximize their presence through social media. If they have a LinkedIn profile, they can link their profile to publications and/or articles they have written and announce upcoming speaking engagements. LinkedIn enables users to add these attachments as well as videos, slides, etc. Written articles and alerts can also be published on a firm's website. Again, this builds a lawyer's reputation necessary for consultative selling.

The 2012 ABA Legal Technology Survey Report states that 88 percent of lawyers said their firms are on LinkedIn and 55 percent are on Facebook. The 2013 In-house Counsel New Media Engagement Survey said "LinkedIn is the social media source in-house counsel uses most to obtain information and expand their contacts." As of January 2014, LinkedIn counted more than 700,000 LinkedIn profiles in the legal industry. Seventy-six percent of consumers go online to find a lawyer.[6] There are many social media platforms available today. If a lawyer's client base is personal injury he or she may want to also have a Facebook page to reach the individual who is not using LinkedIn, although an Internet lawyer search will turn up the lawyer's LinkedIn Profile. Surveys indicate that YouTube videos and blogs are bringing in more new business for lawyers than any other social media platforms. "Social media use is now widespread, main-

---

6   Lawyers.com, 2012.

stream, and more influential than ever," says Monica Romeri,[7] CEO of Darwin Digital Content, in her 2014 article on social media statistics. The key point about social media is that it is important for lawyers to have a strong presence on it so that they can be easily found by search engines and enhance their reputation for skills and knowledge. In consultative selling, you want to be found and be able to demonstrate your legal experience.

Social media statistics:[8]

- 72% of all Internet users are active on social media

- 89% of those between 18 and 29 years old are social media users

- 72% of individuals aged 30 to 49 are engaged in social media

- 60% of people between 50 to 60 years old are active on social media

- 43% of those 65 years old and above are engaged in social media

- 71% of users access social media from a mobile device

## [6.25] V. GOING FORWARD

When in doubt as to what your prospects need, find out by asking them about what keeps them up at night. This conversation can point you in the direction of your prospects' risk fears, competition, employment issues, economic issues, etc. This will lead you to the next step in understanding how you can help them overcome these issues and solve their problems.

---

7   Monica Jade Romeri, New Social Media Statistics, *SocialMediaToday*, www.socialmediatoday.com/content/new-social-media-statistics-you-need-know.

8   *Id.*

# APPENDIX

## Table 1: Consultative Selling Self-Assessment

| Your Behavior | Yes | Maybe | No |
|---|---|---|---|
| Have practice area experience | | | |
| Have practice area expertise | | | |
| Able to resist temptation to "pitch" services or solution | | | |
| Know how to build high trust | | | |
| Know how to build high credibility | | | |
| Understand prospect's business environment | | | |
| Understand prospect's critical business drivers | | | |
| Understand prospect's high priority business initiatives | | | |
| Have good feedback that my value proposition holds water in prospect's specific business environment | | | |
| Can build a compelling business case for my solution | | | |
| Can build a compelling value proposition for "why me?" | | | |
| Have an independent perspective on prospect's business problems | | | |
| Have vision of tough issues that might create risks for prospect | | | |
| Have a finite list of business problems where I have meaningful expertise | | | |
| Able to spend entire introduction or initial meeting building relationship | | | |

## Table 1: Consultative Selling Self-Assessment

| Your Behavior | Yes | Maybe | No |
|---|---|---|---|
| Can provide credible reason for another or next meeting | | | |

Answer each statement as it applies to you. For each *Maybe*, evaluate what you need to do to make it a *Yes*. For each *No*, learn what you need to know in order to change your behavior.

# CHAPTER SEVEN

# KNOWLEDGE SHARING

**Alan Levine**

## [7.0] I. WHAT IS KNOWLEDGE SHARING?

Knowledge sharing is self-explanatory. It is the act of letting others know about what you know. More important and requiring more explanation is why you should care about knowledge sharing. Knowledge sharing has intrinsic value; it is a good thing to share what you know. By sharing your knowledge with others, they benefit from gaining an understanding of information and insight that they did not previously possess. What this chapter will concentrate on, however, is how *you* benefit by sharing your knowledge, and that, in essence, is why we are focusing on it in a marketing publication. The act of sharing can have many potential benefits to you, depending on what knowledge you share, how and with whom. If you share the right information with the right people in the right way, you can gain tremendous advantages for your business development efforts.

The idea is that *before* you start sharing all that knowledge, you give some thought as to what your objective is, what you hope to accomplish by sharing. To the extent possible, in each instance, you should determine your objective because it may not always be the same. In general, however, your objective is to demonstrate that you have an expertise about something—an area of law, a business topic, a particular industry. If you can show that you, more than others, know a topic inside and out, those who are the recipients of your shared knowledge are likely to think of you first when they require such expertise. The concept of becoming a "thought leader" may have become overused, but that is what you are trying to achieve. You want to be ahead of the curve in sharing your knowledge rather than an also-ran. You want to be one of the first people to share ideas on a topic, or to present them in a new and different way. In sharing your knowledge, you want to stand out from the crowd so that people remember you and your distinctive insights when they think of—or want to know more about—that particular topic.

Knowledge sharing comes in many forms, and we will explore these forms in the rest of this chapter. Keep in mind that when you are sharing knowledge in a manner that allows you to somehow personally connect with your audience, perhaps by speaking or presenting to them, this allows you to make a bond with them, thereby creating an even stronger connection between you and them.

## [7.1] II. POTENTIAL PITFALLS OF KNOWLEDGE SHARING

While this chapter will largely focus on how you can benefit from knowledge sharing, there are, in fact, potential pitfalls to letting others in on what you know, and it is important to be aware of them. Just as the benefits have to do with what, how and who, so do the pitfalls. Watch out for them:

*What*—Make sure you truly know what you're talking about. If your audience perceives that your knowledge is shaky (or worse), you will hurt rather than help your credibility.

*How*—Be realistic about your strengths and weaknesses as you determine how you choose to share your knowledge. If you are a poor public speaker, stay away from speeches and seminars as ways to share your knowledge. Remember that your goal is to attract interest in you, not repel it.

*Who*—You may share your knowledge with the wrong people. These may be people who have no interest whatsoever in your topic, or have no interest at all in dealing with attorneys. In some cases, though not frequently, you may share your knowledge with someone whose only interest is taking that knowledge and claiming it for himself or herself. You should understand from the start with whom you are likely to be sharing your knowledge, so you can feel confident that they are people who may be receptive to what you know.

When it comes to knowledge sharing, one concern often expressed by lawyers is the lack of time in their busy schedule. If an attorney wants the benefits that come with knowledge sharing, he or she must commit to putting in the time necessary to provide useful knowledge in an effective way. Half-hearted efforts will generally be recognized as such. It is preferable to do nothing rather than go halfway. There are methods in the marketplace by which you can pay others outside your practice to create the content that will be shared under your name. While the appeal of this approach is understandable, you are urged to consider carefully before having others do this on your behalf. Make sure the information is accurate. Equally important, make sure that the tone conveyed is consistent with how you want to be perceived. Whatever "you" say—as written by someone else—you have to be willing to fully stand behind it.

## [7.2] III. NEW TECHNOLOGIES AND KNOWLEDGE SHARING

Recent years have seen new technologies appear at an astonishing and ever-increasing rate, so there is a growing array of ways to share knowledge. And there is every reason to expect that the pace of change will only accelerate. In fact, chances are that within a short time, this chapter will no longer be entirely current because new forms of technology that we may not even be able to imagine now are likely to present themselves.

For now, though, it is important to recognize that the Internet, telephones and other forms of technology have transformed communication in all aspects of the business world. Equally important, however, is the need to understand that these new technologies have not altered the fundamentals of knowledge sharing. The basic equation is that an individual—for the sake of this chapter, let's assume it is you—has unique expertise that he or she wishes to share with one or more other people. There are now new ways to *share* that expertise, and the sharing may be done a whole lot faster and a whole lot cheaper. But the equation of one person sharing with one or many is, and will remain, unchanged.

## [7.3] IV. METHODOLOGIES

### [7.4] A. Bylined Articles

Lawyers have been writing articles for much longer than they have been consciously marketing their services. Frequently, they get their start while they are in law school, writing for law reviews.

Typically, a lawyer will write an article about something he or she knows about, or a topic he or she chooses to investigate. While law reviews used to be the only game in town, now lawyers have a wider choice of publications for which to write, including:

- Law Reviews—These journals are intended for lawyers with particular interest in a topic. The articles are in-depth and legalistic. Generally, law reviews have less value as marketing vehicles than other, less scholarly, publications.

- Legal publications—These are less learned than law reviews, but the audience is other lawyers, though generally a broad cross-section of lawyers. If there is no benefit to you to share your knowledge with other lawyers, this is not the right vehicle.

- General business publications—These are written for the broad community of people in business. For such publications, you should dispense with Latin terms and footnotes in favor of plain English.

- Trade publications—Virtually every industry you can possibly imagine has specialized publications intended for people in that industry, and many industries have more than one. Writing for such publications allows you to demonstrate your knowledge of topics of particular interest to that industry.

### [7.5] 1. Advantages of Bylined Articles

Writing a bylined article allows you to lay out a well-thought-out investigation of a topic or presentation of a point of view. The "upside" includes:

- Typically you choose the topic. Some publication editors take a strong editorial hand, but others give the authors a fair amount of editorial discretion and edit lightly.

- It is a credential builder, which can be especially helpful for younger attorneys.

- Not only may your intended audience see your article, but other journalists, editors and publishers may also see it, which could lead to other writing opportunities.

- Speaking of younger attorneys, publications usually allow you to include the names of multiple authors. Even if a senior attorney's name appears first in the byline, you should include the names of all attorneys who played a significant part in writing the article.

- The reality is that most people may not see the article when it first appears in the publication. Perhaps of even greater value for your marketing purposes, then, is the benefit that comes from getting or making a reprint of the article. Not only can you post it to your own website, but you can send it, either via mail or email, to anyone who may not have seen it when it was originally published, with a note along the lines of, "In case you missed this, I thought you would find it interesting and useful." The article is and forever will be yours (even if some publications do charge an unconscionable fee for the right to get a PDF or reprint of your article), so you can use the reprint, as long as—and in whatever way—it serves your purposes.

## [7.6] 2. Disadvantages of Bylined Articles

- The biggest downside to an article is that it sits on the page and does not allow you to connect on a personal level with your audience.

- Generally, you have little or no control over the time frame when your article will be published, and sometimes the lead time can be long.

## [7.7] B. Newsletters and E-Newsletters

Many law firms publish regular, periodic newsletters or, increasingly, e-newsletters. They come in many sizes, formats and frequencies, but they are self-published, which means you have control. You determine the content. You make the decision about its length, format and tone. You decide how often you want it to go out. And you choose who receives it.

The scope of the newsletter/e-newsletter should depend on your marketing objectives. Some firms prefer their newsletters/e-newsletters to show the breadth of their practices and cover an array of topics. In other cases, they are more targeted, focusing on a particular area of practice (employment law or trusts and estates), a particular geographic area (New Jersey law) or a specific industry (the pharmaceutical industry).

A printed newsletter is mailed to designated recipients, can be enclosed in packages of information you mail to clients and prospects, and can be displayed in your reception area. An e-newsletter is easily emailed to a designated list of recipients, can just as easily be forwarded to any individual of your choosing and can be posted to your website. And because you do not have to incur actual printing and postage expenses, the cost of an e-newsletter can be very, very low.

There are services that can produce newsletters/e-newsletters for you, with little or no involvement of your attorneys. While that has a certain appeal, and the price does not have to be high, the downfall of many of these newsletters is that they sound "canned" or generic and have little connection to your firm and its attorneys. The positive of having a newsletter can be counteracted when the newsletter feels disconnected from the firm that is sending it out.

## [7.8] 1. Advantages of Newsletters and E-Newsletters

- The biggest advantage is control. Everything is under your control. You can do with it as you please.

- You can set the tone and, hopefully, even show your personality.

### [7.9] 2. Disadvantages of Newsletters and E-Newsletters

- By its definition, a newsletter comes out periodically, and even if you do not set a rigid schedule (monthly, quarterly, etc.), you need to candidly assess whether your attorneys can deliver as promised. If the newsletter does not come out on some kind of regular basis, it loses its value as a marketing vehicle for you.

- More and more firms are choosing the electronic route to a newsletter because it is faster and cheaper to produce and disseminate. This is all true, but in a time when more and more information is conveyed electronically, there is something to be said for a hard copy newsletter that arrives in your mail. As people are besieged by an avalanche of email communications, your e-newsletter could be easily deleted or quickly overlooked. A hard copy newsletter could just as easily be deposited in the trash, but it may also continue to sit on the recipient's desk or find its way into his briefcase. Weigh the benefits and costs of electronic and hard copy.

### [7.10] C. E-Alerts

There is a growing trend toward producing e-alerts. Services like Constant Contact have made it fast, cheap and easy. While there are similarities between e-alerts and e-newsletters, the chief differences are length and frequency. Unlike an e-newsletter, an e-alert should be brief and to the point. A big plus is that there is not an expectation among recipients that it will be produced on any regular time schedule; it is understood that an e-alert goes out only when there is something worthy of reporting or commenting on. The length should be limited to no more than a few paragraphs, and there is nothing inherently wrong with one of a couple of sentences. State what you need to say and then stop. What you need to say can be boiled down to this: what happened that the reader should care about, why the reader needs to know and what the reader should do about it.

### [7.11] 1. Advantages of E-Alerts

- As stated above, e-alerts can be fast, cheap and easy to disseminate.

- They allow you to carefully pinpoint your audience, if you care to.

- They permit a very quick response to rapidly changing developments.

- They allow you to say all that needs to be said, even if it is not very much.

- They can readily be tied to all manner of social media.

**[7.12] 2. Disadvantages of E-Alerts**

- They are fleeting; they do not have a long shelf life. They are typically received, read and discarded.

- If they are not read at the time they are received, they are likely to be forgotten.

**[7.13] D. Blogs**

A blog, short for weblog, is defined by Wikipedia as a discussion or information site on the Internet consisting of discrete entries (posts), typically displayed in reverse chronological order. Most are interactive, allowing visitors to leave comments, and it is this interactivity that distinguishes them from static websites. Blogging is a form of social media. The more successful blogs have a specific focus—on an area of law, an industry or another topic—rather than on the law in general. Although blogs date back only to the late '90s, there are now hundreds of millions of blogs, including thousands of legal blogs.

To give a sense of the proliferation of blogs in the legal world, according to Lexblog, a leading name in law firm blogs, 78 percent of the top 200 law firms in the world have blogs or lawyers blogging. These firms have an average of four blogs per firm. By far the most popular topic for legal blogs is employment law.

**[7.14] 1. Advantages of Blogs**

- They can be an excellent way to maintain regular communication with targeted, interested individuals.

- They allow you to demonstrate your interest in, and knowledge of, a particular topic.

- Unlike most other marketing tools, they also give you a chance to share your views and show off your personality.

- Through search engine optimization, they can provide exposure to people who otherwise would not have been likely to discover you.

- They give you a means of two-way communication with your readers.

## [7.15] 2. Disadvantages of Blogs

- Blogs require a steady commitment of time. They demand consistency and stamina. You need to add posts on a regular basis, at a minimum of once every two weeks. Lawyers typically have a lot of trouble with this, and thus, the world is filled with legal blogs that started with grand ambitions and subsequently crashed and burned. Before you commit to starting a blog, give careful thought to whether you can consistently give it a priority in your schedule. If the honest answer is that you can't, stop before you begin.

- A good blog is a distinctive blog. While distinctiveness is a positive for virtually all marketing tools, it is particularly important for a blog. If you have nothing distinctive to say, the blog becomes generic and tends to fade into the woodwork.

- A good blog needs to be outwardly focused, something that some lawyers lose sight of. If it's all about you and what you and your law firm are up to, the reader sees no need to continue reading.

## [7.16] E. Speeches

A speech is the opportunity to speak at someone else's program or seminar. Your responsibility is simply to address the topic on which you were invited to speak. The other party takes charge of everything else, from inviting guests to handling the logistics to ordering the food.

There are different kinds of speaking opportunities. When you are invited to speak, make sure you understand what you are being asked to speak about, who the audience is and what the objective of the program is. For example, if it is a continuing legal education program to educate other lawyers in private practice, consider whether this serves your business development objectives. On the other hand, a CLE program intended for in-house counsel can have a different level of value. And a continuing professional education program for people in a different profession, like accountants or financial planners, can be valuable for you in a whole different way.

# KNOWLEDGE SHARING § 7.17

## [7.17] 1. Advantages of Speeches

- Unlike other forms of knowledge sharing, giving a speech is just about sharing your knowledge. You are not distracted by having to do anything else.

- Unlike written communication, making a speech allows you to personally connect with your audience. They can gain a better sense of who you are.

- A speech can be great if you are an effective speaker—if you really know your stuff, or if you are engaging, even funny, and can keep your audience's attention.

- When you deliver a speech, remember that the knowledge sharing does not end when your speech is finished. Invite questions. Stay around after the presentation is done. Invite your audience to follow up with questions or ideas. Even better, find a reason to follow up with the people in your audience afterward (make sure to get the email/addresses of all who are in attendance), to maintain your connection.

## [7.18] 2. Disadvantages of Speeches

- If you hate making speeches—and it *is* one of the greatest fears of a great many people—this is not the knowledge sharing opportunity for you.

- If you are a poor speaker—if you are stiff, monotonous or otherwise don't connect with your audience—find a better way to share.

## [7.19] F. Seminars

Unlike a speech, a seminar is a program of your own creation. As with other forms of knowledge sharing, you should start with determining your objective. Why are you choosing to put on the seminar, what are you hoping to accomplish and who are you trying to reach? Once you have answered those questions, you choose the theme, select the speakers, assign individual topics, invite the audience and take care of all the logistical details.

## [7.20] 1. Advantages of Seminars

- While a seminar requires more work than just presenting a speech, it also gives you more control over the agenda and the program. You can shape the program to fit your needs and accomplish your objectives. You choose whom you share your knowledge with and how you do it.

- Like speeches, seminars let you interact—and personally connect—with the people in the audience.

- Seminars permit different formats. You can select the format—or different formats—to suit your purposes. These can include individual presentations, panel discussions, audience involvement, even debates.

- Since you are responsible for all aspects of the seminar, you have information about the registrants, so you can take the opportunity to stay in touch with them.

## [7.21] 2. Disadvantages of Seminars

- It seems to be getting increasingly difficult to attract people to seminars. Perhaps it is because there are so many choices, perhaps because people are busier than ever, but it can be difficult to fill the seats.

## [7.22] G. Webinars

A webinar is a live online educational presentation during which the audience is given the opportunity to submit questions and comments. Rather than the speaker and the audience together in a room where the speaker presents directly to the audience, the speaker is typically sitting in front of a computer in his or her office and the members of the audience are sitting in front of computers at their desks. In many ways, a webinar is like a seminar: you put together the program, decide on your topics and speakers and invite attendees. But, in the end, the program takes place remotely, where everyone stays in his place.

There are a number of companies—WebEx and GotoMeeting are two that I am familiar with—that offer turnkey services that are easy and have very reasonable prices. They allow you to create and promote the webinar, and they take care of virtually everything else for you as well. They allow you to record your webinar, which you can later put on your website or email to those who attended—or those who were unable to attend. They track attendance—letting you know who is expected to attend, who actually attends, even the time that attendees turn off their computers. They can even give you their assessment of how interested a given member of the audience is.

KNOWLEDGE SHARING                                           § 7.23

## [7.23] 1. Advantages of Webinars

- Webinars are inexpensive and easy to put on.

- They require relatively little expenditure of energy on the part of the knowledge sharer. Certainly, he or she will need to craft an effective presentation and PowerPoint presentation. However, since the participants only hear a voice, they will not know if the speaker is delivering the presentation in his or her pajamas.

- They require even less expenditure of energy on the part of the knowledge receivers. They barely have to interrupt their lives to listen in.

- It is easy to take the completed webinar and share it electronically with those who did not take part.

## [7.24] 2. Disadvantages of Webinars

- A big disadvantage is the flip side of the ease with which people can take part. They may not be paying a whole lot of attention to the speaker precisely because they are sitting at their desks and may be multi-tasking. Also, since the speaker does not see the audience, he or she has no real way to "read" the audience and sense how they are reacting to what he or she is saying.

- Unlike seminars, webinars do not give the knowledge sharer the opportunity to personally connect with the audience. Yes, the audience gets to answer questions or make comments, but it is more removed. They are not truly interacting with the knowledge sharer, and the knowledge sharer does not have the chance to interact with those who are listening in.

## [7.25] H. Videos and Podcasts

A video is a short videotape in which the presenter talks about a given topic. A podcast is defined as "a digital medium consisting of an episodic series of audio, video, radio, PDF or ePub files subscribed to and downloaded through web syndication or streamed online to a computer or mobile device." These media permit you to present your information in a visual way that the recipient can choose to view at his or her convenience.

## [7.26] 1. Advantages of Videos and Podcasts

- The presentation has the potential of "coming alive" for the recipient in a way that written materials cannot.

- The recipient can view the information when and where it is convenient, and can see it again and again if desired.

## [7.27] 2. Disadvantages of Videos and Podcasts

- Videos and podcasts do not allow for give and take between the presenter and the recipient. There is no immediate way that they can start a dialogue between the two.

# CHAPTER EIGHT

# SOCIAL MEDIA

**Nancy Myrland**

## [8.0]  I. SOCIAL MEDIA USE AMONG LAWYERS

The world of legal marketing has changed a great deal in the past decade, and even in the past five years. The methods lawyers were accustomed to using to connect with other human beings have now either been replaced or complemented by digital methods of communication. At first blush, this might seem daunting, or even a nuisance. We were used to business development the old way, whatever that means. A second look, however, will help you understand that these tools are far from being a nuisance, and can serve to accelerate and focus your marketing efforts, resulting in a more efficient use of your time and resources.

No longer are you just buying ads in the local paper and phone book. You are, instead, able to stake a claim in the valuable real estate known as the Internet. The wonderful news about all of this is that size no longer has to matter. What used to be reserved for only the largest firms with seemingly endless advertising budgets is now open to individuals and firms of all sizes. The Internet doesn't ask you to fill out an application to prove that you have enormous resources before you can have a presence. Your readers, clients and prospects don't stop reading an article or blog post they find valuable because they discover it has been written by a firm of only three lawyers. Legal trade publication editors aren't unfollowing you on Twitter when they realize the conversation they are having is with a lawyer who just started in practice one year ago, or even 50 for that matter.

Online marketing, sometimes referred to as digital marketing, is the umbrella term for any marketing tactics that are delivered online, or via the Internet. Social media are networking sites on the Internet. These sites are growing in terms of use and importance in the legal profession. The main social networking sites I discuss most with my clients are LinkedIn, Twitter, and sometimes even Facebook and Google+. Your clients are using these social media with increasing frequency, and are, in many cases, years ahead of you in their adoption and use, so it is critical that you understand and integrate social media, and the social networking that takes place on these media, into your existing marketing practices. It is not so important that we like or dislike social media, but whether our clients and prospects like or dislike them. It is our job to meet them where they are, or where we suspect they are headed.

Social media can be the great equalizer. This might sound simplistic, but the only requirements to use them are a commitment to establish your presence on the sites that fit into your marketing and business development plans, sharing advice from others in your area of expertise whom your readers might like to hear from, writing or talking about those topics that are front and center for your clients, and committing to interacting with those whose paths you cross. There are, of course, steps in between all of these requirements that will help you use them wisely and effectively, and we will discuss some of them here, but these requirements are an important foundation to learning and using these tools.

My first rule of the road is for you to not be too hard on yourselves. When learning about social media, it can be a bit like drinking from a fire hose because there is an enormous amount of data and information out there, with more being written every day as the tools change. I will cover a few of the main issues here that I want you to think about as you move forward. Hopefully, by the time you're finished with this chapter, you will either have confirmed, contradicted or added to your perceptions of social media and how these platforms can be used in legal marketing.

## [8.1] II. WHO'S USING IT?

Let's take a look at a few numbers so you have an idea what kind of an impact social media are having on how the world is now communicating in the digital era. In the world at large:[1]

- 1.61 billion people use social media. This number is expected to be 2.33 billion by 2017.

- 22% of the world's population uses social media; 66% from the United States alone.

- Usage is growing fastest among 35- to 44-year-olds.

- The increase in use by 55- to 64-year-olds last year was greater than 100% for Facebook, Twitter and Google+.

- Pinterest and Tumblr are currently the fastest growing global social media.

- Mobile is the key driver in the overall growth of social media.

---

1  Statistics gathered and updated by DMR-Digital Marketing Ramblings, www.expandedramblings.com. Please remember that all statistics change daily, causing some numbers to be outdated the day after this is written.

Every month, users spend an average of

- 17 minutes on LinkedIn;
- 3 minutes on Google+;
- 8 minutes on MySpace;
- 21 minutes on Twitter;
- 89 minutes on Tumblr and Pinterest; and
- 405 minutes on Facebook.

We also need to take a look at the legal profession, so let's see how general counsel are using social media:[2]

- Only 27% say they didn't use social media, meaning 73% do use it, up from 66% in 2012 and 57% in 2010.
- They are using Facebook mainly for personal use.
- They are using work hours to research Wikipedia and firm sites.
- They are using LinkedIn to strengthen professional contacts.
- They are reading industry news on blogs.
- They are quiet or invisible users of social media, meaning they read others' posts more than they broadcast their own thoughts.
- They are turning to digital means of research with the same frequency as they turn to more traditional media outlets such as newspapers.
- They may keep up on industry news by reading legal or other niche blogs.

---

[2] 2013 Greentarget, ALM Legal Intelligence and Zeughauser Group State of Digital Media Content Marketing Survey. Where comparisons to 2011 and 2012 are made, these historic numbers are drawn from past versions of the Greentarget study.

## [8.2] A. Two Goals of Social Media

Although goals can be different from user to user, I summarize the main goals of social media use as follows:

- They help us to find and be found.

- They help us to turn contacts into connections.

If you keep these goals in mind, they can guide your use and strategy for social networking via social media. Let's face it. You aren't using any marketing or communication tactics or channels simply because you enjoy them, or because you're looking for more hobbies to squeeze into your busy days. You are using them to help grow your practices by becoming known, liked and trusted. Social media are outlets you can use to help facilitate those relationships your clients and prospects have a right to when they are seeking legal and business counsel. You can have 10,000 contacts, but if you haven't done anything to connect with them, then they are just names in your digital Rolodex. It is your job to turn these contacts into connections in order to foster relationships that are worthy of your clients' consideration when they are trying to decide whom they want to call to the table to discuss matters of utmost importance in their lives and businesses. If you use these two goals to guide your online activities, then you will differentiate yourself in the minds of those who are searching for people who do what you do.

## [8.3] B. Two Very Important Points

Among many others, there are two very important points about using social media.

## [8.4] 1. They Must Be Integrated

Integrated marketing is just what it sounds like. You need to integrate social media into your existing marketing practices in order for your efforts to be as effective as they can be. It is important to remember that these are just additional tools in your marketing and business development plans. You can integrate them by making sure that your social media use is coordinated and complementary. For example, when you have a new lateral hire, or a new associate joins your firm, you could write a news release, write a blog post, Tweet about your excitement about this person, talk about it on your Facebook page, create a video message, podcast an interview with this person, put the news in your LinkedIn group and company page, write about it in your firm print and e-newsletter, and more. As you can see, what you have done is to *integrate* your news across all platforms available to you in a *coordinated and complementary* way so that the likelihood of your target audiences hearing about the news will increase.

In other words, social media need to coordinate with everything else you're already doing. It should then complement everything else you are communicating. Your online marketing messages don't typically stand alone, although they can when it is necessary and appropriate. Just keep thinking about additional ways you can use these tools to continue spreading your news. Always ask, "Yes, but now what else can we do to amplify and distribute our message to try to reach our target audiences?"

### [8.5] 2. Their Effects Are Cumulative[3]

Very simply, this means that these efforts build over time. We all know that very few initial conversations lead to long-term client relationships. This doesn't always match our determination and patience because we like instant gratification! We need to remember that this is not necessarily direct-response advertising where we throw up a toll-free number and our phones and email go crazy with new clients and inquiries.

I recommend you adopt this framework:

- Start with goals.

- Condition yourself to remember that your online conversations, or content, should be quality but they don't have to be epic. Expecting every word that you publish to be of *New York Times* Bestseller List quality can cause inertia and analysis paralysis as you might not want to say anything because you aren't sure if it is good enough. Don't do this to yourself. As I said at the beginning, don't be too hard on yourself. We're building relationships here, not designing the next unsinkable Titanic.

- Don't forget to follow up with people. If you're having a discussion with them online, remember to ask them about the situation the next time you see them, whether that's online or face-to-face.

---

3   I wrote about these two important points on my blog, Myrland Marketing Minutes, at www.myrlandmarketing.com/2011/05/2-truths-about-social-media-part-one and www.myrlandmarketing.com/2011/06/2-truths-about-social-media-part-two.

- Have patience. If these relationships happen quickly, that's icing on the cake, but it is rare. Client relationships occur because of a series of meetings and conversations you and your potential clients have that, along the way, help them to know, like and trust you.

As I have often said, social networking helps to peel back the layers of unfamiliarity that exist between attorneys and their potential, and sometimes current, clients. It is that unfamiliarity, those often awkward, getting-to-know-you meetings that social media can help you peel back. You can help accelerate the removal of those layers so that you can find and get to know your clients, potential clients and target audiences much quicker, and more thoroughly, than if you had to wait solely for a face-to-face meeting, which can often take a long time.

### [8.6] C. Three Important Characteristics

There are three qualities, or characteristics, that I think are important when using social media. You must be

- agile;
- client-centric; and
- responsive.

The combination of these three characteristics is what makes social media different from traditional media. When we use social media, we are no longer solely throwing up one-way, broadcast ads with the hope our target audience will see or hear them. We are actively involved in this process—in this media buy if you will. It is now a two-way process. Instead of giving our dollars to media buyers and public relations experts, and letting them do the work, hoping traditional media pick up our news releases and print them, or hoping our pleas for exposure are heard, we can take some of the control of sending out our messages in these new media on our terms. We get to decide when some of our content gets distributed on our sites and in social media, which makes these social media very powerful tools, but which also calls for these three characteristics in order to maximize our chances of our words and messages being heard when we deliver them. I am not suggesting we abandon our media buyers and PR professionals as that would not be wise.

*Agility* is about content and conversation. You need to be ready to develop content when your target audiences need or want it. I say need because they don't often understand when they need it because they aren't necessarily as on top of subject matter developments as you are. You are on top of changes that are happening in your areas of expertise—changes that can have an impact on your clients and their business. If you are agile, you can then quickly develop content to be distributed to them to give them the heads-up.

You also need to be ready with the conversation that can come after that content is posted, as well as the ongoing conversation that typically goes along with networking. This online conversation doesn't always have to be driven by a major development. Sometimes it just happens as a result of occupying the same space as someone else. You just engage in conversation to get to know one another. You are agile.

*Client-centric* means that your efforts in online marketing and social media need to always have your clients in mind. If you continue to keep in mind the goal stated earlier in this chapter of being found by your target audiences, then you need to always be thinking about what you can do to help them in these online spaces. You would do this in-person too, wouldn't you? It's not all that different. A helpful personality will provide value whether online or in-person.

*Responsiveness* in social media means just that. You can't just set up shop on these sites, then walk away, hoping for them to be productive for you, your firm and your practices. You have to spend some time watching and observing others, and then you need to interact, or to be responsive, to those you meet.

These three characteristics certainly aren't the only ways I know to be effective in social media, but they are three of the most important. Without them, you will not be remembered, or found, and probably won't have done much to help turn those contacts into connections. What a wasted opportunity.

## [8.7] III. PAY ATTENTION TO THESE THREE SITES FIRST

I could spend the next 25 pages discussing several online social networking sites, discussing why they may or may not be effective use of your time, but I will focus on three.

## [8.8] A. LinkedIn

LinkedIn is the 10,000-pound gorilla of online business networking. It was launched on May 5, 2003, although it was hatched in the living room of co-founder Reid Hoffman in 2002.[4]

LinkedIn is a great way to connect with your target audiences because it delivers a way to find and be found. LinkedIn's CEO, Jeff Weiner, has defined LinkedIn by saying "LinkedIn is about connecting talent with opportunity at massive scale. Tools that enable people to be great at the jobs they are already doing."

Another way to look at the value of LinkedIn for lawyers is to share what J.D. Gershbein of Owlish Communications said, "The spotlight now shines on the brand known as you."[5] What an outstanding opportunity! The good news is that shining that spotlight is now possible for everyone, every team, every office and every business unit within the firm, whether yours is a firm of one or 10,000.

Here is what we know about LinkedIn:[6]

- LinkedIn has more than 313 million members in over 200 countries and territories.

- Professionals are signing up to join LinkedIn at a rate of more than two members per second.

- 20% of all online users use LinkedIn.

- LinkedIn counts executives from all 2013 Fortune 500 companies as members.

- More than 3 million companies [or firms] have LinkedIn Company Pages.

- There are more than 1.5 million unique publishers actively using the LinkedIn Share button on their sites to send content into the LinkedIn platform for others to see.

---

4   press.linkedin.com/about-linkedin.

5   J.D. Gershbein, *What the LinkedIn Changes Mean to You*, Success, www.success.com/article/what-the-linkedin-changes-mean-to-you.

6   The use of "professionals" by LinkedIn is not the same as the use of the word in the legal profession, meaning this statistic is not all about lawyers.

- There are more than 2.1 million LinkedIn Groups, with 8,000 new ones being formed every week.

- LinkedIn is available in 23 languages.

- It has more than 5,700 full-time employees with offices in 30 cities around the world.

- 67% of LinkedIn members are located outside the U.S.

- In Q2, 2014, mobile accounted for 45% of unique visiting members to LinkedIn.

- There are over 39 million students and recent college graduates on LinkedIn. This is LinkedIn's fastest-growing demographic.

## [8.9] B. Twitter

Twitter is another amazing network. I fell in love with it back in 2008 when I discovered CNN anchor Rick Sanchez, an early adopter of social media use on TV, using it during his newscast to discuss the presidential election. In order to add my two cents to the discussion I was watching take place online on a life-size screen behind his anchor desk, I created an account in less than a minute. The Tweets were scrolling rapidly as the Tweets were pouring in from people from all over the world who were discussing the candidates and the election.

I am not a political animal in my discussions on social media, but decided I would join the discussion because he was comparing apples to apples, and I just couldn't have that. Not that he would ever see, read or acknowledge my comment, but having the ability to connect with people all over the world was fascinating, exhilarating, educational and eye-opening to me. I was hooked, and have never turned back. I have formed some of the most meaningful relationships of my career on Twitter, which eventually spilled over to Facebook and LinkedIn, where we connect on many different levels. I have gained new business as a result of building relationships on these sites.

A few facts about Twitter:[7]

- Twitter was established in 2006, then incorporated in April of 2007.

---

[7] Twitter statistics found at https://about.twitter.com/company.

- There are over a billion registered Twitter users.
- There are 271 million monthly active users.[8]
- 78% of Twitter active users are on mobile.
- Twitter supports over 35 languages.
- Twitter is headquartered in San Francisco.
- It has 3,300 employees in offices around the world.
- Twitter's micro-video service, Vine, has more than 40 million users.

## [8.10] C. Facebook

Facebook is the one site of the three we are discussing in this chapter that might take you by surprise. What could a largely *social* network like Facebook, with pictures, pets, people and products, possibly have to do with growing your practice and your firm?

Yes, it is those things, but it is also much more. If you have been led to believe that is all that's happening "over there," then your sources or your eyes have been selling you short. As Facebook states in its newsroom,[9] its "mission is to give people the power to share and make the world more open and connected. People use Facebook to stay connected with friends and family, to discover what's going on in the world, and to share and express what matters most to them." Not only do I admire such a lofty mission statement, and would love to see all of us develop one that speaks to what we do every day, but I also believe it can fit nicely into your business plans.

Facebook allows you the space to create a business "Page," formerly called a Fan Page, where you can build community, share, educate, entertain or whatever else you would like to do that fits ethically into your marketing and business development plans. You may have read how Facebook has been making it increasingly difficult for all of us to gain traction with, and eyeballs to, our Facebook Pages. My observations tell me this is true, and that Facebook is attempting to find ways to monetize

---

8   It has become standard practice to report "active" users as those who use these sites at least once a month.

9   newsroom.fb.com/company-info.

its business platform because it is a publicly traded company, and because it is a very expensive business to run. I can understand this, but also know it can be frustrating to find the time to try to combat these practices of Facebook.

Keep in mind that Facebook also offers an incredibly targeted advertising platform to all of its Page owners. You can not only upload the email addresses of existing business contacts, but you can also tell Facebook the keywords and demographics that you are targeting. In both cases, Facebook will then deliver your ads to these people you have identified. This holds very interesting opportunity to firms and businesses of all types.

I also want you to consider spending time on the personal side of Facebook. With over a billion active users, the chances that you will find your friends, business contacts, influencers in your practice area, media you would like to get to know, and even referral sources, is pretty strong. If you don't want to discuss personal matters, share family updates, talk about what you do in your spare time, then don't. There are no hard and fast rules for what you have to share on Facebook, but there are, as you know, many people who will try to convince you it is a silly platform that has no place in the business of law.

I watch dozens of legal profession contacts share valuable information on a daily basis on the personal side of Facebook via their newsfeeds. I also learn about trending news topics in my area and in the world because of what I see shared on Facebook, both by my "friends" and also by Facebook as they watch to see what I am interested in, and then serve more of that to me. I also watch these same people test the platform as a discussion forum for topics they care about in their area of expertise, offering their perspective, but also doing that which is critical on every social medium that exists, and that is to ask the opinions of others. Sometimes people will join your discussion, and sometimes they won't. Sometimes they will just stop by to click "like," click on an article you've shared in order to save it to read later, or to simply see your name float by in their personal newsfeed. I am seeing real business and personal relationships being developed on Facebook, and it's not necessarily on business Pages, so I encourage you to explore this medium as well. Again, remember that we want to build know, like and trust factors with our potential clients, and Facebook is certainly a strong platform to do so.

A few interesting facts about Facebook:[10]

- Facebook was launched by Mark Zuckerberg and his co-founders on February 4, 2004.

- It then spread from a service focusing on use solely by Harvard students to Stanford, Columbia and Yale the following month, March, of 2004.

- There are 829 million daily active users as of June, 2014.

- There are 1.07 billion mobile monthly active users.

- There are 654 million mobile daily active users.

- Approximately 81.7% of Facebook's daily active users are outside the United States and Canada.

- Facebook had 7,185 employees as of June 30, 2014.

- Facebook launched Chat in April of 2008.

- The Like button was introduced in February of 2009.

- Facebook purchased photo- and now video-sharing site, Instagram, in April of 2012.

## [8.11] IV. HOW TO GET STARTED

To get started on all three of these networks, or any other social networking sites, you need to perform similar activities on each, although they will look different on each site because the platforms have been built to be different, both in appearance and use. I have developed *Seven Stages of Social Networking* to help guide you as you embark upon, or ramp up, your social networking activity. These aren't science, and they aren't anyone's gospel. They are just my observations from many years of use, which I fully expect to change every now and then as I see social media evolve.

---

10  Facebook's Newsroom can be found at newsroom.fb.com/company-info.

# SOCIAL MEDIA § 8.12

## [8.12] A. Preparation

This is where you go through the mechanics to set yourself up to use that site. Reserve your name with no underscores, no clever names that will be hard for your friends and followers to remember, and no tricky monikers or logos. One of the most important reasons not to do this is that some of the sites don't allow it. Reserve your name now on Twitter, for example, before someone else does, even if you aren't ready to use it. Join Facebook with your name, not your firm name. On LinkedIn, only use your actual name that people know you by, not a more formal, lengthy name that might not come up in a search.

## [8.13] B. Build a Good Profile

You have a limited number of characters to describe yourself, so be direct. Let people know what you do when they click on your profile. Again, make sure to give your real name so people know what to call you, where you live, the type of clients you work with, etc. Give a good link to a blog or website where your followers can go to learn more about you, and to find out what you know. Make sure you upload a picture before you ever follow the first person because you will not be taken seriously, and even thought poorly of, if there is an empty spot where your picture is supposed to be.

## [8.14] C. Communication 1.0

The reason I call this 1.0 is that, at this point, you are just dipping your toe in to the communication waters here. You will notice Communication 2.0 a bit further down; however, this stage is where I suggest you post just a few simple messages, updates or comments to your account so that when you begin to follow or connect with people in the next stages, and they go look at your Profile, they will look to see what kind of substance is behind you.

Go ahead and post a few messages, saying something like, "Hi, just joined LinkedIn," or "Just figuring out Twitter . . . looking forward to connecting with others who care about water and air rights," or "Hoping to understand Facebook etiquette through observation so I can understand how and whom to friend. Any suggestions?" This way, visitors to your Profile will understand you are still new, but they see you are humbly setting up your account and learning, and they will often reach out to help you.

## [8.15] D. Connection

This is where you start looking for people you want to learn from, teach, have fun talking to, have as clients, or hire, depending on your goals. On Twitter, you can do this by conducting a search using very specific search terms just as you would on Google. When you find people you think fit into these categories, look at their connections and followers, and whom they are following. You will definitely find more people with whom you would like to connect. On LinkedIn and Facebook, I would suggest allowing the sites to review your email list so you can find out who is already there. You can then choose those you want to connect with from a list. On LinkedIn, always send and accept invitations with a personal note or comment on the site. Don't use their standard, terribly impersonal auto-message.

## [8.16] E. Observation

For a while, observe how others do what they do and how they do it, but also remember that is just their way, not necessarily the only way. You will learn trends and methods; some you will like and some you won't. This is where you begin to form your own method and style for using social media. I don't necessarily recommend my method of using social media to all clients because it completely depends on their situation, what their goals are, and what they become comfortable communicating over time. Everyone is different, and that's okay.

## [8.17] F. Communication 2.0

This is where social networking begins to become fun and useful. Once you have watched for a bit, jump in and say something. You can do this in a variety of ways—either by commenting on something someone has written, a conversation between others (this is fine, and expected on mediums as public as Facebook, Twitter and even LinkedIn), or by simply making periodic statements about what you are working on without revealing any specifics that would harm client confidentiality, cause conflict of interest, or that would sound self-laudatory.

You can also begin doing one of the most important things you can do in social media, which is to share, comment on, and forward what others have said.

## [8.18] G. Education

Another way to communicate is by asking an opinion about something non-confidential that you are working on, or by posting a link to an interesting article or blog post you are reading, or one you have written.

This is not only about educating your followers, friends and connections, but also about being educated by those you follow. There is an incredible amount of information shared via social media. You will be amazed how much you learn that you never knew before, or how much more you will learn about topics with which you were already familiar. These are some of the richest, most amazing growth tools available for our knowledge, as well as our followers.

## [8.19] H. Collaboration

This is where all of your efforts can begin to pay off. When you begin to develop relationships, and often close friendships, with some of your contacts and followers, you might find you become comfortable referring business when you might not have ever met in-person. You might even get to the point where you partner with your followers and contacts to work on projects together.

## [8.20] V. BEST PRACTICES

As we discussed earlier in this chapter, you need to commit to making this work, or it won't. What I have discovered time and time again is that when I put time into social media marketing and networking, I see results. This means when I spend time getting to know others, sharing their content, commenting on what they have written and said, and reaching out to meet new people, I see my network, my community, and my connections, grow. You need to do the same.

Therefore, the best practices I suggest you follow are:

1. Decide you are committed to taking this journey, and giving it a chance to become an integrated part of your marketing and business development plan. If you are not committed, or if your firm is not committed to your involvement, don't even start because you need the tide behind you to support you in this journey.

2. Decide where your weaknesses lie, and strengthen them. That can mean embarking upon your own discovery and learning process,

or it might mean reaching out to experts who can guide you through the process.

3. Decide who will be in charge. Sometimes that means you, but sometimes that means a person whose responsibility it is to oversee these communication efforts.

4. Build a social media marketing plan.

5. Build social media guidelines to help you wade through possible situations that could occur.

6. Communicate, communicate and communicate even more!

## [8.21] VI. A BIT ABOUT ETHICS

We can't talk about online or offline marketing and communications if we don't address the ethical implications of what you are doing. One of the most important points you need to remember is that, if you can't do it offline, then don't do it online.

There are rules written state by state, so research into all of the states in which you practice must be conducted. As additional and important guidance, don't forget what we have learned in the ABA's Model Rules of Professional Conduct, Rule 7.2: Advertising, which states that, "Subject to the requirements of Rules 7.1 and 7.3, a lawyer may advertise services through written, recorded and electronic communication, including public media."

Regarding solicitation, Rule 7.3: Direct Contact With Prospective Clients, also tells us that "A lawyer shall not by in-person, live telephone or real-time electronic contact solicit professional employment [from a prospective client] when a significant motive for the lawyer's doing so is the lawyer's pecuniary gain, unless the person contacted: (1) is a lawyer; or (2) has a family, close personal, or prior professional relationship with the lawyer."

There is much more written in the ABA Model Rules, as well as by jurisdiction, so I encourage you to stay on top of these rulings and changes as online marketing continues to be defined. Remember, it is our responsibility to stay in front of all of these rules, and to operate in the purest ethical manner, in order to help run your practice with the integrity, trust and credentials you have been given.

As lawyers Carolyn Elefant and Nicole Black wrote in their book, *Social Media for Lawyers*,[11] social media change the media, not the message.

Here are my suggestions regarding ethics:

- Always follow the Model Rules of Professional Conduct, and the rules of all governing bodies in the jurisdictions where you practice.

- Maintain confidentiality.

- Don't create an attorney-client relationship by providing legal counsel or responding to facts discussed online.

- Be mindful of conflicts. Sever any ties or connections when you deem them a conflict with any other representation or matter.

- Establish internal social media policies and guidelines, and follow them. Conduct regular training on them to make sure you and others are always up to speed.

- On LinkedIn, watch out for recommendations, and skills and expertise endorsements. Know all local rules governing these areas. If they are gray, or murky, and some are, seek guidance.

- Watch the use of the words "specialties" and "expertise." Understand why and how these are subject to sanction in each geographic area in which you practice.

## [8.22] VII. FINAL THOUGHTS

- Learn social media etiquette.

- Add value when you are online.

- Don't over-automate your content delivery to these social networking sites.

- Create a plan.

---

[11] Carolyn Elefant and Nicole Black, Social Media for Lawyers: The Next Frontier (ABA Law Practice Management Section 2010).

- Integrate social with all other marketing and communication tactics.

- Demonstrate commitment.

- Decide you are in this for the long haul.

- Remember the effects are cumulative. Think long term.

- Think relationships by focusing on turning contacts into connections.

- Don't overthink this, meaning don't make it more difficult than it needs to be.

- Speak to people.

- Listen to others.

- Remember that social networking is a contact sport. You are there to digitally touch others in a positive way.

- Ask questions.

- As with all networking, remember that this takes proper care and feeding to grow your online presence and community.

- You have to practice if you want to become more comfortable with all of this. Remember, this is a marathon, not a sprint.

You have to be patient. This all takes time, which is no different than in-person networking and business development. The reason this is worth it is that there are no more boundaries. Communication is more under your control today than it was yesterday. Relationship-building can be accomplished in ways you've never experienced before. It's time. Start reaching out today.

CHAPTER NINE

# LEGAL ETHICS AND LAWYER BUSINESS DEVELOPMENT

Michael Downey

## [9.0] I. INTRODUCTION

What methods of business development do the New York Rules of Professional Conduct (New York Rules) allow?

Lawyers' business development activities—including marketing, advertising, and soliciting potential clients—are subject to a fairly comprehensive regulatory regime, a regulatory regime more rigorous than the rules governing other profession's advertisements. Nevertheless, I believe the question of what business development methods are allowed is the wrong question to ask. Lawyers are generally permitted to engage in most types of business development as long as certain requirements are satisfied regarding the content, distribution, funding, and retention of advertisements. The only conduct prohibited tends to be soliciting legal work in "real time," using deception to solicit clients, soliciting non-lawyer strangers in "real time" (mainly in person or by telephone), and employing runners or sharing fees with referral sources.

The reference to the "certain requirements" that regulate lawyer business development, however, oversimplifies a somewhat complicated framework of regulations imposed on the content, distribution, funding, and retention of lawyer advertisements and business development efforts. The best approach to understanding this framework is to understand its historic underpinnings, which in turn require an understanding of the development since 1977 of First Amendment protections to lawyer business development activities, primarily advertising. Accordingly, this chapter begins with discussion of the development of constitutional principles governing the regulation of lawyer business development, before discussing what conduct is prohibited and how other conduct is regulated under the New York Rules of Professional Conduct as effective on October 1, 2014.[1]

## [9.1] II. SUPREME COURT PRECEDENT SHAPES THE FRAMEWORK FOR REGULATION OF LAWYER BUSINESS DEVELOPMENT

The ethics rules that regulate lawyer business development in New York are, like the ethics rules in every United States jurisdiction except

---

1   Part 1200 of the Joint Rules of the Appellate Division (22 N.Y.C.R.R. Part 1200).

California, modeled on the American Bar Association (ABA) Model Rules of Professional Conduct (the ABA Model Rules). The framework for the ABA Model Rules governing lawyer advertising and business development, in turn, is based on a series of U.S. Supreme Court decisions that began with *Bates v. State Bar of Arizona*.[2]

For decades prior to *Bates*, New York and most other states prohibited lawyers from engaging in virtually any type of advertising or overt business development activities. In *Bates*, in fact, two Arizona lawyers, John R. Bates and Van O'Steen, faced potential lawyer discipline for placing an advertisement in a daily newspaper, with the headline, "Do You Need a Lawyer? Legal Services at Very Reasonable Fees."

The president of the Arizona Bar filed a bar complaint against Bates and O'Steen on the basis that publication of their advertisement violated Arizona Code of Professional Responsibility Disciplinary Rule (Arizona DR) 2-101(B), which in part stated:

> *A lawyer shall not publicize himself*, or his partner, or associate, or any other lawyer affiliated with him or his firm, as a lawyer through newspaper or magazine advertisements, radio or television announcements, display advertisements in the city or telephone directories or other means of commercial publicity, nor shall he authorize or permit others to do so in his behalf.

Arizona disciplinary counsel prevailed at a hearing, and a minimum six months suspension was recommended. Later the recommended suspension was reduced to one week for each lawyer. Instead, Bates and O'Steen sought review before the Arizona Supreme Court (which reduced the recommended sanction to a censure) and ultimately the U.S. Supreme Court, arguing in part that Arizona DR 2-101(B) impermissibly infringed upon rights protected by the First Amendment to the United States Constitution.[3]

In June 1977, the U.S. Supreme Court agreed that the blanket ban on lawyer advertising imposed by Arizona DR 2-101(B) violated the First Amendment. In reaching this conclusion, the Court rejected arguments that Arizona DR 2-101(B) should be upheld as necessary to protect the

---

2   433 U.S. 350 (1977).

3   *Id.* at 366.

# LEGAL ETHICS AND LAWYER BUSINESS DEVELOPMENT § 9.1

dignity of the legal profession and proper administration of justice, and that lawyer advertising was inherently misleading.[4]

In reaching this conclusion, however, the U.S. Supreme Court limited its holding in four respects. First, the Court stated that it was leaving for another day what limitations could be imposed on statements concerning the "quality of legal services."[5] Second, the Court said the *Bates* decision should not be read as deciding what limitations could be imposed on in-person solicitations by attorneys or their "runners." Third, the Court expressed its view that "false, deceptive, or misleading" advertising was "subject to restraint."[6] And fourth, lawyer advertising could be subjected to restrictions as long as they were reasonable as to "time, place, and manner of advertising."[7] This included that "advertising on the electronic broadcast media" would warrant "special consideration."[8]

In the years following the *Bates* decision, the Supreme Court granted certiorari and issued opinions in several major cases involving First Amendment challenges to regulations restricting lawyer advertising, decisions that helped clarify how states could limit lawyer advertising. We discuss the most significant aspects for our purposes of five of these decisions:

- *Ohralik v. Ohio State Bar Association*, 436 U.S. 447 (1978), where the Court permitted a state to ban direct, in-person solicitation of prospective clients, specifically in a personal injury action;

- *Zauderer v. Office of Disciplinary Counsel*, 471 U.S. 626 (1985), where the Court held a state could not discipline an attorney for "soliciting legal business through printed advertising containing truthful and nondeceptive information and advice regarding the legal rights of potential clients" who might be able to pursue a specific type of case;

- *Shapero v. Kentucky Bar Association*, 486 U.S. 466 (1988), where, reviewing a solicitation letter sent to people facing foreclosure, the Court rejected a complete ban on solicitation letters targeted to potential clients known to face particular legal problems;

---

4   *Id.* at 368–76.

5   *Id.* at 366.

6   *Id.* at 383–84.

7   *Id.* at 384.

8   *Id.*

- *Peel v. Attorney Registration & Discipline Commission of Illinois*, 496 U.S. 91 (1990), which allowed a lawyer to state truthfully that he was certified as a civil trial specialist by the National Board of Trial Advocacy; and

- *Florida Bar v. Went for It, Inc.*, 515 U.S. 618 (1995), which upheld a state's rule that imposed a 30-day blackout period after accidents and disasters before lawyers could solicit victims and their relatives.

Of particular importance for this discussion, the *Bates*, *Ohralik*, and *Shapero* decisions distinguished between (1) *in-person solicitations*, which under *Ohralik* could be banned; (2) *truthful general advertisements*, which under *Bates* had to be allowed but could be regulated as to time, place, and manner; and (3) *targeted, mailed solicitations*, which under *Shapero* could be subjected to greater regulations. These three opinions demonstrate that the level of constitutional protection for lawyers' business development activities is inversely related to the invasiveness of the communication method employed.

Or, as the Court states in *Shapero*, "In assessing the potential for overreaching and undue influence, the mode of communication makes all the difference."[9]

In its Model Rules, the American Bar Association roughly follows this construct, but it does not seek to impose the maximum level of regulations that the Constitution permits. Rather, the ABA appears willing to avoid getting close to constitutional limits, and thus gives lawyers a freer rein to advertise and solicit clients than may be necessary.

A number of states, including New York, however, regulate lawyer business development communications more rigorously, perhaps even to the fullest extent permitted under the Constitution. In these states, as the lawyer's advertising and client solicitations become more targeted at prospective clients and thus more invasive, the state also increases its regulation. The result is something of a narrowing funnel: the more targeted the communication, the more heavily it is regulated.

Several states that impose more strenuous restrictions than the ABA—such as Louisiana, New York, and Virginia—have faced constitutional challenges and claims that their restraints on lawyer advertising and client solicitation are unconstitutional. Ordinarily the lawyer wins these chal-

---

9    *Shapero*, 486 U.S. at 475.

lenges because the state cannot make the necessary showings to justify its additional regulations. The case challenging New York's restrictions on lawyer advertising was brought by Alexander & Catalano, LLC, which won most of its challenge in *Alexander v. Cahill*.[10] New York then amended its lawyer advertising rules, but again imposed restrictions beyond what the ABA Model Rules impose. The resulting regulations may still overstep the constitutional limits on how states may regulate lawyer advertising and client solicitation. My advice to lawyers, however, is that unless they have a willingness to sue the bar they should simply comply with the applicable ethics rules as written. Accordingly, this chapter likewise provides guidance on the New York Rules as written, without regard to whether the various restrictions would pass constitutional muster.

## [9.2] III. ABA MODEL RULES GOVERNING LAWYER MARKETING

As the U.S. Supreme Court was deciding *Bates* and its progeny, the American Bar Association modified the ABA model ethics rules to reflect the guidance on what restrictions were constitutionally permissible. Today there are five rules focused on regulating lawyer advertising. In summary, those five rules are:

- Model Rule 7.1, which prohibits a lawyer from making a false and misleading statement in any communication—including both private communications and advertising—about a lawyer or the lawyer's services;

- Model Rule 7.2, which expressly provides that lawyers may advertise, subject to ABA Model Rules 7.1 and 7.3; establishes a requirement that an advertisement must identify at least one party responsible for the advertisement; and prohibits the payment of referral fees to non-lawyers for referring work to a lawyer (except in limited circumstances);

- Model Rule 7.3, which regulates two types of solicitations, which are communications seeking retention for a specific legal matter. Model Rule 7.3(a) generally bans in-person and real-time solicitations of clients, except where the person solicited is a lawyer or has a family, professional, or close personal relationship with the soliciting lawyer. Model Rule 7.3(b), meanwhile, allows but imposes additional restrictions on lawyer solicitations that are delivered in writing, by recording, or other electronic means—in other words solicitations that are not

---

10   598 F.3d 79 (2d Cir. 2010).

"real time"—including that such communications must be labeled "Advertising Material";

- Model Rule 7.4, which restricts how and when a lawyer may claim to be an expert or specialist in a particular area of the law; and

- Model Rule 7.5, which regulates what name a law firm may use, including allowing the use of trade names and prohibiting certain naming conventions that might be misleading.

These five ABA Model Rules, which I refer to as the "Chapter 7 Rules," are designed to interact. In other words, a lawyer advertisement must comply with Model Rule 7.1 *and* Model Rule 7.2, and a lawyer's targeted solicitation of a potential client generally must comply with Model Rules 7.1, 7.2, and 7.3—Rule 7.3(a) if a real-time solicitation (and thus probably not permitted), and Rule 7.3(b) if not a real-time solicitation.

This chapter will not deal with the specifics of these five Model Rules. After all, like many other jurisdictions, New York has adjusted the ethics rules that regulate lawyer advertising so they do not correspond perfectly with the ABA Model Rules. But it may be useful to understand the ABA Model Rules' framework for regulating lawyer advertising, because it reflects the U.S. Supreme Court decisions listed above as follows:

- ABA Model Rule 7.1 prohibits false and misleading communications, which reflects *Bates*;

- ABA Model Rule 7.2 permits lawyer advertising, also reflecting *Bates*;

- ABA Model Rule 7.3(a) virtually prohibits in-person solicitation, as allowed in *Ohralik*;

- ABA Model Rule 7.3(b) permits but imposes additional restrictions on targeted solicitation letters, which are allowed by *Shapero*, and in fact are often called "*Shapero* letters"; and

- ABA Model Rule 7.4 regulates lawyer claims of specialization, an issue addressed in *Peel*.

## [9.3] IV. NEW YORK RULES GOVERNING LAWYER BUSINESS DEVELOPMENT ACTIVITIES

New York's Rules of Professional Conduct—like the ethics rules of many other jurisdictions that govern lawyer marketing and business development—are based largely on ABA Model Rules 7.1 through 7.5. Yet New York's Rules also make some significant departures from the Model Rules. Much of the remainder of this chapter discusses those Rules, trying to provide practical advice for lawyers on when to observe and how to comply with the New York Rules.

In both the ABA and New York Rules, the so-called "Chapter 7" rules—Rules 7.1 through 7.5—are not the only ethics rules that regulate the content, distribution, and funding of lawyer business development communications. In addition to (both Model and New York) Rule 7.1, several other ethics rules require lawyers to be candid in their communications, including Model/New York Rule 8.4. Further, several ethics rules including the prohibitions on sharing fees in Model/New York Rules 5.4 and New York (only) Rule 5.8 restrict how lawyers can fund lawyer advertising by regulating the sharing of fees with non-lawyers. Finally, Model Rule 5.5 and to a lesser extent New York Rule 5.5 provide some guidance on when a lawyer may face disciplinary consequences for soliciting potential clients in a state where the lawyer is not licensed. This chapter will try to reference those other rules as appropriate, although the focus will be on New York Rules 7.1 through 7.5.

### [9.4] A. Regulation of Firm and Personal Activities

In reviewing this material, the reader may note that there is no separation of firm activities from a lawyer's personal activities. This reflects that the ethics rules that govern lawyer advertising also do not distinguish between firm and personal activities. If a lawyer creates a personal webpage—perhaps by participating in an online social network such as Facebook, LinkedIn, or Twitter—that lawyer's communications about the lawyer's ability and willingness to provide legal services are governed by the same ethics rules that would govern formal marketing efforts by that lawyer's firm. It is becoming more frequent for lawyers to face discipline for information they post on their "own" websites, such as on social media; therefore, even lawyers not involved in a firm's formal marketing efforts should review and be familiar with the ethics rules that govern lawyer advertising, primarily New York Rules 7.1 through 7.5.

## [9.5] B. Content Regulation of Business Development Communications

Turning to New York's ethics rules that govern lawyer marketing and business development efforts, New York Rule 7.1 is—consistent with Model Rule 7.1—the primary tool for regulating the content of lawyer business development communications. But New York Rule 7.1 regulates only *advertising* communications, not "all" communications about a lawyer or lawyer's services like ABA Model Rule 7.1. Further, it does so with a Rule that is much longer and more complicated than the Model Rules that govern lawyer marketing and business development.

New York Rule 7.1 opens with a broad prohibition against deceptive lawyer advertising. Rule 7.1(a) prohibits a lawyer from disseminating any advertisement that "contains statements or claims that are false, deceptive or misleading." This includes a prohibition against deceptive invisible metatags and similar text.

Rule 7.1 also imposes certain requirements on advertisements. All advertisements must include the name, principal office address, and telephone number of the lawyer whose services are offered. In addition, Rule 7.1 requires that any advertisement, other than one on radio, television or billboard or one that appears in a magazine or newspaper, display the label "Attorney Advertising."

Beyond this basic framework, New York Rule 7.1 follows the trend common in other jurisdictions that the following types of communications receive special attention:

- Claims about the lawyer's skill;

- Claims of specialization;

- Discussions of past results;

- Client (or other) paid testimonials; and

- Statements about attorney fees and liability for costs.

Often I warn lawyers that, when dealing with such matters, they should ensure that everything they place in an advertisement, including on a firm or other website, is something they would be willing also to say in an affidavit and to defend under cross-examination from a disciplinary counsel. My advice is quite simple and direct on these points.

# LEGAL ETHICS AND LAWYER BUSINESS DEVELOPMENT § 9.5

Unfortunately, Rule 7.1 is written not in a simple and direct style. Rather, it is a 1400-word rule with 18 parts, numerous subparts, and little evidence of an intent to follow some overriding system of organization. In trying to provide some organization, I believe it is fair to state there are four types of statements generally permitted; four types of statements permitted only when three additional safeguards are observed; and three types of statements that are generally prohibited. There are also a number of provisions that regulate the advertising of lawyers' fee arrangements. To discuss Rule 7.1, I will use these four groupings: (1) statements generally permitted; (2) statements permitted only when additional safeguards are followed; (3) statements generally prohibited; and (4) statements concerning fee arrangements. In using these four groups, I try to respect how Rule 7.1 divides its regulations into these categories, even when this seems somewhat illogical. For example, client identities are treated as permitted statement, although consent is required, but testimonials on pending matters are treated as impermissible, although they are allowed if the fact that the matter is still pending is disclosed.

*Generally permitted statements.* The four types of statements generally permitted and listed in Rule 7.1(b) are:

1. Statements concerning factual information that would typically appear on a lawyer's resume; these statements can be disseminated without complying with additional safeguards or requirements. Specifically, Rule 7.1(b)(1) permits a lawyer to disseminate his or her

   > legal and nonlegal education, degrees and other scholastic distinctions, dates of admission to any bar; areas of the law in which the lawyer or law firm practices, as authorized by these Rules; public offices and teaching positions held; publications of law related matters authored by the lawyer; memberships in bar associations or other professional societies or organizations, including offices and committee assignments therein; foreign language fluency; and bona fide professional ratings.

2. Client identities, as long as the client has provided prior written consent;

3. Information about certain aspects of the attorney's fees, including fees for initial consultations and ranges of fees for certain specified services; and

4. Information about other aspects of the potential lawyer-client relationship, such as acceptable payment methods, nonlegal service providers used, and the lawyer's business or other relationships with those service providers.

*Statements permitted with additional safeguards.* There are also four types of statements listed in Rule 7.1(d) as permitted but requiring adherence to a short list of additional safeguards. Those four types of statements are:

1. Statements "reasonably likely to create expectations about the results the lawyer can achieve";

2. Statements comparing the lawyer's services to the services of other lawyers;

3. Testimonials of current or former clients;

4. Statements regarding the quality of the lawyer's services.

The three additional safeguards required for Rule 7.1(d) communications listed above are:

1. The statement must be factually supported on the date published;

2. The statement must be accompanied by the disclaimer, "Prior results do not guarantee a similar outcome"; and

3. If a testimonial relates to a still-pending matter, the fact that the matter is still pending must be disclosed.

*Generally prohibited statements.* Finally, there are three types of statements that are prohibited by Rule 7.1:

1. Statements that are paid endorsements or made by spokespersons or participants in the advertisement (i.e., actors), unless the fact of compensation is disclosed;

2. Inaccurate representations about the lawyer's firm or law firm affiliations; and

3. Advertisements that appear to be legal documents.

*Statements concerning fee arrangements.* In addition to those four groups, there are numerous provisions that regulate advertising statements concerning attorney fees. Generally, a lawyer is bound by statements concerning fees that will be charged and cannot engage in bait-and-switch tactics such as advertising a fee while knowingly omitting charges for necessarily related services. Yet, beyond these general requirements, Rule 7.1 gets quite specific on fee-related advertisements. If a lawyer advertises a fixed fee for a service, for example, under Rule 7.1(j) the advertised fee must include all services that are "recognized as reasonable and necessary" to complete the advertised task. Also, the lawyer must provide a written statement of the fixed fee agreement at the time the advertisement is disseminated, and must make that statement available to the client at the time of engagement.[11]

Contingency fee lawyers must comply with New York Judiciary Law § 488(3), which directs lawyers handling contingency fee and pro bono matters not to "promise or advertise his or her ability to advance or pay costs and expenses of litigation in such manner as to state or imply that such ability is unique or extraordinary when such is not the case."

Finally, Rule 7.1 imposes requirements on how long an advertised fee must be available. For broadcasted fees, the fee must be available for at least 30 days. For published fees, the published fee must be available for at least 30 days if the publication is republished monthly or more frequently. If the publication is published less frequently, the rate must be available until the anticipated date of the successive publication, or at least 90 days where no successive publication is scheduled.

*Regulations of specific advertising content.* Because of the size and relative disarray of Rule 7.1, it may be useful for a lawyer to have a list of what provisions govern what specific types of content. I offer the following list in the hopes it may help lawyers who find the prior summary somewhat confusing:

- Claims of skill/comparisons—Rule 7.1(d)(1) and (d)(4)

- Claims of specialization—Rule 7.4

- Discussions of past results—Rule 7.1(d)(1) and (3) and 7.1(e)

---

11  *See* N.Y. Rule of Professional Conduct 7.1(j).

- Promises of future results—Rule 7.1(d)(1)

- Client names and endorsements—Rule 7.1(b)(3) and (d)(3)

- Communications about fees—Rule 7.1(b)(3) and (4); Rule 7.1(j); Rule 7.1(l)-(n), Rule 7.1(p)

- Disclaimer—Rule 7.1(f) disclaimer with associated legibility requirements at Rule 7.1(i)

*Targeted solicitations.* The reader should keep in mind that the prior discussion deals only with advertisements not targeted to a person known to have a specific legal need. Where the communication is a permissible uninvited solicitation (*see* "Methods of Delivering Business Development Communications," *infra,* Section III.C), New York Rule 7.3 imposes additional requirements. In truth, however, these requirements are relatively limited. The lawyer must avoid using coercion, duress, and harassment and avoid soliciting anyone who has indicated a desire not to be solicited or who the lawyer knows or should know is unable to exercise reasonable judgment regarding retaining the lawyer. N.Y. Rule 7.3(a)(iv) specifically references that the age or physical, mental, or emotional state of the intended recipient may interfere with the exercise of reasonable judgment, thus preventing the lawyer from soliciting the intended recipient. In addition, N.Y. Rule 4.5 generally prohibits a lawyer from soliciting a potential plaintiff in a personal injury or wrongful death case until 30 days after the date of the incident.

Where a targeted solicitation is permitted, it must include the name, principal office address, and telephone number of the lawyer offering services and file a copy of the communication with the local disciplinary counsel including, if applicable, a list of the recipients. The lawyer must also avoid means of delivery such as certified U.S. mail that might require the recipient to travel to a location other than the ordinary location where the person receives business or personal mail, or that would require a signature.[12] The solicitation must also, where applicable, indicate how the lawyer learned the recipient may need the offered legal services.[13] Finally, any sample retention agreement included in the materials must be marked "SAMPLE" at the top of each in red and a font matching the largest font

---

[12] N.Y. Rule 7.3(d).

[13] N.Y. Rule 7.3(f).

# LEGAL ETHICS AND LAWYER BUSINESS DEVELOPMENT § 9.5

used in the sample agreement, and include "DO NOT SIGN" where the signature would ordinarily be placed.[14]

*Claims of practice focus and specialization.* Again, similar to the ABA Model Rule of the same number, New York Rule 7.4 permits a lawyer to publicly identify an area or areas of practice, or indicate the lawyer's practice is limited to certain areas of law. But the lawyer may not suggest the lawyer is a specialist or specializes in any area of law unless that lawyer has a certification from a certifying body approved by the ABA, and clearly identifies that certifying body. Such a claim of certification also must include the disclaimer, "The [name of the private certifying organization] is not affiliated with any governmental authority."[15] Where the certifying body is recognized by another state (for example, Connecticut), Rule 7.3(c)(2) specifies the disclaimer should read, "Certification granted by the [identify state or territory] is not recognized by any governmental authority within the State of New York."

*Law firm names.* New York Rule 7.5 imposes more stringent regulations on law firm names than the comparable ABA Model Rule. In addition to prohibiting misleading names, New York Rule 7.5(b) also expressly prohibits law firms from using trade names. Only the names of current lawyers at the firm, or firm lawyers now deceased or retired, may be used. Further, when a lawyer assumes public office, the firm shall cease using the lawyer's name unless the lawyer remains actively practicing law and regularly associated with the firm.[16]

Rule 7.5(b) also generally restricts the use of terms like "legal aid," "legal service office," "legal assistance office," and "defender office" to qualified legal assistance organizations. The use of "legal clinic" is also restricted, unless the lawyer's name is also incorporated in the firm name.

*Law firm websites.* Law firms may use domain names that do not include the name of the law firm or a firm lawyer, but all webpages must clearly identify the lawyer or law firm. Also, the domain name may not state or imply "an ability of the firm to obtain results in a matter." Therefore, it would not be appropriate for a New York firm to use the web URL

---

14  N.Y. Rule 7.3(g).

15  N.Y. Rule 7.4(c)(1).

16  N.Y. Rule 7.5(b).

"WinYourCase.com." Finally, the name must not otherwise violate the Rules discussed above.[17]

*Law firm telephone numbers.* Law firms may use telephone numbers that include a domain name, moniker, or motto, as long as the name, moniker or motto does not violate other applicable ethics rules. Thus, again, using 800-WIN-CASE would apparently not be appropriate.

## [9.6] C. Methods of Delivering Business Development Communications

*Advertising in general.* In advertising, Rule 7.1 generally permits lawyers to advertise, as long as the advertisement is not misleading (and complies with the rambling requirements in Rule 7.1 described above). In fact, perhaps unnecessarily, Rule 7.1(r) permits a lawyer to write and speak about legal topics, so long as the engagement is not to give individualized legal advice. A lawyer may also "accept employment that results" from such efforts, from "participation in activities designed to educate the public to recognize legal problems, to make intelligent selection of counsel or to utilize available legal services."[18]

*Targeted solicitations.* With regard to targeted but uninvited[19] solicitations, the New York Rules basically follow the framework sanctioned by the Supreme Court's decisions in *Ohralik* and *Shapero* (discussed *supra* in Section II) that in-person, telephone, and real-time solicitations directed to nonlawyer strangers are prohibited, and that solicitations by other means are heavily regulated.

With regard to permissible in-person and real-time solicitations, Rule 7.3(a)(1) permits such solicitations only to a "close friend, relative, former client or existing client." These terms are not defined; they are also narrower than the scope of permissible solicitations allowed under Model Rule 7.3(a), because Model Rule 7.3(a)(2) allows solicitation of anyone with a "prior professional relationship," not simply clients and former clients.

For other types of solicitations, the lawyer must include the name, principal office address, and telephone number of the lawyer offering services

---

17   N.Y. Rule 7.5(e).

18   N.Y. Rule 7.1(a).

19   N.Y. Rule 7.3(b) expressly exempts responses to a request for a proposal or information from its definition of "solicitation."

and file a copy of the communication with the local disciplinary counsel including, if applicable, a list of the recipients. As in target solicitations, the lawyer must also avoid means of delivery such as certified U.S. mail that might require the recipient to travel to a location other than the ordinary location where the person receives business or personal mail, or that would require a signature.[20] The solicitation must also, where applicable, indicate how the lawyer learned the recipient may need the offered legal services,[21] and any sample retention agreement included in the materials must be marked "SAMPLE" at the top of each in red and a font matching the largest font used in the sample agreement, and include "DO NOT SIGN" where the signature would ordinarily be placed.[22]

### [9.7] D. Retention Requirements

Rule 7.1(k) generally requires a lawyer to retain copies of advertisements for three years from first dissemination. Webpages shall be kept at least one year. Rule 7.1(k) also specifies that websites should be preserved upon initial publication, after any major change in design, and after extensive changes in content, but in any event no less than once every 90 days.

Although the location of the requirement is a bit odd, it appears Rule 7.3(b)(2) requires lawyers to keep a copy of all targeted solicitations, as well as an accurate translation if not in English, for three years after the last date of dissemination.

### [9.8] E. Paying for Business Development Activities

In addition to regulating what a lawyer says to develop business, how the lawyer delivers the message, and whether the lawyer must retain a copy of the communication, numerous ethics rules regulate how the lawyer may pay for promotional activities. Generally, a lawyer may pay reasonable advertising charges, but the lawyer may not share fees with a nonlawyer or pay anyone for recommending the lawyer or the lawyer's services.

In addition, a lawyer may not pay a member of the media for publicity, Rule 7.1(o).

---

20   N.Y. Rule 7.3(d).

21   N.Y. Rule 7.3(f).

22   N.Y. Rule 7.3(g).

Referral fees, meanwhile, generally may be paid only to lawyers, and then as Rule 1.5(g) allows. Rule 7.2 does recognize three exceptions when referral payments may be made: (1) referral arrangements with non-law firm service providers regulated under Rule 5.8 and 7.2(a)(1); (2) payments to qualified legal assistance organizations regulated under Rule 7.2(a)(2); and (3) referrals from groups such as legal aid offices, military legal assistance offices, and certain legal service plans, all regulated under Rule 7.3(a)(4).

### [9.9]  F. Activities Outside States of Licensure

Finally, lawyers commonly question whether they can try to market or solicit business outside their states of licensure. Generally this type of activity creates risks. Specifically, the lawyer may be deemed to be engaging in the unauthorized practice of law, particularly if the lawyer might be deemed to have held himself or herself out as a lawyer licensed in the jurisdiction.[23] Also, the state where the (potential) client is located may attempt to regulate the lawyer's conduct using its rules, which may or may not conform to New York's rules. In fact, New York's own Rule 7.3(i) states that New York Rule 7.3 applies to lawyers who solicit New York residents as potential clients, even if the lawyer is not licensed in the state.

To avoid such problems, it is often beneficial for a lawyer to (1) disclose on business development communications the jurisdictions where the lawyer is licensed; and (2) try to avoid sending solicitations into areas where the lawyer does not reasonably anticipate being licensed to handle the matter, unless co-counsel is retained and disclosed in the business development communication.

Of note, many lawyers will—and the law likely allows lawyers to—send solicitations to potential clients in states where the lawyer is not licensed, as long as the lawyer is soliciting a matter that the lawyer anticipates will be filed in a federal court where the lawyer is properly admitted, for example the federal court in the state where the prospective client is located or in some other state, perhaps as part of a federal multi-district litigation. In such circumstances, the lawyer may want to include information that suggests this intention, however, as it may help the lawyer avoid or gain quick dismissal of any ethics complaint that might arise from the solicitation.

---

23   *Cf.* ABA Model Rule 5.5(b)(2).

# [9.10] V. HELPFUL GUIDANCE FOR THE MARKETING LAWYER

I realize that the Rules are quite complicated and thus the contents of this chapter can be quite dense. Therefore, I thought I would end with a quick list of 12 helpful hints for lawyers as they embark on business development activities, with the reassuring message that, as long as they avoid these problem areas, they will probably also avoid ethics problems for their business development efforts:

1. Make sure that everything you say in any sort of marketing materials, including your resume and social media sites, is the absolute truth, something you would not mind being questioned about by disciplinary counsel.

2. Make sure anything you say about others, or that you ask anyone to say about you, is also the absolute truth.

3. Only write about clients if they authorize it. Even better, send them what you have written before you publish it and make sure they think it is okay.

4. Avoid claiming you are an expert or specialist, unless you can point to a specific, bona fide entity that has certified you as a specialist.

5. Never try to trick, pressure, or harass anyone into hiring you.

6. If you advertise a fee arrangement, make sure that people who retain you because of the advertisement pay only the advertised fees.

7. Pay reasonable advertising costs, but never share your fees—except with other lawyers as Rule 1.5 permits—or pay anyone for sending you clients.

8. You can say thank you to referral sources, and even send them a periodic gift, but never pay non-lawyers to refer you work—even with reciprocal referrals.

9. Avoid real-time (in-person or telephone) solicitations of non-lawyers who are not close friends or current or former clients.

10. Avoid answering legal questions about specific facts, unless you have decided to be the questioner's lawyer.

11. Presume everyone will someday read everything you write. So, if you don't want someone to read it, don't say it in writing (including email).

12. Keep copies of all advertising communications for at least three years, and be prepared to produce them if disciplinary counsel ever requests them.

# CHAPTER TEN

# FIRM CULTURE

### Donna Drumm, Esq.*

---

\* The author would like to acknowledge Tom Sager of Ballard Spahr LLP for his insights in an interview given for this chapter on Sept. 18, 2014.

# [10.0] I. INTRODUCTION

This chapter is written for the lawyer in a solo or small firm who is contemplating taking a leadership role in restructuring the current compensation structure in their law firm. A paramount aspect of changing the structure is considering the current law firm culture, and the impact the compensation system has on the culture. Compensation structure is the number-one influence of a firm's culture. The purpose of this chapter is to analyze the motivation to alter, define your law firm's internal and external culture, outline compensation models and introduce an adoption format to effect change.

Changing how people get paid is not a light-hearted effort. Motivations for shifting the compensation structure may be as varied as the lawyer, and include

- dysfunction or unfairness observed with the current compensation structure;
- desire to be more profitable;
- client pressure;
- new responsibility to change the compensation system;
- entering into a new practice area; or
- merger or acquisition of another law firm with a different compensation structure.

## [10.1] A. What Is a Law Firm's Culture?

Generally culture is, "Any group of people that engages in some activity together will have a set of values, conventions, and ways of being that are unique to that particular group."[1]

> A culture is a set of beliefs, behaviors, implicit agreements, and practices that are so prevalent in a group that they are essentially assumed. Every company and every law firm has a culture. Unfortunately, the culture of most law firms is some version of—or contains some elements of—the business-as-usual culture described above. It

---

[1] Finding a Law Firm that Works: Lawyers Assistance Program Facilitated by Robert Bircher.

contains beliefs, behaviors, and practices that support people operating on their own, competing, gossiping about, and undermining each other. While not spoken directly, the implicit agreements include some version of: "you don't challenge me about my poor work habits and I won't challenge you about yours.[2]

Most articles on law firm culture are directed toward the law student looking for a job and law firm. Culture is an ingredient to the decision making pie. Yale Law School's office of career and development advises its interviewing 2Ls and 3Ls to assess culture in the law firms for which they are deciding to interview:

> Assess the firm's "culture." Is there a sense of collegiality? Are doors in the office open or closed? Are there photos of family, friends or outside hobbies in attorney offices? Are the attorneys of certain political affiliations? How do the attorneys treat the support staff? What opportunities does the firm provide for social and professional interaction among attorneys? Are there opportunities to join clubs or sports teams with colleagues from work? Consider all of these factors in analyzing the firm's corporate culture and your fit within that environment.[3]

Jordan Furlong, in his blog post *Vulture Culture,* offers an insider's view:

> Culture is what people at the firm actually do every day. In harsher terms, it's what people get away with. Culture is what actually happens. A law firm's culture is the daily manifestation *of its performance expectations and behavioural norms*—what is encouraged and what is tolerated.[4]

---

[2] Rich Goldstein and Ron Bynum, Creating a High Performance Law Firm Through a Culture of Collaboration, *Law Practice Today*, January 2013, www.americanbar.org/content/newsletter/publications/law_practice_today_home/lpt-archives/january13/creating-a-high-performance-law-firm-through-a-culture-of-collaboration.html.

[3] Yale Law School, Career Assessing Law Firms: Culture, Clients, Compensation and Beyond, www.law.yale.edu/studentlife/cdoadvice_assessinglawfirms.htm.

[4] Jordan Furlong, Vulture Culture, Law 21, January 22, 2013, www.law21.ca/2013/01/vulture-culture (emphasis added).

# FIRM CULTURE § 10.2

Law firms have scorecards to evaluate their performance. In the most simplistic examples, the billable hour is Hours x Rate = Pay. Tracking hours on a daily basis with billing systems is a transparent record visible to anyone who has access to the program. Performance reports are sent to clients in the form of billing statements. Cases are won or lost based on written opinions. Culture is how the firm performed to reach the result.

Lawyers' behaviors are codified by the New York Rules of Professional Conduct.[5] They are expected to be competent, diligent and confidential in their client communications. Specific duties extend to prospective clients and former clients. Behavior is regulated by judicial sanctions and the grievance process. In law school, students are required to take courses on professional responsibility. The Multistate Professional Responsibility Exam (MPRE) is required for admission to the bars of all but three U.S. jurisdictions (Maryland, Wisconsin and Puerto Rico).[6] To a great extent the culture of a firm and how its members adhere to these behaviors is judged by the community.

## [10.2] B. Internal Culture

Law firm culture is viewed introspectively by those who are working there and outwardly by other attorneys, judges, clients and the community.

The descriptions below identify internal cultures that occur in many small and solo firms. Management determines the compensation structure. Types of management, many times unintentionally, yield predictive roadblocks to shifting compensation structures. The list is not exhaustive rather illustrative.

## [10.3] C. Culture of Management

*Non-management*—no set goals, lack of action plans and ability to implement strategic objectives. Culture is derived from those who work in the firm in no formal manner. Compensation plans are made on a short-term basis depending on monthly income. Different compensation arrangements are made as new associates and partners join the firm.

*Family-run firm*—the leaders are family members, mother/daughter, husband/wife. The "leaders" or those who impact the decision-making

---

[5] Part 1200 of the Joint Rules of the Appellate Division (22 N.Y.C.R.R. Part 1200).

[6] *See* National Conference of Bar Examiners website, www.ncbex.org/about-ncbe-exams/mpre.

process for compensation may be lawyers and/or non-lawyer family administrators. Those who are not family members operate under an unspoken assumption that they are at a disadvantage and will never achieve the influence that the family members have.

*Long-term management*—the firm has been in existence for many years and there is a defined compensation structure. The firm leadership has adopted an "if it's not broke let's not fix it" attitude.

*Friend-run firm*—the founding partners are friends from law school or otherwise long-term friends. Perhaps a lateral hire was made who was one of the founding partner's friends. Merit and client base aside, the management must recognize this assumption by the employees that they have an equal chance in rising through the ranks.

*Management from non-billable legal institutions*—many smaller firms are created by attorneys whose previous positions were in the government or nonprofit organizations. These managers, comfortable with receiving a regular paycheck and benefits enter into running their enterprise responsible for their own profitability. The business model is completely different and compensation structures must be created to support a "for profit" entity. Given the pressures of starting a new practice, the compensation structure is "borrowed" from other similarly situated law firms.

## [10.4] D. Dangers of Overlooking Culture

The cost of not being aware of a firm's performance expectation and behavioral norms affects one's personal career and the success of the firm. A recently hired attorney, who does not know how he or she is being evaluated, or is incognizant to the behavioral norms of the office, will negatively impact those around him or her. Personal work satisfaction will be impaired. Eventually, he or she will leave or will be asked to leave.[7]

Lack of attention to culture at the organizational level can, in the extreme, lead to public humiliation or close down an organization. After a man out on bail jumped over the gate of the White House, entered and was not apprehended until he was within feet of the family quarters, the U.S. Secret Service, the law enforcement agency responsible for protecting the president and his family, was publicly excoriated and the director resigned within 24 hours after a Congressional hearing. News broadcast-

---

[7] A. Harrison Barnes, *A Firm's Culture Is What Matters Most*, Employment Research Institute, Aug. 23, 2011, www.bna.com/a-firms-culture.

ers, Twitter followers and the public were confounded that this elite force trained with the best technology could let this happen. The answer: the Secret Service's work culture fostered complacency and incompetency.[8] The next section will guide the reader toward identifying your firm's internal and external culture.

### [10.5] E. Law Firm Culture Is Not Transparent

The first challenge in identifying your law firm's culture is to acknowledge that culture is not transparent. Very few law firms publicize their culture on their websites or in marketing literature. Ballard Spahr LLP dedicates a webpage to "The Ballard Way":

> Act with Integrity, Decency, and Respect. Humanity underpins our culture. It guides our interactions and decisions at every level . . . We give our attorneys room to explore and our employees opportunities to excel.[9]

Interestingly, well-known corporations—Avaya, Estee Lauder, Home Depot, and Moody's, to name a few—communicate their corporate culture on their Human Resources pages.

### [10.6] F. Assessing Your Firm's Internal Culture

Exercise 1: Walk through your office as a new client would for the first time. What do you see? Does it match with the culture you wish to convey to your clients?

Is your office casual or formal?—that's the culture speaking

Are the office doors closed or open?—that's the culture speaking

Are clients greeted by a receptionist in a warm and friendly manner?—that's the culture speaking

Are attorneys referred to as Mr. and Ms.? Or by first name?—that's the culture speaking

---

[8] Russell Belman, *The Secret Service Is Beset by a Culture of Complacency and Incompetence*, The Atlantic, Oct. 1, 2014, www.theatlantic.com/politics/archive/2014/10/secret-service-director-resigns-amid-bipartisan-furor/381005; Joe Davidson, *Hearing Hits Secret Service Problem: Its Work Culture*, The Washington Post, Sept. 30, 2014, www.washingtonpost.com/politics/federal_government/hearing-touches-on-secret-service-problem-its-work-culture/2014/09/30/6861ff08-48dc-11e4-b72e-d60a9229cc10_story.html.

[9] The Ballard Way, Ballard Spahr LLP, www.ballardspahr.com/the_firm/the_ballard_way.aspx.

What is the dress code for partners? Associates? Staff?—that's the culture speaking

Do you display awards in your reception area?—that's the culture speaking

### [10.7] G. External Culture

Exercise 2: Assessing your law firm's external culture:

What firms would you consider *similar* to your law firm? In what ways?

Do you respect or aspire to their values? Which ones?

What firms would you consider *dissimilar* to your law firm? In what ways?

Do you respect or aspire to their values? Which ones?

Assessing your firm's internal and external culture to ascertain if it connects with the work environment and values you and your colleagues wish to promote is also important to clients. Clients care about a firm's culture. The context within which a lawyer works influences his or her choices and priorities just as the context within which the clients exist influences their choices. The lawyer works within the rules—both stated and implied—set by the firm. So, when a client is looking for a lawyer, the culture of the firm becomes an important differentiator among firms.

### [10.8] II. COMPENSATION

Now that you have begun the exercise of identifying the culture in your firm, let's take a look at typical compensation models to "sync" the culture you wish to engender in your law firm.

Compensation structures foster the financial health of the firm. They create the fundamental metrics to run your law firm because they are inextricably related to the revenues of the firm. A structure rewards people in the firm for their work and gives clear guidelines on how they can succeed financially. We are addressing compensation in the "marketing" section of this book with the premise that organizations that reward their owners and employees for the value of the work they do cultivate a collaborative working environment which includes serving clients at the highest levels and producing an atmosphere to draw in new business from current clients and new clients.

The methods below are adapted from the article *Partner Compensation Systems in Professional Service Firms* by Michael Anderson. The information should briefly familiarize the reader with six prevalent systems used in American law firms. Law firms borrow from these systems and tweak the percentages to reflect their individual financial situations. The description does not address pay for associates or staff. Each method apportions profit—meaning that expenses, including associate and staff pay, have been deducted.

1. *Equal Partnership.* Equal partnership is typically used by small firms. Tiers of partners (Senior/Junior) are identified and a percentage is allocated to each tier. Each person in the tier receives an equal percentage. Billable and non-billable contributions are rewarded. Individual performance is less important than firm performance. It embodies a culture of one for all, and there is reduced confrontation or finger pointing. Weakness—those who work less will be resented by those who work more.

2. *Lock-Step.* Firm profits are divided based on seniority. Partners at the firm longest receive the highest percentage. This method embodies a client-centric culture where partners are incentivized to grow the firm by increasing client base. Individual contributions and initiatives (creating new products and processes) are not rewarded. It embodies a culture of stability for senior partners. It is also attractive to younger associates and partners who value an "I'll pay my dues" and learn-from-the-wisdom-of-the-senior-partners approach. Weakness—those who work less will be resented by those who work more.

3. *Modified Hale and Dorr.* Firm profits are awarded in percentages for each dollar of revenue collected based on four categories: the originator of the business (finder), the person who maintains the relationship with the client (minder), the person who performs work on the matter (grinder), and discretionary percentage for exceptional performance. This method is flexible; each partner can determine where to put his or her talent, and more value is placed on individual contributions. Weakness—it embodies a client-hoarding culture and associates are kept from receiving work assignments.

4. *50/50 Subjective-Objective System.* Fifty percent is awarded to actual billing or receipts (objective) and client generation (objective), and

50 percent is awarded to client management performance (subjective) and other factors determined by the firm leadership. Time spent training associates, marketing, and firm administration are acknowledged and rewarded. It embodies a culture of accountability and innovation. Weaknesses—those uncomfortable with subjective measurements may feel manipulated and confronted by performance perceptions by other partners.

5. *Team Building.* Fifty percent of a partner's compensation is based on how well the firm does financially; 40 percent is based on a practice or group department's performance, and 10 percent is based on an individual partner's performance. This method values the team over the individual; work is pushed down to the associate. It embodies a culture of equality. Time may be devoted to creating and marketing new services and efficient processes. Weakness—an individual does not control his or her financial future.

6. *Eat What You Kill.* Each partner runs his or her own business of clients. The income from client origination and expenses related to supporting the client are paid by the partner. A client's file may be sold to another lawyer in the firm. Typically the originating partner will retain a 10 percent origination fee for the life of client files he or she sold from the billings. This method is effective for the solo firm. It embodies a culture of hoarding files and clients with multiple partners. Weaknesses—no incentive to grow the firm. Team work is almost non-existent and there is scant opportunity for training of associates.

## [10.9] A. The Client-Centric Law Firm and Cross-Selling

The client-centric law firm was developed by Carol Schiro Greenwald and Steven Skyles-Mulligan in their book *Build Your Practice the Logical Way*. The book's basic premise is that the most effective and efficient way to grow your practice and your firm is to broaden and deepen your relationship with a handful of "best" clients, and to create a prospecting campaign for new clients with characteristics similar to these clients. They call current key clients *foundation* clients.

When a firm focuses financial rewards on origination of new clients rather than expansion of current clients, it will be harder to create the client-centric foundation piece: depth of client. When individuals "own" their clients, it is harder to cross-sell services. When compensation is tied to billable hours attorneys have little short-term incentive to spend non-billable hours on business development, even with their own clients.

Cross-selling is providing additional services to an existing client. Examples are matrimonial attorneys who also handle real estate. They know when their divorce clients will be selling or acquiring property. They offer to handle the transaction themselves or recommend someone else in their office who is qualified. Cross-selling is natural in an environment where compensation is based on the success of the firm. Cross-selling is less likely where compensation is based on the success of the individual, even if the talent is available in the firm.

### [10.10] B. Rainmaker to Umbrella

Create a rainmaker culture where everyone working on the client matter is listening for opportunities. Schedule bimonthly meetings to discuss the possibilities and how the opportunities can be presented to the client for the next matter. Collectively, the team can come up with the best approach to bring to the client. There should be clear measures as to who brings up the opportunity.

### [10.11] C. Listening

Some people have photographic memories and can remember names, faces, children's names and hobbies of everyone they meet. Most of us have to rely on our decaying memories, and a few of us keep notes. Begin a practice of building a memory database of the clients you have targeted for additional work opportunities. At each meeting or phone call, listen for three non-work-related facts about your client, such as names of children, the sports they play, or in-laws who live in the same town as your daughter. Write an email to yourself listing the topics. Then at the next meeting or phone call, refer to the email before the meeting, and ask the client about the topic.

### [10.12] D. Warm Opportunities

As we are taught to spot issues in law school, teach your team to spot warm and hot opportunities. A warm opportunity is a building block to a relationship. This is pure pre-social media. You are stepping out of the worker mode—polite, work-only discussions—to the more social discussions. You are listening for common ground: what do you like about the person? What do you admire about the business, its recent growth, its ability to keep employees for decades? What groups are they members of that you are a member of? What is of interest to this person in his or her business life (books, authors, seminars they attend) or social life (clothes, wine, books, TV shows, movies)?

Examples of warm opportunities are sending an article you think clients might be interested in, mentioning a new restaurant in the area or reading their LinkedIn page and sending them a heartfelt message about how much you appreciated their insight. Send a book review of a book you think they might be interested in. (The *Wall Street Journal* publishes daily book reviews and the *New York Times* publishes book reviews in the Sunday paper). Because you share common ground, it's authentic.

As a building block, once you shift the way you communicate with clients, if they respond in kind and show appreciation for your interest, you can continue to engage. If they rebuff, or show no interest in what you've sent, no harm done. Figure out something else.

## [10.13] E. Hot Opportunities

Hot opportunities are matters in the making. This is information you learned from the client or another source that identifies a legal need that your firm, or a colleague you can collaborate with, can fulfill. The art to turning a hot opportunity to a new matter is timing and listening. If you know your client's business you can see the opportunity. For example: You represent a client who runs a successful business selling teeth-whitening strips on the radio. She mentions in passing that she is working with a dentist who wants to expand her business to online education on dental health. You mention to your client you are aware of the new laws in online education and you would like to discuss with them the steps of their business plan and see where you can help them. After a successful meeting (and consulting appropriate ethical rules including a conflict check), the dentist and your client agree to engage you for the new matter.

Even more subtle is the referral. Suppose in the example above that you did not know about the new laws in online education, and after questioning other partners at the firm, you found no one in your firm practiced in that area. But your friend at the bar association has a top notch online practice. You can still maintain control over acquiring the new matter by referring another attorney to the client, and remain involved in the transaction because of your history and experience with the company. Engagement letters can clarify the boundaries of each of your roles.

## [10.14] F. Be the Undesignated General Counsel For Your Client

The General Counsel (GC) to a corporation is responsible for the legal health of the organization. From human resources to emerging technologies, the GC must have a 360-degree knowledge of the organization in order to anticipate liability and support sound leadership. If your clients employ a general counsel or not, take on the role of the GC for your clients. Become aware of their company as if you were the GC of the company. You are looking for all the interests of the company and, of course, how you can help them. Find out what their needs are, and be forward looking to what trends could hurt or benefit them. Consult social media, Google alerts or make contacts with others in the company.

In her coaching practice for New York-based lawyers who have founded—or are contemplating founding—solo practices or small law firms, Carol Kanarek—who is a University of Michigan Law graduate, a former practicing lawyer, and a licensed psychotherapist in the state of New York—discusses the following issues with her clients. Ms. Kanarek's goal in working with her clients is to help them to identify the intersection of what would be satisfying and realistic for them, and to assist them in "branding" themselves in the crowded legal marketplace.

The following are some of the key issues that Ms. Kanarek suggests the reader consider carefully in planning a practice or in evaluating a firm's current practice:

1. Do you and your current or potential partners have the same expectations regarding the importance of work hours and money? Regardless of whether you are contemplating a solo practice or a partnership, be honest in answering the following questions: What do you envision for you/our firm in one year? Five years? Ten years? How much money do you need and expect to earn?

2. What should be the primary substantive focus of your firm's practice? How will you obtain clients? Are there other professionals with whom you can partner (e.g., accountants, other small firm lawyers) to make cross-referrals?

3. Is your proposed pricing and compensation structure realistic and competitive with lawyers who have a similar substantive focus in your geographic area? What is the objective formula by which you will determine how lawyers in your firm are compensated? One

common formula is one third each of net revenues to each of the following: the lawyer or lawyers who originate the business; the lawyer or lawyers who handle the legal work; and overhead (e.g., salaried employees and/or office expenses). There are many ways to set up compensation structures, but it is critical yours makes rational sense.

4. Are there certain areas of your firm's practice where it makes sense to offer some basic services on a fixed-fee basis (e.g., house closings, drafting a basic will, reviewing a severance agreement)? Are your hourly fees realistic for your substantive and geographic area? It is essential to network with other solo and small firm lawyers whose backgrounds are similar to yours prior to establishing your own firm. LinkedIn is one of the best possible mechanisms for identifying relevant individuals and firms with whom to speak. Many solos and small firms successfully serve as outside counsel on a monthly retainer basis to companies that have no in-house lawyers.

5. What is the primary message you want to send in your website and other marketing materials? Can you work out a way in which you can "job share" with actual or virtual partners, contract lawyers, and/or counsel (who may be paid on an hourly basis) so that your clients will have a seamless experience vis-a-vis your firm but you will be able to maintain some control over your own time?

Ms. Kanarek emphasizes that the great news is that clients are increasingly savvy and cost-conscious—and most of the large firms charge far too much in hourly fees to handle more than a tiny percentage of the legal work that needs to be done. Regardless of your area of practice, if you can project the message that your goal is to partner with your clients to achieve the most cost-effective results for them, you will almost certainly be successful. Indeed, many small firms have much higher profits per partner than do a large number of the firms in the AmLaw 200. Clients are in the driver's seat these days. Those lawyers who project both the substantive and emotional intelligence to partner with their clients have been increasingly successful over the past 15 years. The future of the legal profession belongs to readers like you.

# CHAPTER ELEVEN

# LAW FIRM ACTIVITIES THAT SUPPORT INDIVIDUALS' BUSINESS DEVELOPMENT EFFORTS

Carol Schiro Greenwald, Ph.D.

## [11.0] I. INTRODUCTION

All lawyers in private practice, from solos to mega-firms, have a firm structure that deals with the financial, management, risk and technology functions of a practice. As such, the firm—the "shell" around individual practices—can offer significant marketing support and resources because it performs all the business functions and organizes the distribution of personnel. Attorneys should take advantage of firm resources to multiply the impact of their own individual marketing and relationship-building activities.

In this chapter we will look at the kind of business development support a firm can provide. The discussion is divided into the four core areas in the American Bar Association's (ABA) definition of law practice management:[1]

- Finance (see also the chapters on strategic planning and pricing);
- Management (see also the chapters on culture and coaching);
- Marketing; and
- Technology (see also the chapter on technology).

## [11.1] II. FINANCE

Finance includes not only compensation, but also time and billing data, invoicing systems and expenditure approval mechanisms. The finance department can help you develop metrics to measure specific marketing events in terms of both spent time and money, and to track the value of referral relationships.

*Compensation*: People tend to do what is rewarded; money rewards and facilitates activities. This can impact marketing in various ways. Innovative firms also find ways to set a value on marketing time investments and reward attorneys for initiative as well as success. For purposes of this chapter, this is a reminder that client-centricity (previously discussed in Chapter 4) is more likely to lead to increased business when attorneys are rewarded for expanding clients' use of firm services, or for introducing

---

[1] Since 1974, the ABA Law Practice Division (LP) has supplied lawyers and legal professionals with cutting-edge information and resources related to the core areas of marketing, management, technology, and finance, www.americanbar.org/groups/law_practice/about_us.html.

potential clients even if they do not close the deal, or for doing marketing support activities such as blog posts, webinars, newsletter articles, etc.

*Track business development time:* It is important to customize your time and billing system to track business development time. Create custom fields for lead generation, networking, complimentary client time, sales activities such as RFPs and personal pitches, etc. Develop fields that work for you. If you are active on not-for-profit boards or in community activities such as Little League you may want separate categories that track referrals and business from these sources. Or you might want to separate referrals into categories such as from colleagues, others in your firm, current clients, past clients, targeted sources, online introductions, friends and family. These inputs provide data to justify one expenditure versus another. Review a summary printout every quarter to see where your time is most productively spent.

*Budget marketing expenditures:* Everyone needs a personal marketing plan and budget. The firm should be responsible for aggregating these data in order to analyze ROI for marketing expenditures and also ensure that individuals' plans are complementary. In the best of all worlds, individuals' plans will roll up into practice plans, and practice plans into a firm-wide plan focused on branding, targeting, etc. Solos should also create a plan so that marketing activities are cumulative rather than scatter-shot reactions to random invitations.

*Alternative fee arrangements:* Finance is also important if an attorney wants to move toward client expectations regarding pricing and cost of services. Clients are consumers, and consumers typically know the price of most purchases before they use their credit cards. They shop around before they buy in order to find the best price/value deal. So they become uncomfortable when presented with unlimited budgets based on billable hours that accrue only as a matter plays out. This can be unnerving for clients who want price predictability and control over costs.

One way to mitigate the client-firm pricing disconnect is to consider implementing value billing for those matters that tend to be similar in format, fact patterns, and the legal and administrative processes used to resolve the situation. Think real estate closings, basic contracts, insurance defense litigation. To get a sense of the prices you should charge for these services, go back into your time and records billing data and analyze three to six months' worth of matters like the one for which you want to use value pricing. Break the process of resolving the matter into task and timekeeper components and track the hours and fees. Whenever possible, use the codes set out in the ABA's Uniform Task-based Management System.[2] Once the data are collected from multiple matters, get an average for each task segment. This gives you a time/cost baseline for setting a value-based fee, and a sense of staffing requirements if you want to make a profit. (See example in Table 1.)

### Table 1: CLIENT: SUPERCORPORATION MATTER: *Superman v. Gotham*

| Task | Timekeeper | Level | Date | Time Spent | Rate | Total Dollar Value |
|---|---|---|---|---|---|---|
| Initial meeting | D. Smith | Partner | 2/12/14 | 1 hour | $475 | $475 |
| Fact investigation/development | S. Jones | Paralegal | 2/13/14 | 6 hours | $165 | $990 |
| Analysis/strategy | D. Smith | Partner | 2/14/14 | 4 hours | $475 | $1900 |
| Pleadings | D. Smith | Partner | 2/12/14 | 4 hours | $475 | $1900 |
| Totals | Two Timekeepers | | | 15 hours | | $5445 |

Alternative fees are typically defined as any pricing arrangement not based strictly on the billable hour. The alternative fee discussion begins by understanding the clients' objectives, their definition of success and how they want to share the risks and rewards. Focusing on the outcome leads into discussions concerning matter budgets, timing, process efficiencies and shared technology. Alternative fees not only create a shared-risk situation but also create a shared-win opportunity which gives you, the attorney, a chance to be rewarded for your intellectual acumen and legal skills.

---

2 See the Uniform Code at www.americanbar.org/groups/litigation/resources/uniform_task_based_management_system.html.

When you think about it, the goals conversation can be so important to cementing the client relationship that it has a value all its own. Michael Gruber, a partner at Gruber Hurst Johansen Hail Shank LLP, said, "The way for [AFAs] to be successful is for lawyers and clients to find a way to negotiate a win-win situation. . . . The goal of any AFA should be a lasting relationship between lawyer and client."[3]

*Billing as a marketing tool*: Billing systems should be configured to produce invoices that strengthen the client connection by focusing on progress rather than hours. Even if you keep time by a sixth of an hour, the client cares less about the calendar/hour sequence and more about "what for." To answer the "what for" and show progress toward agreed-upon goals, group time by activity. For example, group all discussions with opposing counsel together—by conversation rather than by date/time and then explain the sequence—what happened and when. This way the client can see not only where the most money went but also what remains to be done.

## [11.2] III. MANAGEMENT

While publicity focuses on AmLaw 100 initiatives to respond to a more client-centric world, in reality it is easier for solos and small firms to adapt to the new normal: Less bureaucracy, fewer silos. Let's look at two such firm initiatives that support individual business development activities: legal project management and customized service packages.

*Legal project management*: Legal project management has been defined as "a proactive, disciplined approach to the management of legal matters using tools, skills, knowledge and systems to enhance efficiency and meet client expectations."[4] Breaking the legal process involved in resolving a matter into segments facilitates exposure of inefficiencies, redundancies and unnecessary steps. It also increases process transparency via-à-vis the client and lends itself to the use of prior work products.

---

3   Deborah McMurray and Paul Bonner, Alternative Fee Arrangements That Work for Clients and Lawyers, *Law Practice*, May/June 2014, p. 36.

4   Susan Raridon Lambreth and Carla Landry, *Can Lawyers Be Trained as Project Managers?* Hildebrandt Baker Robbins Whitepaper 2010, p.1.

# ACTIVITIES THAT SUPPORT BUSINESS DEVELOPMENT § 11.2

Every expert has a different approach to segmentation. We will use the basic approach suggested by the American Corporate Counsel Association.[5] This involves four steps:

- Scope—sets goals and deliverables: what the client wants to accomplish and how the attorney thinks it can be done. Includes establishing a communications plan: whom to speak with, when, about what, etc.

- Schedule/people/budget—establishes a project plan encompassing project scope, milestones, schedules, responsibilities and estimated cost. Determines the activities sequence—establishing phases and itemizing tasks within each phase.

- Conduct of the legal matter—focuses on management of the team, ongoing assessments of activity against plan and, when necessary, discussion of adjustments.

- Review—discusses outcome with the client and team meetings to get their evaluation, lessons learned and areas for improvement.

Using this approach allows implementation of the value-added conversation that underlies modern client relationships. It establishes the client's role, sets activity and pricing expectations and provides a formal framework for ongoing communication so there are no surprises. The final stage, review, cements the client relationship by asking for and implementing their suggestions regarding what worked and what needs changing.

Solos and small firms that undertake legal process management will find that it frees up time which can be spent providing the creative value clients want to pay for. There are many project management software programs available at all price levels, but to begin, attorneys can launch their program with paper forms. Redo your client intake form to include questions as to client's goals, expectations, preferred role in the proceedings, etc. Create matter (project) budgets, spreadsheets, schedules, and communication plans. Replace the billable hour focus with an outcome focus that looks to do the best job possible given the available time, resources and money.

---

5    ACC Value Challenge, American Corporate Counsel Association, www.acc.com/valuechallenge/resources.

## [11.3]  IV.  MARKETING

Of course, this whole book is focused on marketing and business development. The firm supplies the money in most cases for everything from networking lunches to conference sponsorships. Here, we will look at three marketing initiatives that are best expedited at the firm or practice group level: client teams, cross-selling programs, and client-friendly service packages.

### [11.4]  A.  Client Teams

According to BTI Consulting Group,[6] 92% of law firms said they are targeting existing clients, but only 33% said they fund client teams as a way to invest in them.

> The funded team can (and does) perform client research, develops client-specific tools and educational platforms, spends more time with clients outside the context of current matters—all key components of a client-centric growth strategy. The most powerful ingredient in any client team is the client. Your ability to leverage your client's needs, objectives, preferences and priorities drives success.[7]

Client teams include everyone who is currently working on a project or has a legal expertise that might be of use to the client. Teams are run by a team leader, usually the client relationship partner, who holds regularly scheduled meetings to discuss trends in the client's world and of the client itself, competitive news, progress on client matters and ideas as to how to deepen the relationship by introducing new attorneys to the client or making a case for the client's need to use additional services.

Boutique firms and solo attorneys can adapt the concept by creating service relationships with resources outside their firms. These might include attorneys with other areas of expertise that the client could use or other service professionals such as accountants and financial planners who can enrich the current services used by the client. Teams enable attor-

---

6   *Law Firms Hyper Focus on Existing Clients: Only 1/3 Mean It*, BTI's Blog: The Mad Clientist, March 19, 2014, www.btibuzz.com/buzz/2014/3/19/law-firms-hyper-focus-on-existing-clients-only-13-mean-it.html.

7   *Id.*

neys to provide forward-thinking advice—the value-add clients are willing to pay for.

## [11.5] B. Cross-Selling

Client teams are an institutionalized way to foster cross-selling. But even without them, firms can create programs to foster a cross-selling culture. The programs begin from the assumption that you can't sell if you don't know. Often attorneys are only superficially friendly even with the attorney who sits next door to them. Several programs can mitigate the "no knowledge" problem:

- Create a series of cross-selling breakfasts or lunches at which a designated practice area or sub-area reports on what it is doing, whom it is doing it for and what kinds of situations would suggest the need for their services. This gives those in the room a better sense of when to offer these services as well as stories about how their colleagues have handled similar situations.

- This program should be paired with a "take an attorney to lunch" program that encourages one-on-one meetings with individuals whose skill sets are relevant to the inviting attorney's client base.

Armed with this kind of knowledge cross-selling becomes more comfortable.

Cross-selling is also a proven technique for increasing the likelihood that clients will remain with a firm. In a 2007 study, the Redwood Think Tank[8] found that retention improves when:

- The client gives the firm a large percentage of its legal work;

- The client has a mature, well-established relationship with the firm;

- When the firm works with the client in two or more practice areas;

- When more than two partners in the firm work with the client's management team.

---

8   Kris Satkunas, *Client Attrition Analytics: Firms Can Control Whether Clients Stay or Go*, Redwood Analytics: 2007 Business of Law Review, 5.

Again, smaller firms or solo attorneys can adapt the cross-selling mindset to their situation by creating value-links with other providers. Use a worksheet like the one below to analyze those key clients worth this kind of investment and plan how to make cross-selling happen.

### Table 2: Cross-Selling Action Grid

| Client name/key contacts | Client's needs | Relevant trend, happening, new law or regulation | Services to offer them | Reasoning behind the offer, specific value-adds | Action Plan: goals, responsibilities, time line |
|---|---|---|---|---|---|
| | | | | | |
| | | | | | |
| | | | | | |

## [11.6] C. Customized Service Packages

Where is it written that the services offered to clients should reflect the organizational set-up of a law firm? Wouldn't it make more sense for a client-centric firm to create customized packages of services, often with a flat fee, in order to build a relationship with depth?

Assuming the answer to the first question is, "Nowhere," and the answer to the second question is "Yes," the question then becomes how to create such packages. Begin again from clients' needs.

- For example, a divorcing spouse needs not only a divorce agreement but quite possibly lawyers to deal with a real estate sale or lease, changes to his or her will, a review of the tax implications of the divorce, etc.

- A tech start-up may need not only corporate contracts, but also an intellectual property attorney to protect its idea and a tax attorney to help it use the "Silicon Alley" tax advantages in New York City.

Attorneys in full-service firms can create multi-disciplinary marketing groups that combine the services into one package and then create joint marketing materials to sell them as a value-add of working with the firm. Attorneys in one-practice boutiques or solo attorneys can form informal groups to create the same package approach. In both cases the client is saved the bother and stress of finding and vetting additional lawyers, and the attorneys have the service advantage of working with others who will treat the client with a service that matches its own.

## [11.7] V. TECHNOLOGY

Remember the *New Yorker* joke showing two dogs at a computer? One says to the other, "On the Internet, nobody knows you're a dog." So too technology levels many playing fields, allowing small firms to compete with much larger firms as well as online competitors. Usually clients relate to "their" individual attorneys and pay little attention to the firm itself. Using technology to streamline, systematize and accelerate routine processes allows attorneys to enhance that connection.

According to Altman Weil, "Ninety-four percent of U.S. law firm leaders . . . agree that a focus on improved practice efficiency is a permanent change in the legal landscape."[9] Six in 10 reported that they are using technology tools to replace human resources.

Similarly firms see technology as a tool to increase productivity, manage costs and improve the transparency of the firm's legal processes. Here are some examples of tech substitutions for human routine, time-consuming and/or expensive activities:

- Document management systems with imaging capabilities replace finding, copying and storing paper documents.

- Networked computers, the Internet and the cloud permit attorneys to be connected to work from anywhere as compared to the 20th century where people had to be in their office to do office work.

- Research materials are available online as are form banks with computerized search functions that facilitate shared workflows and client access to written work product through client portals or online work rooms.

- Time and billing systems, most of which include a mobile app to track time while out of the office, make it easier to capture time, align it with the nature of the work completed and report it out in a meaningful way on the client's invoice.

---

9   Altman Weil, "2014 Law Firms in Transition Survey: Highlight on Efficiency," p. 3.

- Virtual firms and firms that use hoteling, where attorneys in the office on a particular day are assigned a cubicle where they can plug in their devices and work, both eliminate the need for large investments in real estate. Attorneys practicing without formal office space can rent meeting rooms in an office suite when they need to have in-person meetings.

- National practices are facilitated by video-conferencing, online meeting capabilities, etc. that negate the need for in-person meetings. Global practices are possible through the Internet.

- Process management creates a level of standardization that mitigates the problem of inconsistent work product, and also increases productivity by establishing "a system of repeatable and efficient processes for accomplishing work."[10]

- Technology has given attorneys a host of new marketing tools from websites to podcasts.

Attorneys will match specific tools and services to their own pocketbook, comfort level and the requirements imposed by their clients and practice areas. However, the impact from a business development point of view should be the same. Freed from routine and time-consuming detail work, attorneys can focus on providing the advice and service that clients really value. Time-saving work routines allow more time to invest in learning about the client, sharing information and providing customized approaches to each client.

---

10  Clyde A. Szuch and Wendy Weisbrod Loder, *Keeping Up With The Client*, Law Marketing Exchange, November 1994, p. 9.

CHAPTER TWELVE

# CLIENT FEEDBACK

Laura Meherg

# [12.0] I. INTRODUCTION

The market for legal services has never been more competitive. In more than 1,400 client interviews conducted by Wicker Park Group Consultants[1], clients almost always commented on the vast array of choices they have in selecting outside counsel from the enormous pool of talented, capable and smart lawyers vying for their business. Often, when clients are not fully satisfied with one attorney or firm, they will simply call another one for the next matter. Unless there is a strong relationship already in place, it is rare that a client will take the time to initiate a conversation about performance or even "fire" a firm. Here are some of the comments:

> "There are 100 lawyers capable of handling every matter that crosses my desk."

> "If a matter goes badly, we just go elsewhere. We're like a bad boyfriend. We just stop calling."

> "Smart is what got you in the door. How you manage the relationship is what keeps you inside."

# [12.1] II. BENEFITS OF CLIENT FEEDBACK

One of the most frequently cited traits of the successful lawyer or law firm-client relationship is a willingness to seek feedback and act on it. Yet more than 50 percent of firms surveyed by LexisNexis Martindale-Hubbell and Wicker Park Group admit they are not regularly soliciting client feedback on their firm's performance. The primary reasons firms do not seek feedback, as identified by survey participants, are a lack of staff or resources, cost, an unwillingness to respond to feedback and that it is just not a priority of firm leadership. However, firms that do seek feedback can reap great benefits and extensively develop business. Some of the benefits from client feedback include:

- preventing potential erosion or loss of work;

- understanding client's businesses, needs, pressures and decision-making processes;

- identifying opportunities for growth and market trends;

---

[1] The author is a partner and founder of Wicker Park Group Consultants, which facilitates client feedback.

- demonstrating service credibility;
- seeking competitive intelligence/market research;
- measuring performance;
- understanding important client initiatives;
- defining communication standards;
- aligning resources for maximized value and efficiencies;
- creating client promoters; and
- making better strategic decisions.

Clients also greatly benefit from client feedback by receiving more customized and focused service delivery, having better-managed expectations and achieving greater efficiencies.

## [12.2] III. CLIENT FEEDBACK TOOLS

Most experts agree the most effective method of seeking client feedback is through face-to-face conversations at the client's place of business. The interviews may be conducted by managing partners, client-relationship attorneys, administrative staff, marketing or business development staff, outside consultants or a combination of any of the above. While the client-relationship attorney should be seeking informal feedback on an ongoing basis, more formal client interviews are more successful when conducted by someone who does not have a regular working relationship with the client. As the general counsel (GC) of an auto manufacturer said in one comment, "To have someone who is not involved in the day-to-day matters seek our feedback allows for a different perspective and gives us the chance to step away from the day-to-day and think about the relationship in a different way."

The interview is only as effective as the interviewer. Skilled interviewers listen more than talk, are able to ask probing follow-up questions and quickly build trust and rapport with clients to garner the most productive and candid feedback. In reality, most lawyers and law firm leaders are already doing the jobs of several people. The time and resources necessary to do client feedback interviews well tend to take a backseat to the most urgent and immediate problems of the day. Third-party independent consultants as well as marketing, business development and client service professionals in law firms are extremely adept at conducting client feedback interviews on behalf of law firms and often can get more candid input than lawyers.

Electronic and telephone surveys are often good solutions for organizations not quite ready to make the investment in face-to-face interviews. Firms frequently choose to ease into the client feedback process using one of these "less-threatening" methods in an effort to demonstrate to their partners the value of the feedback collected and to create a benchmark for future initiatives. If conducted properly by skilled research professionals, these methodologies can help ease the transition to face-to-face interviews and provide useful client feedback in the process.

Telephone interviews are a very effective way to check in with clients earlier in the relationship, to check in at the end of a matter or project and to reach clients in diverse geographical locations. Electronic surveys are excellent for mid- and end-of-matter surveys, conducting market research and prioritizing clients for in-person or telephone interviews. Both telephone and electronic methodologies allow firms to reach more clients. While telephone surveys allow for give-and-take in conversation, the electronic survey is strictly a one-way conversation. Caution should be taken to keep electronic surveys at a completion time of two to three minutes and to include no more than 10 to 12 questions.

## [12.3]  IV.  BEFORE THE INTERVIEW

### [12.4]  A.  Client Selection and Prioritization

Only interview the clients you want to keep! Unless you have unlimited time and resources, it will be impossible to interview every client of the firm or even just the ones you'd like to keep. Start with a manageable number of clients. Pilot the effort with a practice area, industry group, client service team or partners who are willing participants. In addition to the firm's largest clients, also talk to clients who are new to the firm, have significant increases or decreases in billing or are undergoing organizational changes. Acting on tips or hunches can also prevent potentially catastrophic client relationship problems.

### [12.5]  B.  Research

The more you know about the client and the relationship with the firm going into the interview, the more successful your interviews will be. Thorough preparation is a critical component of a successful client interview. External research resources, company websites, social networking sites, litigation tracking tools, CRM systems, experience databases and accounting records are excellent resources to create a client dossier or briefing book. Most importantly, talk with the attorneys and staff who regularly work with the client to get a complete snapshot of the history and depth of the client relationship. Ask the client's regular contacts about the client's communication style and personality traits.

The relationship partner should make the initial contact with the client to give the client a heads-up that someone will be in touch to schedule the interview. This is a great opportunity to keep the relationship partners involved in the process and allow them another positive point of contact with their clients. Provide the attorneys with a brief script outlining the purpose of the interview, the names of the interviewer and/or scheduler and the next steps.

## [12.6] V. CONDUCTING THE INTERVIEW

### [12.7] A. Approach and Demeanor

Well-prepared and effective interviewers can get clients to open up to them almost immediately. Some interviewers are naturally engaging and can build trust and rapport very quickly. Others may require interview training to develop better listening skills. One tip offered by an effective managing partner who interviews at least four or five clients every month is to reassure the client right off the bat that any criticism or suggestions for improvement will be handled in a constructive manner.

Be sure to adapt your communication style to the interviewee's communication style. Mirror and match the client's pace and level of directness as discussed in Chapter 2. Watch for non-verbal cues like crossed arms or other defensive body language as signs that a client may be holding back. He or she may be hesitant or uncomfortable providing feedback and will require additional encouragement to be candid.

Begin the interview by thanking the client for taking time out of his or her busy schedule to meet with you. You'll be amazed how delighted the vast majority of clients are to share their opinions. Most in-person interviews can be conducted in 45 minutes to one hour, and clients are often happy to extend the interview if they still have more to share. For telephone interviews, we suggest scheduling a 30-minute call. Make sure you plan accordingly and respect the time commitment you have made with the client. Today there are frequently multiple points of contact in a client's organization, so be sure to include those contacts who have significant experience with your firm in the interview process. The less senior legal counsel or paralegals may have more interaction with attorneys than the GC and in many businesses, both small and large, a wide range of professionals interact with outside counsel.

## [12.8] B. The Questions

A good interviewer will use open-ended questions and expand on the interviewees' responses with good follow-up questions. Typically, an interviewer should spend 85 percent of the time listening and the remaining 15 percent of the time asking questions and rewording responses to confirm understanding. The research conducted in advance will allow interviewers to craft client-specific questions regarding

- industry trends;
- trade publications;
- associations and conferences;
- competition;
- regulatory needs;
- specific projects, matters, individuals;
- strategic plans/goals; and
- pet projects or community and charitable involvement.

Other questions can be more general and may be grouped into categories based on service delivery, relationships with attorneys and staff, communication, technology, legal fees, billing and how the client works internally as well as with outside counsel. The questions "What does the firm do well?" and "What should the firm do differently?" allow the interviewer to find out not only what's on the client's mind but what issues are most important. A comprehensive list of questions is included as a resource at the end of this chapter. Some other favorite questions of Wicker Park Group interviewers include:

- What do other law firms do that impresses you?
- What can outside counsel do to make your life easier?

- How do you define responsiveness? Using that definition, how does our firm perform?

- How can we add value that doesn't end up on the bill?

- What are the three greatest challenges facing you/your organization in the next 18 months?

Staying focused on the task at hand—seeking candid feedback about your firm's performance and service—can be quite a challenge. The initial reaction is to immediately defend your partner or firm, seek an immediate solution or jump on a new opportunity. Remember you are there to seek information first and then follow up by looking for the best ways to correct any problems or taking advantage of opportunities uncovered. The legitimacy and sincerity of your claims are at stake when you rush to react. It's usually best to take careful notes and save serious "sales" attempts for a future conversation. That said, there are exceptions to every rule. If the situation requires a quick solution, then deliver it.

Making clients aware of your firm's other or new locations, services and special skills may also be appropriate based on the context of the conversation. It is shocking how little law firms' clients really know about the firms they hire beyond their primary contacts. In countless interviews, clients have said they did not know the firm has an office in a particular city or country.

### [12.9] C. Dealing with Difficult or Delicate Feedback

The majority of clients interviewed by Wicker Park Group have significantly more praise for their outside counsel than criticism. In fact, most complaints about law firm relationships typically result from failing to manage client expectations or other common communication breakdowns. On those rare occasions when you do receive surprising negative feedback, it is always better to be prepared. Here are five tips for dealing with difficult feedback during client interviews:

1. *Ask more questions.* Use open-ended questions to dig deeper and uncover details about the problem. Saying "Tell me more about…" is a great way to get the client talking.

2. *Seek the client's input for possible solutions but recognize that you don't have to propose a solution immediately.* Some good ques-

tions to ask are: How would you like to see this problem resolved? What steps can we take to correct course?

3. *Don't get defensive or make excuses.* If deadlines are not being met, the last thing a client wants to hear about is how "busy" you are with other bigger clients or more important projects.

4. *Listen.* Recognize that sometimes clients just want to vent, and you may be the only person they talk to that day who is *willing* to listen.

5. *Clarify any immediate action needed.* Let your client know when and how you will follow up.

### [12.10]   D.   Capturing the Information

Effective note-taking is a critical part of the interview process as well. A legal pad and pen are the simplest tools for in-person interviews, but an iPad or laptop can be appropriate with younger, more tech-savvy clients. In either case, the more you can maintain eye contact during the interview the better, so select the method that will work best for you. Recording interviews may seem like a simple solution but usually just inhibits the interviewee and is not recommended. Having two interviewers allows one person to ask questions while the other makes notes. Just remember that anyone participating in the interview should be engaged in the conversation and not participating just to take notes.

### [12.11]   VI.   AFTER THE INTERVIEW

### [12.12]   A.   Creating a Report

The most critical component of the interview process is the follow-up after the interview. If there are two interviewers involved, it's best to compare notes and make sure their recollections correspond. An extensive written report should be prepared, including suggested action items to correct any service issues or to take advantage of new opportunities. A typical client feedback interview report includes an executive summary, any numerical or ratings scores, common themes and key trends across multiple interviews, individual interview summaries with direct quotes, suggested actionable follow-up strategies, client budget information and client preferences.

## [12.13] B. Disseminating the Information

Determine in advance of the interviews when, how and how much information will be disseminated in the firm. Wicker Park Group typically advises law firms to share the report with any and all members of the client service team (including attorneys and staff), industry or practice group leaders, executive committee members or others responsible for compensation and the marketing and business development team. Others who may benefit from this shared knowledge include professional development and recruiting partners and staff, human resource directors, office managing partners and other key administrative leadership.

The client service team and key relationship partners should have an in-person debriefing with the interviewers after the report is completed. A best practice from Wicker Park Group clients is to preemptively schedule this meeting three to four weeks out from the date of the scheduled client interview. This session is used to address the critical action items and to develop plans to address any other concerns raised in the interview. Firms with successful follow-up strategies identify a partner or business development professional with the authority and ability to make sure action items are completed. If there are problems, check back frequently with the client to make sure they are being addressed appropriately from the client's perspective.

## [12.14] C. Addressing Difficult or Delicate Feedback Internally

When problems are uncovered, immediately involve the appropriate leadership, which may include a supervising attorney, practice group leader or managing partner. With that leader, determine the best messenger(s) to deliver the feedback and remember that face-to-face conversations are always best if possible. Be sure to emphasize any positive feedback provided and keep the conversation regarding negative feedback on constructive solutions to address problems and prevent a recurrence. Address immediate actions needed and establish a follow-up plan and time line. While we don't advise firms to over-sanitize reports, it is important to be sensitive when sharing any negative feedback. When possible, personalize the positive and de-personalize the negative. Before including information in a report, a rule of thumb is to ask: "How will this be constructive?"

## [12.15] VII. COMMON THEMES AND KEY TRENDS IN CLIENT FEEDBACK

Evaluating key trends and themes from a series of client interviews can also be beneficial and provide valuable information for firm planning activities. These results as well as positive highlights from individual client interviews should be shared at firm meetings, at associate and staff meetings and in other internal communications.

Critical performance areas most frequently addressed by clients in interviews are related to communication skills, managing expectations, succession planning, complacency or taking the relationship for granted, and efficiency. At the end of the day, clients want outside counsel to:

- Proactively engage in discussions about VALUE and how to implement practices focused on value;

- Demonstrate an understanding of the enormous COST pressures facing clients and focus on efficiency;

- Provide TRANSPARENCY through better communication, project management and planning;

- UNDERSTAND your client's business, industry, culture, politics, pressures and preferences; and

- Build long-term relationships by MAKING LIFE EASIER for clients.

Ask clients what they need and how they want to work with you. Deliver on those preferences in an extraordinary way. Then go back and ask how you did.

## [12.16] VIII. CASE STUDY

The following case study outlines assumptions made about a client in advance of the interview, facts learned during the interview and suggested follow-up strategies.

### [12.17] A. Assumptions

The relationship partner has represented the client for more than 40 years. This partner is nearing retirement and was a personal friend of the founder and his family. The company founder's son-in law was named

CEO after the death of the founder two years ago. The relationships with other company executives—CFO, COO and other key business people—remain very strong, but the client has had several bad experiences with a litigator at the firm. The COO considers himself the company's GC despite not being a lawyer. When the relationship partner called to schedule the interviews with key company contacts, he learned that the company had recently hired its first GC.

How should you approach and prepare for these interviews? What questions should you ask?

## [12.18] B. Facts

Despite the relationship partner's efforts to introduce other attorneys at the firm to key contacts, the client does not see a clear successor to the relationship partner and is worried about the future. The GC position was not created as a cost-cutting measure but to improve communication and gain control over strategic legal issues. The company is in the process of developing a new strategic plan. The new CEO is highly risk averse and fears risk associated with the company's lack of a strategic contract management system. The new GC has a sales background and has been in private practice but has not been an in-house counsel before. He has a favorable view of the firm and wants to get to know more about it. The CEO's best friend's son is a new associate at the firm. The company is currently using another small local firm for litigation because of the bad experience.

What are some suggested action items?

## [12.19] C. Follow-up Strategies

- Developed a monthly meeting schedule with topic-driven agendas for the new GC to meet the attorneys and gain a better understanding of the firm and its capabilities.

- Provided best practices for the new GC around litigation and contract management and helped facilitate networking with other clients since he is new to the role and wants to learn from his peers in other companies.

- Formed client service team and invited GC to attend meetings.

- Formally apologized for the litigator's behavior and assured he would not work on future cases.

- Worked with GC to foster a better relationship with the CFO and created new billing practices protocol.

- Hosted strategic planning sessions at the firm to give the company a cost-effective "offsite" location for minimal distractions.

## SAMPLE CLIENT FEEDBACK QUESTIONS

1. Customized introductory question that relates to relationship history—and who are your regular contacts?

    a. Selected by RFP: How or why was the firm selected?

    b. Inherited: How well did we manage the transition from your predecessor to you?

    c. Unknown: What's the genesis of your relationship with (firm)?

2. How satisfied are you with the service and relationship?

3. How likely are you to refer others to (firm)? (Net Promoter Score (NPS) rating scale) Why?

4. What do you like about working with (firm/attorney)? What do we do well?

5. How have we best served you? How has another firm best served you?

6. What can we do differently?

7. Have you ever had a service/billing problem with (firm)? How was the problem resolved?

8. What other law firms do you regularly use and which ones stand out as providing extraordinary service? What distinguishes them from the average firms? Or—Whom do you consider the superstar attorneys/firms?

9. What frustrations have you experienced working with outside counsel?

10. Do you feel you are getting value for the fees? How can we improve the billing process? How do you define value?

11. How do you prefer to communicate with outside counsel? How satisfied are you with our communication regarding the status of projects, legal updates, etc.?

12. What advice would you give (firm) to improve its services/products/people?

13. Who else on your team would it be valuable to talk to in this format?

14. How can firms add value to the relationship in ways that don't show up on the bill?

15. What are your three greatest challenges in achieving success/goals—department/company/personally?

16. What have I not asked you that you'd like to discuss?

## INTERVIEW BEST PRACTICES/TIPS

- **Smile and enjoy your visit.** This will show your clients you enjoy spending time with them and have a genuine interest in learning more about their business.

- **Be prepared.** Review the research provided by the marketing department and be alert to news about the specific company and industry. Rehearse.

- **Ask open-ended questions using How, What, Why?** Respond to their answers with follow-up questions when relevant and possible.

- **Listen more than talk.** You should listen 85% of the time and spend 15% of the time asking questions or follow-up questions and re-phrasing their responses to clarify understanding.

- **Don't be defensive or make excuses.** Offer a quick apology to criticisms and move on.

- **Don't criticize** their business, their superiors, their opinions or other firms.

- **Don't sell.** Ask questions to gain a better understanding of potential needs. Offer solutions in a follow-up meeting.

- **Don't offer solutions.** Ask more questions to create a tailored response and solution later.

- **Take notes.**

- **Schedule a follow-up** conversation or meeting as appropriate. Address any problems with a time line of agreed next steps.

- **Write a thank you note!**

**CHAPTER THIRTEEN**

# THE PRICING OF LEGAL SERVICES

**Christine S. Filip, Esq.**

# THE PRICING OF LEGAL SERVICES § 13.0

## [13.0] I. INTRODUCTION

"The billable-hour system is the way most lawyers in big firms charge clients, but it serves no one."[1]

Take a look at yourself in a mirror. What do you see? A neatly composed professional or a dollar sign? The crux of pricing for lawyers is this: your (prospective) clients see you as a neatly composed professional until you mention money. Here is why: we have made it difficult to understand value for money.

It is an ironic commentary on an articulate profession that we have made the pricing of legal services abstruse and, some would say, anachronistic. Where our commercial colleagues speak of pricing pressures, value adds and discounts, lawyers have alternative fee arrangements (especially during recessions), blended rates, flat rates, and hourly fees, as if, like automatons, we have fashioned our profession to the standards of intellectual time and motion studies. And, at the onset of every economic downturn, the profession spends far too much blather presaging the death knell of the hourly fee.

Each of us knows, however, that "price" represents a value that we consider extremely important in our lives as consumers, and we all are now well equipped to enter a pricing negotiation for a car or a home or a vacation package using Internet tools. Likewise, our legal clients are similarly enabled to pierce the archaic veil of law firm pricing using comparative Internet tools to ascertain competitive price ranges for most types of legal matters, leaving aside the bet your life or bet the company scenarios in which a client might pay most any price for a good result to avoid those horizontally striped togs.

If a prospective client can know the competitive price range for a type of legal service, it might be worthwhile to simplify our response when asked, "How much will this cost?"

This chapter is not meant to be a complete exegesis on law firm pricing strategy. It is written as a practical guide to improving your financial results by changing how you answer the following question:

Q: What's in a price? A: Economic value.

---

[1] Steven J. Harper, *The Tyranny of the Billable Hour*, The New York Times, March 28, 2013, www.nytimes.com/2013/03/29/opinion/the-case-against-the-law-firm-billable-hour.html.

## [13.1] II. WHAT'S IN A PRICE?

Back to the image in the mirror. A price represents you. It is a numeric symbol of your reputation and your worth. It is one of the most important elements of business development because it can accelerate or negate a client's acceptance of establishing a working relationship. For all of these reasons, the easier to understand we make the rationale behind the pricing for services, the faster we facilitate price acceptance and practice growth.

When you declare a number for your fee *with no more explanation*, the client "sees" a (your) second house on a beach front, a new luxury car, a child going off to college or just unreasonable greed. Is this what you want? It certainly does not accelerate getting to yes.

Like any other negotiation, the negotiation of a price does not usually take place in a single instance. It is typically discussed or articulated throughout a number of conversations with a current or prospective client as you discuss the matter at hand.

Basic pricing strategy says that for any price, there is a reference value, which is the comparison of competitive prices for a product or service in the marketplace. This is the starting point, or benchmark, for the successful negotiation of your fee. You need to know the "average competitive price" in your geography for the services you are proposing so that you have a starting point to discuss your own price. I am going to use "average competitive price" as the starting point for the price discussion based on using economic value analysis (EVA), a form of principled negotiation. Before that discussion, however, let's look at the basic financial structures of setting prices.

## [13.2] III. PRICE STRUCTURE

William E. Sansone, CPA, partner and chair of the law firm practice at the accounting firm WithumSmith+Brown, suggests these items to consider when pricing a job or calculating a billing rate:

- Direct cost—payroll, payroll taxes and benefits (401k, health insurance, etc.);

- Overhead cost—calculate an allocation factor to your billing rate (usually one-third of the billing rate). Major overhead items to consider = payroll and related cost, rent and insurance;

- Profit factor—usually one-third of the billing rate;

# THE PRICING OF LEGAL SERVICES § 13.2

- Market conditions—what other attorneys are charging

- For fixed fees—budget anticipated hours x billing rate

- Risk/reward—will this be a long term client? A referral source? Use business judgment when determining your fee.

A decent price should yield a profit that allows your practice to flourish. What is a decent price, and what is a sufficient profit?

A price is the cost of your doing business as a lawyer plus a markup, which is your profit margin. In simpler terms, profits are the dollars left over from your price once you have paid costs of doing business. Profit is derived as

> *Price* you charge (in accounting terms, "revenue")
>
> *Minus* the cost of services, such as payroll, payroll taxes and benefits, office costs, including rent, equipment, insurance
>
> = *Profits*

If you are starting a practice or reviewing your current pricing structure, the first place to start your analysis is researching the average competitive prices for the client matters you or your firm handles. In the same way that you would research the price of a car, home or other personal buying decision, use the Internet and your colleagues. Law journals and other legal publications frequently print the prices or hourly rates of firms in your area. Do the research. You will find some articles on point and some guidelines.[2]

Secondly, talk to your colleagues, including your accountant. Ask them what they know about prices for matters you handle in similarly sized firms, with the caveat that neither of these approaches, Internet research or gossip, compensates for your tenure or experience in the profession.

---

2   Some guides to law firm pricing include Thomas S. Clay, 2013 Law Firms in Transition, Altman Weil, www.altmanweil.com/dir_docs/resource/2d831a80-8156-4947-9f0f-1d97eec632a5_document.pdf; N.Y. Rules of Professional Conduct, www.nycourts.gov/rules/jointappellate/NY-Rules-Prof-Conduct-1200.pdf; Patrick on Pricing, www.patrickonpricing.com; How to Price Legal Fees, FindLaw, http://practice.findlaw.com/financing-a-law-firm/how-to-price-legal-services; Toby Brown and Vincent Cordo, Law Firm Pricing: Strategies, Roles, and Responsibilities, 2013.

What you are analyzing is the average competitive price, not the exact price you should charge.

Once you understand the average competitive price for services in your area, because prices vary by geography (consider New York City versus Poughkeepsie), you have a benchmark to construct your fees, which will vary up or down by your level of experience.

Lawyers and firms construe prices into various forms:

- Hourly rate: your price (cost plus markup) multiplied by the number of hours you worked the matter;

- Blended rates: a price somewhere between what a partner and an associate would charge per hour;

- Contingency fee: used in certain types of cases (e.g., personal injury, malpractice), in which the client pays nothing (sometimes ordinary expenses along the way) until a result, when the lawyer takes a percentage of the judgment or settlement;

- Flat fees: one price estimated on the number of hours a matter will take to complete multiplied by the hourly price. Flat fees can be used for both transactional and litigation matters and become popular during economic downturns. If you have a historical record of handling a type of work, you can derive estimations for the hours it will take you to work the matter. There are lawyers and firms who use flat fees;[3]

- Alternate fee arrangements (AFA), which can be any construction of fees that demonstrate a discount for the client or a financial incentive for the attorney. These are popular during economic downturns, and if the recession is long and broad enough, AFAs may change the pricing landscape long term, particularly with regard to the downward pressure on pricing.

---

3   *See* Rachel M. Zahorsky, *Facing the Alternative: How Does a Flat Fee System Really Work?*, ABA Journal, March 1, 2012, www.abajournal.com/magazine/article/facing_the_alternative_how_does_a_flat_fee_system_really_work; Frederick J. Esposito, Jr., *Planning for Flat-Fee Billing*, Attorney at Work, May 24, 2011, www.attorneyatwork.com/planning-for-flat-fee-billing; Amy Miller, *GCs, Law Firms and Flat Fee Arrangements: A Matter of Trust*, The American Lawyer, June 9, 2009; www.corpcounsel.com/id=1202431310403; Michael Sherman, *Fixed-Fee Engagements in Litigation Cases: Why and How* (divorce litigation), Law Practice Today, July 2010, http://apps.americanbar.org/lpm/lpt/articles/ftr07104.shtml; Andy Daws, *Five Questions About Fixed Fees You're Afraid to Ask*, Attorney at Work, March 21, 2014, www.attorneyatwork.com/five-questions-fixed-fees-youre-afraid-ask.

# THE PRICING OF LEGAL SERVICES § 13.2

When you start your practice, the first puzzle is what to charge for a given matter. This is not a conundrum, nor is it rocket science. Remember: Google and gossip. And, let's not forget the ethical guidelines of the profession.

You may recall from law school that there are Rules of Professional Conduct. Rule 1.5 of the Rules of Professional Conduct[4] sets out eight factors that are determinative of whether a fee is "excessive" and is based on a "reasonable lawyer" standard. More importantly, the Rule in part (b) says that "A lawyer shall communicate to a client the scope of the representation and the basis or rate of the fee and expenses for which the client will be responsible," and that such an explanation be made in writing. It is worthwhile looking at the rule in print, not just as a hyperlink you may or may not consult.

## RULE 1.5: FEES AND DIVISION OF FEES

(a) A lawyer shall not make an agreement for, charge, or collect an excessive or illegal fee or expense. A fee is excessive when, after a review of the facts, a reasonable lawyer would be left with a definite and firm conviction that the fee is excessive. The factors to be considered in determining whether a fee is excessive may include the following:

(1) the time and labor required, the novelty and difficulty of the questions involved, and the skill requisite to perform the legal service properly;

(2) the likelihood, if apparent or made known to the client, that the acceptance of the particular employment will preclude other employment by the lawyer;

(3) the fee customarily charged in the locality for similar legal services;

(4) the amount involved and the results obtained;

(5) the time limitations imposed by the client or by circumstances;

---

[4] www.nycourts.gov/rules/jointappellate/NY-Rules-Prof-Conduct-1200.pdf.

(6) the nature and length of the professional relationship with the client;

(7) the experience, reputation and ability of the lawyer or lawyers performing the services; and

(8) whether the fee is fixed or contingent.

(b) A lawyer shall communicate to a client the scope of the representation and the basis or rate of the fee and expenses for which the client will be responsible. This information shall be communicated to the client before or within a reasonable time after commencement of the representation and shall be in writing where required by statute or court rule. This provision shall not apply when the lawyer will charge a regularly represented client on the same basis or rate and perform services that are of the same general kind as previously rendered to and paid for by the client. Any changes in the scope of the representation or the basis or rate of the fee or expenses shall also be communicated to the client.

## [13.3]  IV.  THE EFFECT OF DISCOUNTING

Every recession teaches clients to demand, and usually get, a discount on attorney fees. Discounts are expected and generalized from low price clients to sophisticated in-house counsels. The problem with giving a discount without using a financial rationale to explain the discount is that the lower level of pricing becomes the norm. The financial effect of a discount is this: for every dollar you discount, you lose multiple dollars in profits. Case in point:

> A good client comes to you with a commercial matter for which you ordinarily charge $300/hour, and you estimate will take you 20 hours. This would yield a final bill of $6,000. Your firm's cost basis is $3,000. Profit = $3,000. In light of the stressful times, you give a 10% discount, or $270/hour or a final bill of $5,400 minus the $3,000 cost basis, and your profit is $2,400. This is a 20% loss of profit margin.

However your firm's cost basis is constructed, every dollar in discount costs you multiples in profit margin dollars. The numbers may differ (billing rate, cost basis), but the effect is always the same. Over time and usage, continuing to discount will vastly change your financial future.

## [13.4] V. PREVENTATIVE MEASURES: ECONOMIC VALUE ANALYSIS (EVA)

In our personal lives, while we may be proud of our expert negotiation skills, we will still pay extra for items or features that we value highly. The extra dollars we pay, known as a premium, are well known to luxury goods makers; otherwise they would be out of business, and while their prices may decrease some during recessions, they are still above the average lot of non-luxury competitors. You may have paid a premium for a product—a house, car, college education, household appliance, clothing, hair stylist—but you had little remorse because you *valued* the product or service you received. Premium services, products and their prices are recession-proof.

The vast majority of law firms don't tout "premium services," meaning high prices. The very few impute premium price value by their white-shoe status. The ability of all other law firms to build dollar value into their prices and to decrease the need for discounting can be accomplished by using a principled negotiation technique called Economic Value Analysis in the course of discussing a matter with a longstanding or a prospective client.

Reaching agreement on a price with a client is not usually one instance in time. Rather it happens throughout the discussion of a legal matter. The important issues to remember in using EVA are (1) you need to do your research so that you know average competitive prices and (2) you must be able to articulate real reasons why you are worth more than that average price.

EVA is a principled negotiation technique that has three steps and it works as well with new clients as it does with long-term clients. The dollar signs ($$$) imply relative values, meaning $$ is a higher price than $. This EVA conversation may occur in stages over time or at the final decision point. The following are the progressive steps in the EVA negotiation process.

1. Articulate the average competitive price = $

    a. The buyer will already know this so do not fear talking about "it" or a range of competitive prices;

b. If you are just beginning a professional practice, do your research; the range of average prices for a service is not a state secret and is frequently published in professional journals.

2. Tell and demonstrate to the buyer why your services and buying from you or your firm have important, unique values, which match the client's needs and interests, that make the price higher = $$$.

Unique values, those attributes that *validly* differentiate you, are not merely service benefits—you need to dig deeper. The strongest differentiator is another client's direct recommendation, not a testimonial from your website, but direct, live testimony. Here are some other supporting differentiators, with the caveat that these are generic. You need valid proofs appropriate to the buyer's interests:

a. Client recommendation;

b. An objective industry/professional accolade;

c. Your track record, especially results in similar matters.

3. Reduce the risk: lower the price for new buyers, high volume or long-term clients = $$. Note that this price is higher than the average competitive price ($).

The third step may *appear* to be a discount, but if you start at a higher than average price level as in the second step, your revenue and profit yield will be higher than you have gotten historically. A prospective client may need an inducement to switch lawyers, literally to reduce the risk, and a long-term client may need to be recognized for its loyalty. Similarly, because in the second step you are demonstrating valid differentiators about your skills, you give clients a reason to stay with you over time because they feel they made a good decision. Long-term clients who return with the next matter are also likely to recommend others to you; this type of loyalty behavior is a direct contributor to profitability.[5]

## [13.5] VI. SPEED BUMPS

Using Economic Value Analysis as a principled negotiation strategy, while effective in supporting higher prices, is still a negotiation, which means you will get objections, surprises and less-than-sterling behavior

---

5   Frederick Reicheld, The Loyalty Effect (Harvard Business School Press, 1996).

from your client. These tips allow you to deal with those bumps in the road to success.

Most negotiation training counsels you to "solve" objections when, in reality, one cannot make the conflict disappear. My experience has shown that understanding the reason for the roadblock will allow you to trade concessions and make the deal work.

When you hit an impasse, try three steps, with the caveat that you do not go to #3 unless you're ready to fold the tent:

1. *Be Conciliatory:* "I realize this issue is important to you, but I need more information about why it is. Can you tell me more so I can understand?"

2. *Do the Columbo:* "I must be missing something here. I'm confused. Tell me why you absolutely need X."

3. *Bring in the Judge:* "So what you are telling me is (paint the best picture from their view) you want X, Y, and Z. If I did that, how would I explain that to my judge (my managing partner, my accountant, the ethics board, my dog—any absent judge)?" This makes the other party stand in your shoes in front of your judge. Use this as a *last* resort. It can kill a negotiation or add enough levity to move on.

When you know the reasoning, you have a basis for tradeoffs and concessions.

Use factual data to support your view, and if you do concede something, make sure you ask for something in return (SIR) of equal value, even if that's hard to calculate, but you must explain a rational basis for that dollar value. For example, if a client asks you to produce an employee handbook *and* to train management staff on frequent employee issues, the training is a value add (and a concession) for which you should charge, or if you don't, you should know the cost basis (and profit mark up, i.e., the final price) and ask for something in return of similar financial value, like another pending matter, a faster payment, payment of past due items, a referral to another potential client or something else of value to you.

Forgetting to ask for something in return (SIR) is typically where you lose money and lower your price without getting a concession from the other side. Preparation is key: you need to have the cost basis of any concession at your fingertips and a credible list of SIRs.

### [13.6] VII. MANAGEMENT CONSIDERATIONS

If you are a managing partner or a solo, you need to treat your negotiated client matters as a portfolio of investments. Simply put, if you have too many matters in which the SIR has a longer time horizon, you will impact cash flow. As a result, inspect your client agreements as you would your investments. You need some faster yield agreements to balance against longer term investments. Not all SIRs have delayed financial yields, but those that do will need your attention and planning as you continue to acquire new matters and clients, especially if you have other lawyers working in your firm.

Finally, you need to inspect your realization rate to understand whether your agreements are being honored.

Over the course of the recession, realization rates reported in Peer Monitor[6] dropped in the United States from 92 percent in 2007 to 83.5 percent in 2013. Your realization rate, what you actually get paid as opposed to what you bill a client, should improve or stay at expected levels if you are using EVA, but noticing a decline in actual fees collected should point you to interventions with those clients shorting your invoices and perhaps to consultation with the lawyer(s) involved.

### [13.7] VIII. EVERY SUCCESSFUL SALE *MAY* PRODUCE A LOYAL CLIENT

To produce better-than-average revenues and margins, you need to fulfill the expectations set during the sales process. Clients who are loyal, meaning they continue to buy from you, send you referrals, and act as a direct, live proof source for prospective buyers, underwrite positive financial results that are unparalleled. The research on the financial effects of loyalty, many of which are normed over a variety of industries, will help you change your behavior around the price conversation. Net net, how you act by using EVA, affects the price outcome. Make the decision to say "yes" easier for your clients and prospects.

---

6   *Law Firms: Charging More, Getting Less*, The Economist, June 18, 2014, www.economist.com/news/business/21594317-lawyers-biggest-customers-are-discovering-they-can-haggle-charging-more-getting-less.

# CHAPTER FOURTEEN

# WHERE DO ADVERTISING AND PUBLIC RELATIONS FIT INTO MY BUSINESS DEVELOPMENT ARSENAL?

Marcia Golden

## [14.0] I. WHY DO LAWYERS MARKET?

To generate business. Period. End of story.

Marketing, as it pertains to lawyers and law firms is the *process* or act of communicating the value of a firm, practice or practitioner to clients, prospective clients and referral sources in a manner which encourages engagement.

## [14.1] II. WHO MARKETS?

Everyone—big firms, small firms, solo practitioners. You, even if you are unaware of it. From the suit you wear, to your business card and briefcase, your website, your networks, clubs, memberships, and affiliations—everything you do and say or don't do and say delivers a clear business communication about the way you practice law and why clients should retain you.

Advertising and public relations—the focus of this chapter—are marketing tactics drawn from a huge and rapidly evolving arsenal of business development weaponry. They are two among many in an ever-growing collection of conventional and electronic communications tools—whether it is social media and blogs, or direct- and e-marketing, networking, conferences, websites, etc. And more tools and tactics come online every day.

## [14.2] III. ADVERTISING VERSUS PUBLIC RELATIONS OR ADVERTISING + PUBLIC RELATIONS?

The answer is yes.

Why do small firms or solos invest in advertising and/or public relations?

1. To level the playing field.

2. To become better known.

Should you invest in advertising and/or public relations? It depends on your goals and your budget. Let's start with public relations.

## [14.3] A. What About Me?

How do you outwit clever reporters and convince them to write about you, your practice and/or your firm instead of your competition? Even when that competition is a mega-firm?

To paraphrase the late David Ogilvy, of the eponymously named advertising agency Ogilvy & Mather: You don't have to be better than your competition; you just have to say why you rock better than your competition. You just have to say what makes your firm worth retaining better than your competition—large and small.

## [14.4] B. What Does That Look Like?

Wikipedia, that font of free information, defines public relations (PR) as the practice of managing the spread of information between an individual or an organization and the public.[1] For lawyers and law firms, the aim of public relations is to disseminate useful information to the media that the media believes will be useful to its audience. The goal: To position you and your firm as expert resources in the media read, viewed, or listened to by clients, prospects and referral sources.

So how do you make that happen? This section on public relations discusses what makes real news, how those stories happen, the relationship between the reporters and your firm, how to deliver news media can use, and a case history analysis of what a former San Francisco law firm shared with a New York City business reporter to generate media exposure for its satellite office (and basically eating the local competition's lunch).

## [14.5] C. What Is Real News? You Know It Because You've Seen It

You watch the morning business news, read your daily newspaper, weekly trade journal, online news provider, or newsfeed, and you see reports and articles on topics squarely within your area of expertise . . . quoting somebody else.

How did that happen? Why did the reporter call them, instead of you?

---

1   en.wikipedia.org/wiki/Public_relations.

Because someone (the competitor, one of their representatives, or, perhaps their public relations consultant) picked up the phone and made a phone call. But not just any call—a *sales* call.

That's right, public relations is sales. But not a sales spiel pushing your firm's great service or depth of expertise, or a lot of puffery about why you/your firm is so far superior to your competition. It's benefit selling. Getting the media to cover you has less to do with you, than the clear communication of how what you do benefits that news outlet's audience.

## [14.6] D. What Does That Mean?

Ask yourself: How will that news outlet's audience *benefit* from what I have to share? These might be stories about trends in family law moving from litigation to mediation, or exposures real estate investors must address when expanding into triple net leasing, or even "miracles" you've produced on behalf of your clients.

Before you pick up the phone to contact a reporter, ask yourself: How will that news outlet's audience *benefit* from what I have to share?

## [14.7] E. News They Can Use

So how do you get *your* number into the right reporters' hands?

First rule of sales: Know your customer. Understand that the reporters you want to reach are your "clients," so interact with them accordingly. Give them what they want: News they can use, which translates into news their readers/viewers/listeners can use.

## [14.8] F. What Does That Look Like?

Look in any issue of the *New York Times,* your local newspaper (print or online), the *Wall Street Journal, Crain's New York Business,* or industry-specific trade media appropriate to your practice—*Industry Week, FierceCFO, Corporate Counsel, Medical Economics, HR Magazine*—to see who's quoted and note the thread common to all of them. In nearly every case, the firm profiled or the attorney quoted gave the reporter news he or she could use and was featured in an article as a result.

For example, there was a profile that ran long ago in *Crain's New York Business,* touting the rapid rise of the (now defunct) Silicon Valley law firm Brobeck Phleger & Harrison in Manhattan's Silicon Alley. In the article *Frisco Lawyers Click With Internet Firms*,[2] Alexander Lynch, a partner in the firm's Manhattan office interviewed for the story, tapped into an industry trend, shared real world experience in the field, named names (of clients), discussed facts (including numbers and market position), unique business strategies, and the competition.

The attorney shared real information, including his

- Numbers: "Brobeck's 9-year-old office [in NYC] is outhustling other law practices in the grab for new media clients. . . . Last year, the New York office took in $20 million in revenues, or about 8% of the entire firm's gross . . . billed a total of about $1 million for the three IPOs it worked on."

- Unique business strategy: Brobeck shared two: (1) To rise above the stiff competition to secure DoubleClick, Mr. Lynch started work on a draft version of the IPO prospectus, free of charge. Weeks later, "he had a completed document and relationships with DoubleClick's top two executives. He won the job hands down." (2) One controversial idea Brobeck imported from California is to accept stock as part of its legal fees, a "notion . . . catching on in Silicon Alley."

- Clients by name: In addition to DoubleClick, he offered up several other clients by name: Juno Online Services, Agency.com, Miningco.com, Multex.com, and Jupiter Communications. More important, DoubleClick's General Counsel even went on the record to say nice things, noting, "The New York firms just don't get it."

- Predictions: "Like many believers in the Internet, Brobeck is betting that its cadre of high-tech clients will . . . provide a big payoff."

- Market competition: "[Brobeck's] niche is under invasion from several New York-based firms, including Dewey Ballantine, Proskauer Rose, and O'Sullivan Graev & Karabell."

### [14.9]  G.  So What About You and Your Firm?

In the world of media relations, it's all about paying it forward. You must give reporters "news they can use" to get the coverage you need to grow your practice. This means providing reporters with substantial,

---

2  Matthew Goldstein, *Frisco Lawyers Click With Internet Firms*, Crain's New York Business, Feb. 15, 1999, p. 3.

detailed information to create a foundation upon which he or she can build a story.

Deliverables include:

1. A clearly identified market trend. In employment law, it might be the hidden silver lining in recent tech layoffs. In family law, it might be the return to litigation from mediation. For intellectual property law, it might be the challenge of protecting assets stored on employee thumb drives. And so on.

2. A statement outlining your unique business strategy or strategies. For an article targeting healthcare, hospitals and medical practices, it might be your firm's willingness to conduct intern and resident "lunch 'n' learns" to discuss recordkeeping and other documentation. Or that your real estate practitioners conduct pre-bid property reviews of commercial developments. And so on.

3. Case histories. These are "miracles" you've produced on behalf of your clients. Litigations won. Businesses saved. Along with client names if requested by the reporter, plus solid information on what you did for those clients.

4. Facts about your competition in the market—big and small—and even earnings and fees.

## [14.10] H. Now What?

Now that you've been quoted and the interview/article has appeared, keep the ball rolling.

The old adage that "today's *New York Times* is tomorrow's fish wrap" is truer than ever—especially given the quick story turnover of online media.

Public relations must do more than simply generate buzz about you and your firm. It can and should generate a tangible result—make the phone ring, shorten sales cycles, and attract unsolicited lead funnels.

But that can only happen when you take the stories that result from all the seeds you've planted in the media and

- reprint the articles;

- post reprints onto your website;

- share it on LinkedIn and via Twitter (linking back to your website);

- email and snail mail reprints to your database of clients, prospects and referral sources. (And yes, snail mail—even Google sends out mail with a stamp, so they must think it's worth the money.);

- add relevant reprints to your sales material, proposals and presentations, etc.;

- and then go out and do it again. And again. And . . .

## [14.11] I. A Note About Press Releases—What Are They *Really* Good For?

Nothing will ever replace picking up the phone to contact a reporter with a story specific to his or her audience, and following up with a short email pitch.

Historically, press releases are a tool for mass dissemination of general news—awards won, new hires, industry updates and the like. Broadly circulated—whether via snail mail or email—they are less likely to be considered "news" and are de facto admission to the reporter receiving them that he or she is not sufficiently special to warrant a story pitch specific to them. Except in small media markets or some trade media, press releases typically end up as space fillers.

However, they do have another, more elegant function: client/prospect/referral source outreach.

While reporters receive press releases all the time, your clients, prospects, and referral sources rarely do. Send your press releases to them and most will read them.

Press releases can also be used to increase your "Google juice"—the information on you, your practice and your firm that resides on the Internet.

Search online for "Free Press Release Distribution" and note the dozens and dozens of resources that permit you to post your press release on their distribution site and circulate it through the web for free!

Snagged a speaking engagement? Create a press release about it, then post it on your website, tweet a link to it, post it on LinkedIn and then circulate it through as many of these free distribution sites as you have time for. Set up a "Google Alert" for your name and your firm's name and then see how often you pop up. Any client/prospect/referral source searching for your firm online also will see more than just your website. You'll look as significant as you are!

### [14.12]   J.   What About Advertising?

Lawyers and law firms are latecomers to the advertising party. It seems like a lifetime ago that marketing beyond referrals or a business card could get one disbarred. Then in the 1970s, the Supreme Court ruled such "commercial speech" by lawyers was protected by the First Amendment and opened Pandora's Box. And then the state bars weighed in.

This is not a screed about "tasteless attorney advertising." You can always Google "attorney advertising" for that.

According to Wikipedia, that font of free wisdom: "Advertising is a form of marketing communications used to encourage, persuade or manipulate an audience (viewers, readers, or listeners) to take or continue to take some action."[3] In Latin, *ad vertere* means "to turn toward."

In the age of *Mad Men*, advertising most conventionally referred to print (newspapers/magazines/billboards) and/or broadcast (radio/television) media, with a little direct mail thrown in.

Today, advertising messages appear everywhere—digital *and* the usual print and broadcast outlets, on theater screens, taxi backseat monitors, Internet searches, websites, mobile devices, online/offline, golf balls, etc.

No matter where you see it, the one question you must ask yourself before diving in is, "Does advertising make sense for my firm, my practice, me?"

Here is a brief guide to figuring out the answer that's right for you. It reviews the questions:

- WHO advertises?

- WHAT do they say in their ads?

---

[3]   en.wikipedia.org/wiki/Advertising.

- WHEN does it make sense?

- WHERE do they advertise?

- WHO's your market?

- WHY should YOU advertise? (Or not.)

- HOW should you advertise?

If you are an attorney considering advertising, you have one goal: To raise your visibility among prospective clients and referral sources by clearly communicating a single, compelling reason the recipient of your marketing message should engage (or refer) *you*.

### [14.13] K. So Who Advertises?

Firms looking to brand or raise the visibility of their names or practices in their markets, as well as firms soliciting direct contacts by end-users (prospective clients). Big firms and little firms and solos.

### [14.14] L. Who's Your Prospect/Market?

Who are your clients and how do they come to you?

Your market is B2B (business to business) if you are an attorney representing businesses, large or small, for profit or nonprofit—corporate law. For example, if your employment law practice represents corporations sued by former employees, your referral sources are likely to be other businesses or professions—other attorneys, accountants, bankers, insurers, etc.

Your market is B2C (business to consumer) if you represent individuals or families—personal law. For example, if your employment law practice represents individuals suing former employers, your referral sources may be B2C *and* B2B. The B2C employment law practice who seeks *referrals* from former clients and/or other professionals and advisors is both B2C—for clients and "friends and family" referrals *and* B2B—for referrals from other professionals and advisors.

### [14.15] M. What Do You Say?

When a prospective client seeks representation, it is a given that your firm and its competitors all satisfy that prospective client's *stated* criteria.

It is understood that you and your firm do good work. It is understood that many of your competitors also do good work.

All things being equal then, the decision of which lawyer or firm to retain typically is based on *intangibles*. This area—the clear *communication* of intangibles, or what separates your firm or your practice from all others—is important.

So how do you separate your firm or your practice from the crowd? Talk about a clearly defined benefit you bring to the client who engages you. And limit yourself to communicating one strong benefit in each advertisement or marketing communication.

For example, suppose you're an intellectual property specialist who handles the full spectrum of IP law—patents, trademarks, counsel, and litigation. If you run an ad that says, "We do everything IP," or "We can handle all of your intellectual property needs," how does that make you different than another IP specialist or a generalist with an IP practice?

Because when you say the same thing these mega law firms say, what the prospective client hears is, "Hmmm. All things being equal, I choose the bigger firm."

So take a closer look at your practice and ask yourself two questions:

1. Where do I best the competition?

2. When does size matter?

## [14.16] 1. Where Do I Best the Competition?

For the former Cohen Pontani Lieberman & Pavane, it was the firm's nearly perfect win rate. So even though they "did all things IP," every marketing communication—advertising, public relations, practice development, client pitch—led with the firm's strong suit: IP litigation and some variation on the following:

> CPLP is unique in its focus on intellectual property litigation that infuses every aspect of its IP work in prosecution of patents, trademarks, and copyrights; in drafting opinions and licenses, and in due diligence and transaction work. It is CPLP's philosophy that no legal activity is so routine that it does not have the potential to become the weak link in IP protection, resulting in legal exposure

or porous rights. Hence, the firm views all IP matters as potential litigations to be won or avoided and is positioned to provide world-class litigation services, as well as other highly skilled IP services to achieve wraparound IP protection at the highest level.

Because the firm's professionals were such skilled litigators, they approached every aspect of IP with an eye toward avoiding litigation (tighter patents, trademarks, counsel). And when litigation was unavoidable, who did you want in your corner? CPLP with its stellar win rate or . . . ?

They found a chink in the marketing armor of their bigger competitors, and took possession of the battlefield.

**[14.17] 2. When Does Size Matter?**

When it's your home-court advantage. This mandate holds for attorneys with consumer practices (personal injury, trust and estates, family law/matrimonial, individual debt default, elder care, etc.), or corporate practices: find the key distinguisher in your practice—the benefit you bring to your client's table—and communicate it clearly.

It's easy to laugh at the broadcast ads run by Lowell "The Hammer" Stanley. But his message, that for 30 years he has pounded on slow- or no-pay insurance firms to get them to cough up cash for his injured clients, is simple and resonates with his target audience—angry individuals who have been disabled and unable to collect from insurers. He's the hammer and insurance companies are the nails, and even his phone number 459-CASH reinforces it.

Size does matter! It's your job to explain *how* it matters.

## [14.18] IV. WHEN DOES ADVERTISING MAKE SENSE?

Advertising is one component of a well-thought-out marketing or practice development plan that should also include networking, speaking, blogging, and other visibility and practice-building initiatives.

- One advertises to raise one's visibility before a target market.

- One advertises to add heft. If you *can* (afford to) advertise, you must be big enough.

- One advertises to credential oneself and one's practice—avoiding the "I'm sure they're good, but . . ." conversation.

- One advertises out of guilt or charitable obligation.

Regardless of why one advertises, the message communicated must always deliver a clearly defined benefit (even in charity ads) and serve a clear purpose.

For B2B practices the benefit of advertising can be as simple as making you visible to potential referral sources. Or, to blunt the "damning with faint praise" conversation that may occur when in-house counsel asks, "Do you know these folks?" of general outside counsel, who responds, "I'm sure they're very good, but I don't know them."

For consumer practices (divorce, personal injury, bankruptcy, class action, etc.), it may be the only way for you to reach prospective clients.

Media outlets for B2B advertising range from industry-specific business or "trade" outlets that match your practice (*Industry Week, HR Magazine, Corporate Counsel, Telephony, Restaurant News, Real Estate Weekly,* and others), the business section of local newspapers, or business media *(Crain's, Westchester Business, Adirondacks Daily Enterprise, Bloomberg,* even business/industry-specific blogs).

Media outlets for B2C advertising are even more wide-ranging—from newspapers, magazines, radio and television (cable, online, conventional), to outdoor (billboard, mobile and bus ads), direct mail (snail and email) and even hyper-specific e-zines and "mommy blogs (attention family lawyers)" among them.

## [14.19] A. What About Ads of Obligation?

These are advertising opportunities difficult to refuse. Also called "Journal Ads" or sponsorship banners, these media investments are not in vehicles offering direct benefit to you, your firm or your practice.

Your client asks you to take a Journal Ad to support a charity or sponsor an event. You say yes, as it's really not a request. You've got to do it. How you do it, though—the message you communicate—is up to you.

## [14.20] B. Original Ad

In one instance, a firm took an existing ad and redirected the copy to support both the charity and/or client in a manner that made the firm memorable—meeting its own marketing needs. A win-win!

## [14.21] C. What About Me? Should I Advertise?

You already do. From your business card and offices, to your website. From the suit you wear, to the car you drive. All of that delivers a clear communication of who you are and what you can bring to a client's table.

## [14.22] D. Does That Include Public Relations?

Yes. Half of the battle in new business development is being top of mind when a need arises—top of mind to potential clients and referral sources. Advertising and public relations are two tactics among many.

The goal of advertising and public relations is to position you, your practice and your firm to best advantage in your prospect's or referral source's mind exactly when that need arises.

It's rare that a client will "test drive" an attorney. One cannot offer a fancy giveaway or coupon to draw clients to your office. In the law, as in business, repetition and reinforcement (you deliver your message once, you say it again, and then you say it again a little differently) are key to developing your practice and growing your firm. Individuals will do business with companies/law firms/attorneys they "know"—whether they've "met" them in an ad or by reading an interview in a media outlet they trust.

If they don't know you're out there, they can never retain you.

# APPENDIX
## FOUR BASIC "TRUTHS" ABOUT THE WAY PEOPLE BUY

1. **Clients seldom understand a product/service as well as the company/firm selling it.** You know everything that goes into your business and the services you provide. Clients/customers, by contrast, usually having only a fleeting and superficial relationship with that product/service, are relatively ignorant. And they may not even be interested. Unless you can put yourself in the shoes of your "ignorant" client, you cannot claim to be market-oriented.

2. **Clients will perceive the product/service you offer in their own terms.** Given their imperfect knowledge about your business and the services/products you provide, they have to select some attribute relevant to them (the *salient* attribute) on which to base their perception. This usually will be the attribute most obvious to the customer in the use/application of your service and the delivery of its benefits, even if it actually is peripheral. While a firm might believe its ability to guide a client along the fine line between noncompliance and over-compliance is the reason it was selected, the client might say, "I chose this firm because the partner I met with did not make me feel stupid." For example, the owner of a mid-sized creative firm interviewed three different general practice law firms. She chose the firm where the presenting partner was the only one not wearing a Rolex. She related to his lack of "showiness."

    Different clients will choose different salient attributes as important to their decision-making process. There is no single way to perceive a product or service. Every customer has a personalized view and in most cases, this is *not* based upon the attributes that you, the service supplier, would naturally use to describe the product or service.

3. **Client perception will focus on benefits, which often are intangible and can seem almost irrational to people in supplier companies.** This is because clients focus on what a product or service can do for them rather than on what the benefit actually is. Benefits, of course, are intangible—but that doesn't mean they aren't real. Employment law litigation, for example, *may* carry extra benefits if handled by a mega law firm. But very possibly, the key benefit to the decision-maker who has to justify that decision to a

higher-up (and later cover his or her butt should the firm not deliver) is being able to say, "Well, I went with the biggest. How could I possibly have known that would be a mistake?"

4. **Client perception is not always at the conscious level.** If you ask a client why he or she chose you, you may get a rational answer, but it may not be the whole story. Feelings behind buying decisions are not always easily articulated because they are complex, emotional and based upon a long-term relationship.

Understanding these four points is more important than most "specialized knowledge about technicalities." The quality of your product/service may be as good as, and even superior to, that of your competition. But that's probably not exactly why your client chose to go with your firm.

Branding is about the way people *perceive*, not about a product or service in isolation.

**CHAPTER FIFTEEN**

# COACHING

**John Rumely**

# [15.0] I. INTRODUCTION

Coaching—the pre-arranged series of meetings between an attorney and an advisor—can be one of the more rewarding career experiences for both parties. As a legal marketing professional, I have had the privilege of being assigned as a coach to attorneys at all stages of their careers, and I can say that these engagements have been among my highest-value accomplishments. Some of my coaching clients have come to me afterward to say they found the sessions very rewarding. (Although at times—particularly during the process itself—I'm sure they felt differently!) This chapter will serve as a brief description of the coaching process: what to expect, what to avoid, how to prepare, how to make the most of your time during the engagement, and how to keep the process alive after the sessions end.

Key takeaways from this chapter:

1. *The value of coaching.* Readers will understand the value of coaching and how it can enhance an attorney's practice, regardless of the size of the firm or where the attorney is in his or her career.

2. *Rationale for coaching.* Law firms offer coaching for a variety of reasons. It's possible the decision to enter into a coaching engagement might be the result of several factors, but it's good to identify them upfront.

3. *What coaching is NOT.* Coaching can take many formats, depending on the experience and preferences of the participants. But it's important to recognize that coaching has its limitations and there are many activities that should not be confused with coaching.

4. *"Size does NOT matter."* Coaching works in small and large firms alike. The process and resources available might be different, depending on the firm size, but coaching can be valuable regardless of the firm setting.

5. *How to commence the process.* The success of the coaching engagement depends greatly on a good start, which will set the tone for the entire process. There are a few simple steps to getting started that will minimize problems later on.

6. *How to keep the process going.* Coaching works best when it instills a set of habits that continue beyond the sessions. There are ways to

keep the coaching process alive after the sessions are completed.

## [15.1]  II.  THE VALUE OF COACHING

For an attorney at almost any stage of his or her career, coaching can be a valuable exercise. As a legal marketing professional, over the last dozen years I have coached attorneys in many different settings and at all ages. Here are some of the advantages I see for an attorney to engage a coach.

### [15.2]  A.  Coaching Formalizes the Career Development Process

Many things are taught in law school, but career development is not one of them. A formalized and articulated approach to managing one's career is not part of the curriculum, which many law schools consider "trade-related." The implication is that career management is one of those things you "learn by doing." This is not surprising, because most attorneys emerging from law school are open to any of several career options. Likewise, many law firms, large as well as small, prefer to rotate young attorneys through a number of assignments to see where there is the best fit—based on skills, personality, and ability to work with any particular team. Many firms also assign young attorneys to where the work is coming in, regardless of what might be an individual attorney's long-term career goals. So in the end, an individual attorney's goals for his or her career are considered subordinate to just getting the career itself underway (not to mention getting the debts from law school paid off!). Coaching is a way an attorney may take control of his or her career and set it along a pre-determined direction.

### [15.3]  B.  Coaching Is the Answer to "Career Drift"

Mid-career drift is another problem. After several years in practice, an attorney may find his or her career moving along a certain path and one morning look in the mirror and ask, "How did I get here? Was this type of work what I really wanted to do?" Or, the assignments given by the firm may have been so diverse that the attorney asks, "Where am I?" There is no clear direction to what the next step might be. Finding one's career going in the wrong direction, or having no direction whatsoever, causes confusion in terms of how an attorney should direct business development energies.

- How do I know which industry associations to support?

- Which gathering should I frequent to look for new clients?

- Which trade publications should I read and where should I submit articles?

Coaching is a way to understand where the drift (or the lack of direction) came from and can put some direction back into the career.

### [15.4] C. Coaching Encourages a Healthy Self-Evaluation

We brush our teeth every day, but that doesn't mean we don't need to go to the dental hygienist for a periodic checkup. Many of us know how to exercise, but that doesn't mean we don't look for a trainer when we go to the gym. Likewise, engaging a career coach gives attorneys an opportunity to step back and review where they are in their career. In doing so, attorneys will have the opportunity to reflect on the recent engagements that "fit right" in terms of long-term interests, personal preferences, and the type of work best suited to their skills and preferences. The coaching sessions will focus on those engagements and deconstruct them:

- What made the engagements I'm proud of go well?

- Why was I engaged in these particular matters?

- Where do I find more?

Likewise, the sessions should focus on the engagements that didn't go well:

- Was it a matter of personalities?

- Is there something inherent with a particular type of work that just doesn't work for me?

- Was it the wrong team?

### [15.5] D. Coaching Focuses on the Business Plan

Many law firms require a business plan from every partner, generally asking for them annually. If the truth be told, these plans are often set aside and forgotten as soon as they are submitted. In most firms, business plans are considered a nice idea, but generally not taken seriously, except maybe for attorneys whose practices have declined and may be under firm scrutiny. It's my belief, however, that business plans work when they're taken seriously. And if you want to take a business plan seriously, get a coach. Coaching brings the business plan into focus so it's front and center, and it provides a basis for ongoing discussions and periodic updating.

## [15.6] III. RATIONALE FOR COACHING

There are many ways to justify the time and expense involved with a coaching engagement. Here are the ones that I find most compelling.

### [15.7] A. Coaching Builds on Successes

Coaching sessions provide the opportunity for an attorney to select what was successful in the recent past and ask the important questions:

- How did I get this work?

- If it came from a referral, did I thank the source or somehow acknowledge my gratitude? How do I pay back the referral?

- What did I like about the engagement? What did I hear from the client about my work? Is there more where that came from?

### [15.8] B. Turnaround in a Career That Has Stalled

Let's face it: all attorneys have occasional lulls in their work—slow periods between major engagements that might occur for any of the following reasons:

1. *Major engagement just finished.* Marketing professionals always advise attorneys that "the best time to market is when you're busy"—advice that's not so easy to follow, of course. For those attorneys who can't or won't focus on the pipeline, there is often a lull after a major engagement. This is particularly true for litigators, who become completely absorbed in the matter in hand: "Winning today is everything; tomorrow will take care of itself." When tomorrow comes, as it inevitably will, the litigator has to start all over again.

2. *Major client went away.* It's a fact of life—all good things come to an end. There are plenty of reasons we lose clients, and most of them aren't good reasons. But we do lose them. And when we do, we have to regroup, examine where we are, and look for new business opportunities. This is precisely when coaching can be most valuable. Coaching is forward-focused and forces the attorney to forget the lost client and create new ones, or grow the existing ones.

## [15.9] C. Mid-Career Adjustment

Many attorneys embrace coaching as a way simply to review where they are and compare (or contrast) that with where they want to go. Coaching is a "time out" in the career-building process which is reflective, analytical, critical, and ultimately forward-looking.

## [15.10] D. Preparation of Senior Associates for Partnership

Many law firms—large or small—begin working with promising senior associates two or three years before their expected induction to partnership by introducing them to the process of pursuing their own clients and growing the relationships of clients they've inherited. Coaching is ideal for these candidates.

## [15.11] E. Integration of Lateral Hires

When a firm brings over an attorney from another firm, or hires an attorney from "in-house," coaching is ideal in terms of integrating the new attorney into the firm and accelerating the integration process.

## [15.12] IV. WHAT COACHING IS NOT

I've been called into coaching situations where I've immediately realized "this isn't going to go anywhere." There are plenty of misconceptions surrounding coaching and it's best to get them out in the open before an engagement gets under way. Here are examples where coaching is not applicable.

## [15.13] A. Coaching Is Not Mentoring

Many firms, large or small, have a formal mentoring program—where experienced attorneys work with junior associates to "show them the ropes" and guide their career development. This is laudable and, when done well, is a hallmark of an excellent firm. But mentoring is not coaching. Mentoring focuses on the "big picture" questions: "Do you like practicing law within a firm, or would you prefer to go in-house? Are you maintaining a healthy career-life balance? Are you running into any ethical dilemmas?" Coaching is more focused on the tactical: "Whom do you know who might be able to utilize my services? How do I grow my practice? How do I expand into new areas to develop more business for the firm?"

## [15.14] B. Coaching Is Not Training

When we think of training, we are usually dealing with an agenda that is predetermined and coursework or particular exercises that have been set in advance. Training is often mandated and required for certain certifications or to master some new skill. Also, training is generally not interactive and usually does not involve feedback from the attorney. Coaching, on the other hand, is open-ended in terms of what might be covered, and the attorney usually sets the goals. Coaching ideally should be voluntary (or offered as a reward to promising attorneys). Coaching is attorney-focused and enables the attorney to build on his or her capabilities. Most important, coaching (unlike most training) should be interactive—providing plenty of opportunity for feedback and mid-course corrections in where the sessions go next.

## [15.15] C. Coaching Is Not Part of the Formal Evaluation Process

Most firms conduct some form of evaluation each year where attorneys are reviewed (and compensated, presumably) based on a number of criteria: fee revenues from existing clients, new business generated, new clients introduced to the firm, pro bono activities, office support, and overall contributions to the good of the firm. Attorneys are often asked to generate a business plan at the beginning of the year and this plan might be the starting point for the evaluation: Did it accurately lay out the year's activities? Coaching should not be part of the evaluation process, but coaching might be a consequence of the evaluation process. In other words after an evaluation is completed, one of the recommendations might be coaching (as a reward, hopefully—not a remediation).

## [15.16] D. Coaching Is Not Marriage Counseling

Coaching typically does not involve aspects of an attorney's life beyond the office, unless those activities somehow impinge on the attorney's practice. If there is a sense that problems at home (as a result of long hours in the office, frequent travel, or general stress) are straining a relationship with a spouse or others at home, the coach should refer these problems to a professionally trained counselor and not try to handle them within the confines of the coaching relationship. If necessary, put the coaching on hold until these other issues are addressed. If they are not addressed, it's more than likely to negatively affect the success of the coaching relationship.

### [15.17] E. Coaching Does Not Address Personal Problems

Likewise, problems that affect performance such as drinking or substance abuse, obsessive and compulsive behaviors, or disruptive personality traits such as outbursts of anger, depression, or extreme anxieties, ought not to be tackled by the coach, except to identify them and refer the attorney to a qualified counselor. Again, if these traits are distracting enough to affect the coaching engagements, sessions ought to be postponed until there is sufficient evidence they have been addressed.

### [15.18] F. Coaching Is Not Easy—It's Going to Be Hard

Making changes in one's habits and patterns—particularly forming new habits—can be very difficult. That's why we don't try to do it alone. A coach is there to remind us of our promises, discourage old ways of addressing problems, reinforce new patterns, and cheer us on when we succeed.

## [15.19] V. THE SIZE OF THE FIRM DOES NOT MATTER

Whether the coaching takes place within a large firm with hundreds of attorneys, or in a small partnership with only a few partners, the basics are the same.

### [15.20] A. Coaching in a Large Firm

Larger firms have a certain amount of flexibility in how they promote and support a coaching program. Many firms maintain a list of pre-approved consultants and assign them to the attorneys they want to take part in a coaching program. Other firms hire coaches and keep them on staff, either reporting to human relations or the marketing department. Some firms put their business development professionals through a training program. In such a program, the trainees are typically given an introduction to the value of coaching, taught how to initiate sessions, and then are usually put through role-playing exercises that simulate a real coaching engagement.

The advantages of utilizing outside consultants are several:

1. The coach's role is clearly defined and there is no confusion on the part of the attorney as to why the coach is there—coaching is all this person does for the firm and for the attorney.

2. The coach, as an outsider, can provide the anonymity and discretion that many attorneys would require as a condition to entering into such an engagement.

3. The coach should have few distractions in terms of day-to-day deadlines.

4. The attorney can expect honest feedback from the coach. An outsider is less concerned with office politics and treating the attorney like a "boss."

The advantages of utilizing in-house staff as coaches are several:

1. The coach knows the firm and its resources and knows what is realistic in terms of what the firm and marketing team can deliver by way of support to the attorney.

2. The coach knows other attorneys within the firm who might be helpful as allies in the coaching process and development of business.

3. The coach is more accessible and can be called on at a moment's notice when an occasion arises to execute on a business opportunity. A coach can drop by the attorney's office on a regular basis to assess and provide positive feedback and to ask and answer additional questions.

4. The coach, familiar with others among the firm's marketing team, can keep abreast of what's working with other attorneys who are in coaching engagements.

## [15.21] B. Coaching in a Small-Firm Setting

Small firms (which we shall define as having fewer than 50 attorneys) encourage coaching for the same reasons as large firms. However, it's rare that a small firm can afford a coach on staff. In such a situation, the coaching is generally conducted by an outside consultant, but may also involve peer-to-peer consulting.

## [15.22] C. Coaching Can Be Done by Peers

Regardless of the size of the firm, the coaching role can be assumed by other attorneys who are properly prepared and are willing to make the commitment. This might be the solution for some attorneys who simply insist on coaching by someone of similar rank, or don't trust the process to "outsiders" or non-attorney staff.

## [15.23] VI. HOW TO COMMENCE THE PROCESS—GETTING STARTED

How the coaching engagement is commenced has a great influence on the sessions' eventual success. Here are some things to keep in mind:

### [15.24] A. The Coach Must Be Trained and Qualified

Coaching involves special skills and temperament. It doesn't require a law degree or an advanced degree in psychology, but a coach ought to undergo a formal training process, where many of the principles discussed in this chapter are reviewed, digested, and (hopefully) integrated into the process. Having a poorly trained coach, or one with bad intentions, is worse than no coaching at all. Fortunately, there are plenty of consultants who can "coach the coach" in terms of advising someone in a firm who aspires to be a coach.

### [15.25] B. Choice of the Coach

Beyond being properly trained and qualified, the coach must be trusted by the attorney. Ideally the relationship between the attorney and coach will be built on trust and confidence. If the coach is selected from the business development staff, he or she should have some level of familiarity with the attorney. If an outside coach is to be utilized, this relationship will have to be established at the outset; it is a prerequisite for a successful engagement.

### [15.26] C. Agreed-Upon Principles

When discussing whether to proceed with a coaching relationship, the attorney and coach ought to agree on several important points:

1. Both participants agree to commit the time for this effort. This will not be easy, as most attorneys probably feel they "give 110%" to their practices. So coaching might seem to be above and beyond what is normally asked by the firm. Ideally, both parties will agree upon the number of sessions, frequency, and what might be required in terms of the commitment of extra time.

2. Normally, attorneys are expected to "know everything" about a matter or case, and they're good at being cautious and defensive when embarking on something new. For those who think "I'll never be good at business development," the coach ought to reassure them that such skills can be learned. The attorney must be willing to trust the coach as more experienced in business development and, therefore, to take the coach's advice. This also involves trusting the coach to suggest new ideas and approaches.

3. Both parties must be willing to follow up on agreed-upon activities in a timely manner. If the attorney needs research or background information on an idea, will the coach see that these are delivered? If the attorney agreed to make phone calls to prospects or set up a meeting, will those calls be made?

4. The attorney should be willing to recognize that this is for his or her benefit and therefore should take ownership of the goals, embrace the process, and commit the energy to ensure it moves forward.

## [15.27] D. Assess the Attorney's Position in the Firm

"One size does not fit all" definitely applies to coaching. A good coach will adapt the sessions to the attorney's level of experience and rank within the firm. A more senior attorney should be focusing on long-established relationships among existing clients and building on past accomplishments. Coaching sessions with a younger attorney, on the other hand, might be more free-wheeling in terms of where to look for new business. A lateral hire newly arrived at the firm might require a whole different set of priorities, depending on age and experience. In fact, many firms assign a coach to lateral hires for this very purpose.

## [15.28] E. Set the Schedule

When setting the frequency and timing of the sessions, a sports analogy might be useful: coaching shouldn't be a marathon, but it definitely shouldn't be a sprint either. Maybe it's best to think of coaching as an aerobic exercise—one geared to the attorney's rhythm and weekly patterns. Here are some suggestions on scheduling:

1. *Agree on number of sessions.* There are plenty of opinions on this subject. Some say five sessions are all you need to schedule. Some say many more—15, 20. I personally believe 10 sessions are enough to know how it's going. After 10 sessions, ideally the bad habits have

been banished, the new habits are taking over, and enough time has lapsed to measure progress.

2. *Agree on the frequency and dates.* If both sides are serious, there ought to be specific dates set on the calendar during session #1. Some coaching engagements agree on weekly meetings. Others think bi-weekly meetings provide enough time between sessions to actually get the to-do lists done. Somewhere between weekly and bi-weekly ought to be where it's settled. Monthly meetings are simply too infrequent, in my opinion.

3. *Schedule can vary.* Both parties should be realistic and not kill themselves just to keep to the schedule. If the attorney is bogged down on a particular day, the session can be postponed until later in the week. The parties should be honest with each other—session #3 ought to take place as session #3 (and not just slide into session #4). Both parties should know where they are in terms of the number of sessions lapsed and the number yet to come.

## [15.29] F. Location, Location, Location

There are many considerations when deciding where to hold the sessions. Most attorneys would naturally expect to hold them in their office, with the attorney behind the desk, as usual, and the coach sitting in the visitor's chair. This is logical, because the attorney may want to refer to items in the files or on the computer. But the problem with this choice is obvious: it reinforces the attorney's previous way of doing business, which might need to change. The attorney's phone is nearby, which raises the chance of "Oh, I've got to take this call," interrupting the sessions. And it also places the attorney "in charge" in terms of power in the coaching relationship.

Coaching is about change, and the sessions should be a team effort and collegial. Therefore, it's best to reject any setting that reinforces old ways of doing things, or does not imply equality between the attorney and coach in the context of the coaching relationship. If doing the sessions in the attorney's office reinforces the "I'm in charge" position that most attorneys prefer to have, then change the location. There may be times when it's most efficient to work within the attorney's office for the reasons mentioned above, but this should be acknowledged and should not apply to all of the sessions. Instead, move them around—to a neutral setting like a conference room or, as discussed below, over lunch at a restaurant.

## [15.30] G. Agree on Goals and Objectives

One of the key components of a good beginning is agreeing to goals and objectives. Here are some suggestions:

1. *Keep it simple and doable.* The attorney ought to have control of the to-do list, which should focus on a set of goals that are realistic, objectives that support the goals, and specific tasks that can be achieved. The coach will know whether this list represents progress and potential new business, or the attorney is just going through the motions.

2. *Stick to the business plan.* If the attorney has a business plan, it ought to serve as a starting point for the discussion. Session #1 might include rewriting the plan completely, if that's what ought to be done. But the business plan ought to be the backdrop for the sessions. If the attorney does not have a business plan, one ought to be developed at the outset. In terms of writing a business plan, there is no "right" way of doing it. Some are just simple lists of clients and prospects with suggested tactics for building more business with each. Others can be quite elaborate, and read more like briefs—in-depth descriptions of all of the attorney's important relationships (business and personal). Regardless of the style and format, keep in mind that the business plan is just that—a plan. It's similar to a blueprint, which no one would confuse with an actual building. Coaching sessions focus on *execution* of the business plan, and should therefore not get bogged down in excessive rewriting of the plans themselves.

## [15.31] H. Ground Rules

There are several key points that ought to be explicitly mentioned, discussed, and agreed upon:

1. *Confidentiality.* This is a tricky subject. Many attorneys will insist on complete confidentiality, and they have a right in doing so. On the other hand, coaches, whether they're from the outside or they are in-house staff, are paid by the firm. Many practice group leaders or managing partners want to keep track of how the process is going and might want progress reports. For some attorneys, having the group leader know of the session progress would be fine. For others, maybe not. This has to be worked out between the attorney and coach.

2. *Is there a budget?* Coaching costs the firm money, period. If it's an outside coach, there are fees associated with the contract that can amount to several thousand dollars. If the coach is from business development staff, there are commitments of resources and salary expenses implicated by the engagement. Either way, the firm has expended resources and this should be acknowledged. In addition, there ought to be a budget committed to the coaching engagement that can be used for reasonable expenses associated with executing the business plan, such as client/prospect entertainment, conference registration fees, subscription fees, travel expenses, etc. Some (or maybe all) of these funds could come from the attorney as a show of good faith in the process. Regardless of where the funds come from, however, there ought to be an acknowledgment that "it takes money to make money." Best to raise this question with the firm before the sessions begin and put this on the agenda for session #1.

3. *Is there a termination clause?* Any attorney who writes up a contract knows there are termination clauses. It may be a very simple reason: "We agreed on 10 sessions; we made real progress in 10 sessions; now it's time to move on." Sometimes the work schedules simply become overwhelming. And sometimes it's simply chemistry—the style of the coach does not fit the attorney's expectations. Regardless of the reasons, there ought to be an explicit agreement that coaching is not "going through the motions" of just another office obligation. If it's not working, do something else with your time.

## [15.32]  I.  Make It Fun

Coaching sessions can be stressful. Let's face it: reflecting on one's professional career and work habits isn't easy. Oftentimes the sessions might take on the onus of a chore. Ideally, they should be welcomed by both parties as a project that could be fun and creative. So don't get bogged down looking at coaching as yet another "assignment." Sure, there will be homework involved, but it's extra credit homework. Remember getting extra credit assignments in school? They were considered a privilege or an opportunity to get a better grade, weren't they? Same thing with coaching.

1. *"Let's do lunch."* Arrange a few (or maybe all) of the sessions so they include lunch—whether brown-bag or at a nearby bistro. Breaking bread and strategizing go well together. In fact, lunches can serve as "dress rehearsals" for sessions with clients. As a coach, imagine looking across the table and asking your coaching client: "So, tell me

about your practice." I have done this with many attorneys with great success. Most attorneys think they have their elevator speech down pat. Try it with the coach.

2. *Snacks.* Maybe there isn't money for lunch with every session. So bring snacks—even if it's coffee. Just make sure the term "coaching" is associated with "fun." There have been times when an attorney I coached came to me afterward and said, "I miss our sessions—I associate them with those cookies you used to bring!"

## [15.33] VII. HOW TO KEEP THE PROCESS GOING

Coaching is about change: we introduce new habits; we discourage old habits that we agree are dysfunctional; and we impose fresh perspectives on the attorney's practice. Once the sessions are complete, there are ways to keep bad habits from creeping back in.

### [15.34] A. Working the Business Plan

One of the important things to keep in mind about coaching is the sessions should be "action-oriented." Having a business plan or a to-do list every week is essential. So have it handy and refer to it throughout the week. The attorney should break down the tasks into what is going to be accomplished and checked off *today*. If progress isn't being made on the plan or the list by session #2, it is important for the coach to offer to call or stop by the attorney's office between sessions just to check up:

- Did you make that call today we agreed on?

- Did you compile that list of contacts you promised?

- Did you review your old proposals for that list of deals you want to highlight?

### [15.35] B. Follow Up

After each session, the coach ought to send a quick email to the attorney reflecting on the meeting—noting who promised to do what task, the deadlines, and the schedule for the next meeting. By session #5, the attorney ought to be generating these to-do lists, not the coach.

## [15.36] C. Monitor and Reflect on the Progress

It's important for both parties—the attorney and the coach—to be frank with each other and ask: "Is this working?" Maybe not at the second session, or the third or fourth, but at one point, it's important to reflect on how it's going and whether the sessions are worth the effort and time. If not, why not? Who's not doing their part? Are the plans you're working on not appropriate? The coach might ask: "Am I pushing too hard?" Whatever the reasons, get them out on the table and discuss them. It's unlikely they're insurmountable. If both parties feel the process is valuable, then make whatever changes are necessary and continue. Experiment and adopt new ideas. Keep moving and keep meeting!

## [15.37] D. Stay in Touch

Many of the plans put into motion during coaching sessions may take months to play out. The sessions themselves may only spread over two or three months, so a periodic check-up might very well be in order. The promise of a check-up will keep a little pressure on the attorney not to let the process die. A check-in will allow the coach an opportunity for a "post-mortem" on the sessions. Coaches need to learn, too, and reflecting on the sessions may provide them with some insights on the coaching technique used. What worked and what didn't? In other words, the coaching and learning goes both ways.

## [15.38] E. No Excuses

We said at the outset of this chapter that change is not easy. Imposing new patterns on how an attorney conducts business can be one of the most difficult things to do. Just like when you're working with a coach at the gym, it's okay to complain, grunt and plead "enough!" But don't give up. Work through the assignments; engage in the process; and put in the effort. You'll see changes.

# CHAPTER SIXTEEN

# TECHNOLOGY TO SUPPORT GROWING YOUR PRACTICE

David J. Rosenbaum

# TECHNOLOGY TO SUPPORT GROWING YOUR PRACTICE § 16.0

## [16.0] I. INTRODUCTION

The effective use of technology is critical to the operation and success of any modern law firm. With so many options and products to choose from, and with so many conflicting claims about what solution is best, how is an attorney to intelligently decide what to buy and implement? This chapter is not intended to recommend specific products or solutions, but rather to help you to understand the choices that are available, the issues that you need to consider, and how to make a smart decision as you select and implement technology to support the growth of your practice.

## [16.1] II. THE IMPORTANCE OF REGISTERING A DOMAIN NAME

Your domain name, the part of your email address after the @ sign, may be the first clue a prospective client has about who you are and what kind of firm you have. Consider the impressions that the following email addresses create: *billysmith@aol.com* versus *bsmith@gmail.com* versus *bill@callusifyouarehurt.com* versus *bsmith@smithlawfirm.com*. To me, the first two examples suggest a solo practitioner working from home, the next reminds me of an advertisement on the side of a bus, and the fourth sounds like the email address of a name partner in a law firm. What image are you trying to create for your practice? This isn't a question of right or wrong, but rather one of marketing and image consistency.

Registering a domain name is easy—connect to the website of a domain name registrar (e.g., networksolutions.com, register.com), enter the domain name you'd like to use, and if nobody's yet registered that domain name, then for a small annual fee it's yours.

Once you have your domain name, it's time to build a website. Prospective clients will likely visit your website to learn more about you. It's not necessary to spend a lot of money on your website, but it is important to be sure that your website clearly communicates who you are and what services your firm offers, and does so in a way that's consistent with the image you're trying to present. Many domain name registrars have do-it-yourself tools for building websites. There are also lots of websites where you can use their tools to build your own website (e.g., wix.com, doodle-kit.com, yola.com). Or consider hiring someone to do it for you.

Your email and website need be hosted on a server that's Internet accessible. If you're doing this all yourself, then check with the domain name registrar where you registered your domain name; they'll generally offer hosting services and provide assistance with establishing the hosting configuration, especially if you've used their tools to build your website. Or if you've used another website's tools you'll often find tips on how to establish hosting for the website you've built. If you've hired a developer to create your website, ask that person to establish the hosting for you.

### ACTION PLAN

- Select and register a domain name that's consistent with the image you're trying to create, and that will resonate with the clients you're trying to attract.

- Build a website using tools provided by the domain name registrar or available elsewhere on the Internet, or hire a developer to build a website for you.

- Establish hosting for your email and website.

- Spread the word about your new email address and website.

## [16.2] III. CREATING AN OPTIMAL INFRASTRUCTURE

Now that you've created your online persona and website presence it's time to create an optimal infrastructure for your office. Infrastructure refers to the hardware and peripherals that you'll use, along with the communications that will connect you to the rest of the world.

The first question you'll need to consider is the extent to which you'll choose to store your data on file servers within your office or whether you'll store your data externally in the Cloud. While both in-house and Cloud-based solutions work and can provide similar functionality, there are significant differences between the two approaches. Purchasing your own file servers requires an expenditure of capital and requires you to provide for ongoing maintenance and support of your systems, but gives you the greatest control of your data, including control over the confidentiality of client information. Utilizing the Cloud (e.g., Microsoft Office 365, Google Apps, Zoho Docs) reduces or eliminates the need to purchase file servers, but replaces up-front acquisition expense with monthly operating fees that may cumulatively exceed the capital costs of outright purchases. Beyond just cost comparisons, the Cloud provides you with much *less direct control* over data security and confidentiality than you have with in-house file servers.

# TECHNOLOGY TO SUPPORT GROWING YOUR PRACTICE § 16.2

As you make your decision about whether to use physical servers in-house or virtual servers in the Cloud, carefully evaluate the anticipated capital and operating costs of each option over a three-to-five-year period, allowing for the impact that changes in Cloud-based pricing could have on your analysis. While the major Cloud providers are actively competing to offer their services at lower prices than their competitors, the current pricing structures may be artificially low, and significant price increases combined with high costs to change providers may be on the horizon.

Beyond just comparing costs, attorneys must very carefully consider the security and confidentiality implications of storing client data on in-house servers where the firm has direct control and responsibility for assuring data protection and confidentiality versus storing client data in the Cloud, where third parties are providing the security—arguably at a more comprehensive level than the firm could achieve, but yet outside of the attorney's control or oversight. Research and pay careful attention to your local Ethics Committee guidelines regarding your obligations to perform due diligence regarding any Cloud providers you may consider using.

Determining where you'll store your data has significant cost and security considerations; selecting your computer is much easier. Start by identifying the software you'll use within your practice (more on this later in the chapter). If the software runs only under Windows, then you should buy a PC (or a Mac with Parallels, but that's a different story); if the software runs on a Mac, then you'll need to buy a Mac. In other words, the choice of software should determine the computer hardware platform.

Desktop computers tend to be comparatively less expensive and more durable than equivalently configured laptops, but laptops are portable. Select a desktop computer if you don't need the computer to be portable, either because you primarily work in a single location or because you plan to buy separate computers for each place where you work. Pick a laptop computer if you want to take the computer with you. Tablets are even lighter and more portable than laptops—they can be great for email and online research but generally don't have good enough keyboards to use for extensive word processing; opt instead for a laptop if you need portability and want to use the device for drafting. Smartphones combine the portability benefits of tablets in an even smaller size with the ability to make and receive telephone calls, but are generally too small to use effectively for drafting or research. Expect to purchase several devices to be used in the office and on the road, each optimal for an intended use.

When selecting your computer(s), disk drive capacity represents the amount of data that you can store on the device, and RAM affects the computer's speed when multiple applications are open at the same time. If your practice requires you to deal with large amounts of data be sure to purchase a computer with a large disk drive—at least 500GB or 1TB. If you like to have multiple applications open simultaneously, select a computer with lots of RAM—at least 4GB and preferably 8GB.

Despite years of industry efforts to achieve a "paperless office" most law firms still do extensive printing. Buy a fast printer with a "duty cycle" rating that's at least twice the maximum number of pages that you expect to print in your busiest month. There are few things more frustrating than working with a printer that's too slow or unreliable. Emailing of attachments has largely reduced the reliance on faxing; buy a scanner that's capable of handling the types of documents you need to transmit. If you need to scan marked-up contracts, pick a scanner with a document feeder that's designed to handle the number of pages in your typical contract. If you need to scan images or odd-sized pages, pick a scanner with a flatbed where you can place the originals on the glass and scan individual images.

The ability to access the Internet quickly and reliably is critical for law firms. Fortunately many fast, inexpensive options are available including high-speed Internet offerings from local telephone companies, cable TV companies and in-building Internet service providers in "lit buildings." While price is important, focus more on speed and reliability. The more extensively you rely on the Internet for email or for accessing Cloud-based services including research services, and especially if you've placed your own data in the Cloud, strongly consider installing two separate Internet circuits from different carriers for redundancy. If you intend to remotely access your computer or an in-house file server from outside your office, be sure to order your Internet circuit with a "static IP address."

Computers require electricity to run. Protect your computers and peripherals with surge protectors to help prevent spikes in electrical power from damaging your equipment. File servers need to be further protected with Uninterruptable Power Supply (UPS) units. UPS units provide a few minutes of backup battery power to the equipment, allowing it to continue operating during a momentary power outage, and provide sufficient power to allow the server to be shut down cleanly in the event of a longer power outage. If your office is in an area that experiences frequent power outages (even momentary ones), consider purchasing UPS units for your desktop computers as well as for your file server. Tip: don't plug laser printers into UPS units—the power that laser printers draw will damage a UPS and render it useless.

Computers, and especially file servers, need to be operated in cool environments. You don't need to place your computers or file servers in heavily air-conditioned raised-floor rooms, but ambient air temperatures where the computers are being used should not be permitted to exceed 85 degrees Fahrenheit. Be aware of excessively high temperatures outside of normal business hours, especially in office buildings where building air conditioning is often turned off overnight and on weekends.

While the importance of telephones has diminished with the widespread use of email, don't forget that you'll also need to speak with clients. For some practitioners a cell phone is all that's needed; for others a more sophisticated system is necessary. Select a telephone system that provides you with the features that you need—from the basics, like voicemail, to capabilities like call-forwarding and conference-bridging. If you're considering relying on a cell phone be sure to verify that you have good cell phone coverage where your office is located.

### ACTION PLAN

- Determine whether to store your data on an in-house file server or in the Cloud; purchase or subscribe to an appropriate solution.

- Purchase computer equipment and peripherals based on the software you'll be using and the devices that best match the way you work.

- Implement Internet service that's fast and reliable; consider redundant circuits, especially if your data is in the Cloud. Remember to secure static IP addresses if you'll need to access your systems remotely.

- Provide adequate power protection and cooling for your computers.

- Select a telephone system with the features that you need to work effectively and efficiently.

## [16.3] IV. PROTECTING DATA—YOURS AND YOUR CLIENTS'

As an attorney you have an ethical and legal responsibility to protect the confidentiality of your clients' data. You also have a personal and business responsibility to protect the confidentiality of your own data.

Along with the responsibilities regarding confidentiality, you also have a responsibility to preserve and assure accessibility of data. If all of your data was destroyed in a fire and no longer existed, it'd certainly be "confidential" but would no longer be accessible, which isn't good for you or your clients.

## [16.4]  A.  Password Protection

The first step in protecting confidentiality of data is to password protect your systems. Use passwords that are easy for *you* to remember and hard for others to guess or figure out. Don't use names, birth dates or words from the dictionary; use combinations of upper and lower case letters along with numbers and special characters (e.g., #/$%~+). One technique is to develop a standard "passphrase" that you combine with a unique suffix for each system. For example, if your standard passphrase is "I'm a great New York attorney" (and if you therefore select *IaGr8N/YA* as your password root), your TimeSlips password could be *IaGr8N/Ya-Timeslips!* while your password for Westlaw could be *IaGr8N/Ya-Westlaw!* Whatever you do, don't write your passwords on pieces of paper that you attach to your monitor.

## [16.5]  B.  Network Firewall

Since your computers will be connected to the Internet, you need to protect the perimeter of your network with a firewall. Purchase and install a firewall that includes both "port filtering" and "stateful inspection"; consider one that also includes virus, malware and intrusion prevention capabilities (e.g., WatchGuard, SonicWall, Cisco).

## [16.6]  C.  Backup System

There's an old IT saying that there are two kinds of people in the world—those who have lost data, and those who will. The best way to protect your data and your clients' data from loss is to implement a good backup system. Traditionally, backups relied on tapes and disk; current backup methods still use tape and disk, and also add online Cloud-based backup options (e.g., Carbonite, BackupMyInfo!, CloudBerry). Backups should be run on a regular basis (i.e., daily), and multiple generations of backup sets should be retained in order to adequately protect against a complete loss of all data (i.e., following a fire, theft or disk drive crash) and to protect against a partial loss of data (i.e., the overwriting of a file that's not discovered until several weeks later). Backup sets should be stored in a location that's separate from where the data that's being protected resides, so that a breach in your office doesn't compromise both your original data and your backups. And backups need to be tested on a regular basis; messages indicating successful backup completions don't assure that there's actually recoverable and usable data within the backup sets. When planning your backup strategy be sure to consider your firm's need to retain data for extended periods of time, which may be stipulated in your client engagement letters, as well as your firm's need to destroy data after specified periods of time. This is also the time to do some disaster and business continuity planning—what would happen to your practice if there was a fire in your building and you couldn't get into your office for several days, or if there was an earthquake and your office was destroyed? These are not eventualities that we want to think about, but are an important part of planning for continuity of your practice and of responsibly meeting your obligations to your clients.

## [16.7] D. Software Updates

System software and utilities need to be updated regularly. Microsoft, for example, releases updates to its software to resolve security vulnerabilities and to correct bugs on a monthly basis. Many software vendors (e.g., Adobe, Java, Skype) similarly issue regular updates. Failure to maintain your computers with up-to-date patches exposes your data and your clients' data to loss, corruption and breach of confidentiality.

## [16.8] E. Antivirus Software

Two important tools in the fight against hackers are antivirus software and antimalware software. Viruses and malware are variants of unwanted software that become installed on a computer, often through a malicious email attachment or via a miscoded or infected website. Viruses and malware may lead to degraded system performance, to deletion or corruption of files and data, and to dissemination of confidential information. All computers and file servers should be protected with antivirus/antimalware software (e.g., Symantec AntiVirus, BitDefender, Trend Micro), and the software should be kept up to date, often on a daily basis. Additionally it's important to follow the principles of safe computing—don't open email attachments that you weren't expecting even if they appear to be from someone you know (if in doubt pick up the phone and call first), don't click on links if you don't know where they lead to, don't respond to an email inquiry from your bank/broker/utility asking for your password since they "lost" it, and be very aware that hackers have become exceptionally skilled at posing as someone else. Social engineering techniques have become much more sophisticated and pervasive, where a hacker, for the purpose of encouraging you to divulge confidential information, provides personal information (e.g., your date of birth, your spouse's name) to suggest that he knows you or has an existing relationship with you. Be wary.

**ACTION PLAN**

- Use complex passwords, with different passwords for each application and system. Consider using a passphrase prefix and unique suffix.

- Implement a firewall to protect your Internet connection.

- Implement *and test* regular backups including offsite copies. Consider retention and destruction requirements in your backup strategy.

- Update your system software regularly.

- Deploy and maintain antivirus/antimalware software.

- Be wary. Be very wary.

## [16.9]  V.  SOFTWARE TO OPERATE AND GROW YOUR PRACTICE

Software comprises the set of tools that you'll use to manage your practice, generate work product and get paid for it.

The basic tools you'll likely use most extensively are word processing and email software. These products, along with spreadsheet and presentation software, are often economically licensed as part of an office suite. There are currently several different ways you can license this core software. Microsoft offers its Office Suite as traditional shrink-wrapped products that you can purchase online or off-the-shelf, then install onto your computer; the advantage of licensing software this way is that when you replace your computer the software can be uninstalled from your old PC and reinstalled onto your new one. There are also variations on the shrink-wrapped product licenses that provide for installing the single license onto two or three computers. Microsoft also offers a software "rental" option in conjunction with its Microsoft Office 365 online solution, allowing you to pay for the software on a monthly basis rather than paying a one-time upfront licensing fee. Visit Microsoft's website (microsoft.com/Office) for the latest information about its software solutions and licensing options.

# TECHNOLOGY TO SUPPORT GROWING YOUR PRACTICE § 16.9

Corel's WordPerfect Office Suite includes WordPerfect, which has long been a favorite word processor for attorneys. This suite doesn't include an email client (so you'd need to separately implement an email client like Microsoft Outlook or Gmail), but does include legal-specific solutions like Bates Numbering in the Standard and Professional Editions, and Corel® Perfect Authority Table of Authorities software in the Legal Edition. WordPerfect Office is not available as a monthly rental. Visit Corel's website (wordperfect.com) for the latest information on the features and benefits of its solutions.

Google Apps for Work (www.google.com/enterprise/apps/business) and ZoHo Docs (www.zoho.com/docs) offer online rental models only, with Google Apps including both of the core products (word processor and email software), while the ZoHo Docs solution doesn't include an email client, relying on you to separately implement a product like Microsoft Outlook or Gmail.

If you're buying a new computer, the least expensive way to license office suite software for it is often to buy the software preinstalled under an OEM license. Note that an OEM license grants permission to use the software on one specific computer and cannot be transferred to a different computer, so under this model when you replace your computer you'll need to license new software.

Time and billing software is used to capture and track your time and disbursements, to invoice clients for your services, and generally to track work-in-progress and accounts receivable information. There are many products to choose from including solutions that are installed in-house on your computer or file server (e.g., Sage TimeSlips, TABS3, PCLaw) and products that run from the Cloud (e.g., TurboLaw/Cloud, Time59, Bill4-Time). When selecting time and billing software, start by considering how you will bill your clients (i.e., hourly, flat fee, retainer, contingency), the degree of flexibility you need in adjusting time entries (i.e., write-ups, write-downs, write-offs) and how you want to present your invoices (i.e., detailed time logs, summary statements), then carefully evaluate each product's ability to meet *your* specific requirements. Review the reporting capabilities of each product (i.e., work-in-progress, services rendered versus client budget, aged accounts receivable) and how the reports will help you to manage your practice and your clients. Consider each product's ability to capture information directly from your calendar to simplify the process of time entry.

Whereas the time and billing software enables you to track your time and bill clients for your services, bookkeeping software is used to manage your business income, expenses, assets and liabilities. Products like Intuit QuickBooks, Sage 50 and Cougar Mountain Denali will help you to record and pay bills, reconcile your bank account, evaluate your firm's profitability and keep an eye on your cash flow. While bookkeeping may seem like a clerical task, the information provided by a good bookkeeping system can be invaluable in helping you to keep your business healthy.

A calendaring or docketing system will help you to keep track of upcoming appointments, court appearances and filing deadlines, and will provide a tool to record for billing purposes how you've spent your time. Your calendar can be as simple as the one that's part of your email client (e.g., Outlook, Gmail), or can be more sophisticated to address coordination of multiple attorneys' schedules who are working together on a matter. If you are frequently faced with deadlines based on filing, service or trial dates, investigate systems that provide rule-based scheduling (e.g., Aderant, Deadlines.com, MA3000) with the ability to calculate dependent dates when an independent date is entered, and to update the dependent dates when an independent date changes. Some insurance companies *require multiple* redundant calendaring systems before they'll issue a professional liability insurance policy to reduce the risk of claims due to missed filing deadlines. As mentioned above, consider whether time entries in the calendar can feed directly into your time and billing system.

Technology and the availability of online research services (e.g., Lexis, Westlaw, Loislaw) have materially reduced the need for attorneys to maintain in-house libraries of physical reference books. Although subscriptions to these online services can be expensive, access to reliable statute and case law is critical to the practice of law. Don't rely solely on the results from Google searches; just because information appears on a website doesn't mean that it's current or accurate. Confirm that the subscription you're considering provides access to all of the materials you'll need for your practice. Compare costs of ownership and usage—not just prices, but also how efficiently you can use each product; a product that you're not comfortable using will slow you down and may compromise the results you achieve. Subscription prices may be negotiable.

Case management software (e.g., Clio, Amicus Cloud, Needles) can help you to keep track of information about your clients and matters (i.e., client contacts, related party details, task list management, conflict checking) and to share that information with others in your firm in a centralized, uniform manner. Case management may be integrated or bundled with time and billing, calendaring, docketing and bookkeeping functionality as an all-encompassing practice management solution.

Depending on the type of law that you practice and the needs of your clientele, your documents and work product may always be handcrafted and unique based on each specific situation. More likely, however, your documents consist of both newly crafted and previously drafted language that you combine to leverage what you've done before and to create work product more efficiently and effectively. As you identify the documents, paragraphs and clauses that you'll use repeatedly, take the time to establish your own forms library. Designate a set of folders on your network where you'll store documents that you plan to reuse. Don't mix forms and client work product in the same folders. Whether you create your forms from scratch or derive the forms from work that you've done for clients, save forms with blank spaces in lieu of client-specific data in your forms library folders; this will both simplify your ability to locate the places in the form where data needs to be inserted, and will reduce the risk of releasing a document for one client that still contains information from a different client. Beware of "metadata" in all documents, especially within your forms; metadata may contain details of previously edited or deleted text within the document. Most word processors include the ability to delete metadata from within a document. If your forms are designed to be used with the simple insertion of information (i.e., client names and addresses, applicable dates and dollar amounts), teach yourself how to use the mail merge functions of your word processing software to merge data into the forms, or investigate document assembly software that both merges data into the forms and adds the ability to combine sections from multiple forms into a single resulting document.

Forms are not the only files you should organize carefully on your network. Take the time to consistently organize your client files and your practice (non-client) files, especially if others within your firm are collaborating with you on client matters. Use your case management software to assign client/matter references. Use the same client/matter references in your time and billing software. Designate an area on your network where you'll create folders for each client and subfolders for each matter. Structure your files within the subfolders, perhaps by year or by type of document (e.g., correspondence, contracts, pleadings), or by whatever structure may be appropriate for each particular matter or for the area of law you practice. The more care you take in saving your documents in an organized fashion, the less time you'll waste trying to find documents later. Designate an area on your network where you'll save useful non-client-specific articles, again organized in a way that will facilitate finding information when you need it.

### ACTION PLAN

- Purchase software that will help you to effectively and efficiently track your clients and matters, produce work product, bill for your services and manage the productivity and profitability of your firm.

  The basics—word processing, email

  Time and billing

  Bookkeeping

  Calendar/Docket

  Research

  Case management

- Begin to establish a forms library.

- Organize your files so you (and others you work with) can find them easily.

## [16.10] VI. PUTTING IT ALL TOGETHER

There's a lot to think about as you select and implement technology to support and grow your practice—everything from establishing your online image, to building an in-house or Cloud-based network, to protecting your data and your clients' data, to selecting and buying a variety of software tools—all in addition to your need to focus your time and energy on the practice of law. The whole thing can be daunting! Fortunately there's a way to approach the process that's logical and proven to be effective.

### [16.11]  A. Determine Your Needs

Don't worry (yet) about what's available, what various products can do, which product is "better" than other products, or what products will cost. Assume for the moment that everything's possible and that everything's free. Think about how you work and what would help you to work more efficiently and more effectively. Think about how you manage your time and how you'd like to manage others. Think about who your current clients are and about the types of clients you'd like to have. Think about how you charge for your services and how you'd like to (or need to) present your invoices so that your clients will pay you for your work. Think about what you'd like your practice to look like a year from now. Think about what information, statistics, trends or analyses would help you to grow your practice. Based on this process of active thinking, write down everything that you think or wish technology could do for you. Use bullet points, write paragraphs or draw pictures—the format doesn't matter. The objective is to develop an understanding of your needs and a document that lists those needs, i.e., a "Needs Analysis Document."

## [16.12] B. Select the Software

Software is the technology toolset that you'll actually *use* as you work toward meeting your needs and achieving your goals. Don't select software simply because you know lots of people who use it or because it received great reviews. With your Needs Analysis Document in hand, start to evaluate software products specifically in terms of how well each product meets the needs you've identified. Your evaluation will be both quantitative and qualitative. Quantitatively, for example, if you bill your clients against a specific budget and a software product doesn't support this functionality, then it's probably not the right product for you. Qualitatively, if a product feels like it will be confusing to understand or difficult to use, then it may not be right for you. At this point in the process it's time to start considering cost. A product that matches all of your needs but costs more that you're prepared to spend may not be viable for you, but neither is a product that doesn't meet your needs, even if it's inexpensive or free. By understanding which of *your specific* needs each product does or doesn't meet versus the cost of each product you can make an informed business decision about what's the best fit *for you*.

## [16.13] C. Finalize the Platform

Having selected your software based on your specific needs, you can now determine what infrastructure will be required in order to operate the software. If your ideal products are Cloud-based, then you can proceed to make infrastructure and hardware decisions consistent with a Cloud-centric environment. If you determine that in-house software will meet your needs better than Cloud-based software, then you'll start to look at a file server and consider the environmental requirements that accompany it.

## [16.14] D. Iterate, Review and Reflect

Reconfirm that the software products and platform you've selected address the needs you've identified in your Needs Analysis Document, and that data protection is adequately addressed by the solution. Even if you've never selected technology before, trust your gut; if the solution feels wrong or worrisome, iterate through the process again. Selecting software and hardware can be intimidating, and even a well-considered decision can be scary, but the decision should feel right, not wrong. If you're still unsure of your decision, seek a recommendation from a computer consultant who works with other attorneys and law firms. Select a consultant who charges for his or her time and doesn't sell the products he or she recommends, so that you can be assured of receiving unbiased advice.

## [16.15] E. Procure It, Implement It and Use It

Invest time and energy to learn the software products thoroughly. Use the analytical capabilities of the time and billing and bookkeeping software to understand and manage the business side of your practice. Study the information in the case management software to understand where your clients come from so that you can use these insights to develop more business. Leverage the capabilities of the word processing software or document assembly software to improve the efficiency with which you create work product. View the technology not as just a necessary overhead expenditure, but as an important set of tools to help you manage and grow your practice.

# CHAPTER SEVENTEEN

# SUCCESS SUPPORTS

**Terri Pepper Gavulic**

## [17.0] I. INTRODUCTION

As you've seen in the preceding chapters, successful legal marketing and business development require a multitude of tools, systems, and processes, coupled with appropriate expenditures of time and money, the right attitude and demeanor, and a splash of good luck and good planning to ensure you're in the right place at the right time. These resources are mostly finite so in this chapter we'll discuss how best to leverage the time, money, and resources expended to maximize your chances for success, as well as discuss commonly experienced obstacles and how to overcome these impediments to success. While there is no "one size fits all" approach to marketing and business development, there are critical success factors and best practices that have been well honed by the rainmakers who've come before, and we'll explore these factors, too.

## [17.1] II. OVERCOMING OBSTACLES

Before a discussion of the factors that will make your marketing and business development successful, let's uncover and dispose of the most common obstacles and impediments. If you are unable to put aside these potential stumbling blocks, no amount of planning or activity will ultimately lead to maximum success, even if you accidentally experience modest successes along the way.

- Compensation—Some lawyers don't actively participate in marketing or business development because their firm's compensation system doesn't suitably pay directly for these activities. Rather, the compensation system might most highly value production (e.g., billing time). Even if the firm rewards unevenly for business development, it's still essential for long-term success and an obligation of partnership. It's compelling to take charge of your career, too. By bringing in your own clients and matters, you can have control over the quality and quantity of work you perform. Managing a client relationship that you've brought in provides cache that is hard to achieve in other ways. As partners—a/k/a owners—it makes no sense not to bring in quality work and clients that keep the firm profitable and viable for the long term. Each time you receive a partner distribution (or a paycheck if you're a non-equity partner), you are getting paid directly or indirectly for *everything* you do, including marketing and business development—after all, there would be no billable work if someone wasn't finding and minding clients.

- Time—Not having enough hours in the day to work on client matters *and* conduct marketing and business development activities is another common impediment. There are a few tactics that help overcome the time crunch. One such tactic is to schedule your marketing activities as you would any other important business meeting by deciding what you're going to do and how much time you're going to spend, then blocking out that time on your calendar. Another thing that can help overcome the time crunch is to select marketing or business development activities that you enjoy doing, so that you don't procrastinate and put off doing them.

- The final obstacle that we'll cover here is that of a lack of skill and knowledge about the marketing or business activity that you're embarking upon. The best suggestion is to make sure that you select activities that you enjoy, as mentioned above, and then become as skillful as possible through training, coaching or regular practice. For example, if you like to write consider writing for trade or industry publications that will be seen by people who might hire you. Then work on crafting your articles, news releases or legal alerts in the best and most user-friendly manner, giving advice and suggestions that your readers can actually take. Always ask someone you trust to review your piece before you submit it for publication, and be willing to accept feedback and constructive criticism. If you enjoy public speaking you might want to join a group such as Toastmasters or look for speaking opportunities that give you practice presenting to an audience.

No matter the obstacle, remember that it is easy for an obstacle to become an excuse for not doing what you know must be done to be successful. Successful marketing and business development professionals don't allow these obstacles or impediments to stop them; they are successful in spite of these things.

## [17.2] III. LEVERAGING RESOURCES

Quite often, marketing and business development are conducted as solo activities, especially in smaller firms. But they perhaps should not be so—even sole practitioners can leverage some of the resources described below. Partnering with other people is especially effective so that you can share the work and minimize the time commitment involved. It's a good idea to understand all of the various resources, including people, tools and technology, that you can leverage to enhance your marketing and business development success, and we'll discuss some of those here.

*People*—John Donne had it right when he said, "No man is an island." Why go it alone when there are any number of people who could help you be successful? Let's consider a few of these human resources that you can (and should) tap into.

*Partners in your firm*—Your partners can serve many important roles in the development of your marketing expertise. Here are a few ways to leverage your partners:

- As role models—Do you have a partner who's an excellent speaker, writer or business closer? Take that partner to lunch and ask him or her to share what and how he or she developed his or her expertise.

- As mentors—Ask a successful partner to take you under his or her wing and guide you to success on a par with his or her own. We've seen many lawyers who are reluctant to do this for fear of exposing personal weakness. *Au contraire*—you will likely be more respected for seeking to enhance your skills and knowledge. If you are reluctant to reach out to an individual, then find a more creative way to achieve the goal of learning success secrets from others in your firm. One excellent way to do this is to offer to organize and moderate a "Rainmaker's Roundtable" luncheon, where the firm's most successful marketers share their best tips and tactics with all the lawyers in the firm.

- As referral sources—If you've identified a company, contact, trade association or other group for which you want to gain access, see if another partner can make an introduction for you. By doing so, the other partners are imbuing you with any goodwill they've generated with that individual or group.

*Younger lawyers in your firm*—Have you ever heard the expression, credited to Frank Oppenheimer, that "the best way to learn is to teach"? Become a mentor or role model for a younger lawyer and you will be forced to learn before you teach as well as get out and do things to show you're not all talk and no action. Often these mentor and mentee relationships become mutually beneficial. You very likely might learn something as well. One way to ensure this happens is to mentor someone who has different strengths than you do. For example, you might teach a younger lawyer how to be an effective public speaker and that younger lawyer might teach you all about using social media to your advantage.

*Other professionals*—Leveraging other people is not restricted to people in your firm (especially if you're a sole practitioner without others in the firm). Professionals in a host of industries often team up on marketing or business development. This could include lawyers pairing with other lawyers in non-competitive practices, accountants, bankers, engineers, or real estate brokers, to name a few. Here are some ideas of ways to partner successfully with other professionals.

- Co-host an event, such as a client seminar or party.

- Form a networking group with regular get-togethers to introduce each other to invited guests.

- Form a marketing lunch group at which you meet regularly to discuss successful marketing and business development activities.

- Partner on initiatives to entice and/or welcome new people or entities to your community. This could include things such as economic development seminars or the development of a company or individual welcome packet.

*Consultants*—There is an entire industry filled with legal marketing consultants; professionals who have worked with scores of lawyers just like you and who can help you take a shortcut on the path to success. Consultants can be identified through a variety of methods including word of mouth and recommendations, through your local or state bar association (as well as the ABA), via an online search, or through the Legal Marketing Association (www.legalmarketing.org). There are many ways consultants can help such as serving as your coach (which is a great way to hold you accountable and keep you from spinning your wheels on unproductive activities). Consultants can also help you develop an effective marketing plan and assist in conducting the research to support that marketing plan. Another way that outside consultants can help you is to interview your clients and give you an objective understanding of the opportunities, threats and perceptions from the client's point of view, as well as help you understand the client's immediate and future needs. Keys to success when working with consultants include:

- Spell out the details of the engagement on the front end, including the specific scope of work, expected fees and format of payment (e.g., hourly fees, monthly retainer, etc.).

- Get references up front and check these references to be sure the consultant has the requisite specific expertise for the assignment.

- Read what the consultant has written or find a chance to hear him or her give a speech. This is a good way to "kick the tires" before making a commitment and ensure a good fit.

*Legal marketing support staff*—If your firm is fortunate or big enough to have legal marketing support staff they can also be contributors to your business development and marketing success. For example, they can put together marketing materials for you and customize these materials when you go out to meet with prospective clients. They can also help to develop and track your marketing plan. Legal marketing support staff might conduct market research for you, and organize client or referral source events for you.

*Non-lawyer personnel in your office*—Other non-lawyer personnel in your office, besides legal marketing support staff, can also be a big help in your business development and marketing efforts. For example, the billing or accounting staff can analyze data for you for fee proposals. This is particularly helpful when proposing alternative pricing structures, which are becoming much more common in today's marketplace. Administrators of your firm can help organize events and meetings, and might even be able to introduce you to referral sources or other trade associations or network contacts. Clerical staff can take on some of the back-end work needed before you go out on a marketing-related meeting or event by producing materials or putting together prospective client fact sheets, tasks which are not necessarily productive uses of your time.

## [17.3] IV. OTHER RESOURCES TO LEVERAGE

*Groups and Associations*—Participating in relevant groups or associations, such as bar associations or trade and industry groups, can provide many benefits to your marketing efforts, such as:

- Access to decision-makers seeking legal services.

- Identification of topics and issues of concern to your target clients, which you can then speak or write about.

- Promotion of your personal brand by associating you with a particular industry or area of expertise.

- Networking opportunities with prospective clients or referral sources.

- Writing, speaking and/or leadership opportunities.

*Online Resources*—Anyone with a computer can also access a vast array of online resources that can inform and support your marketing and business development activities. Here are a few examples of the information and/or assistance you can get online: market research, trend spotting, and an understanding of what your competitors are up to. You can get ideas about marketing activities that worked well for others that you might wish to try, you can have access to free or paid training, you can get ideas or graphics for marketing materials and events, you can blog or participate in group discussions (for example, on LinkedIn) and access a whole host of other resources that are available online.

## [17.4]  V.  MATCH MARKETING WITH CAREER DEVELOPMENT

Now that you know how to identify and overcome the common obstacles and impediments to marketing success, and you have a better understanding of the resources that you can leverage in your own efforts, it's time to talk about matching your marketing efforts with your career development. Marketing and business development are always more effective when a lawyer understands what might work best at his or her given stage of career and professional development. For example, a first-year associate should not go into a prospective client pitch alone (or maybe not at all). You'll get better and more results by focusing on tasks and activities that are appropriate for your stage of development. There was a time when young lawyers were told they should not focus on marketing at all for the first three to five years of their career, but rather they should spend the time focusing on honing their skills as a lawyer. Nowadays, that will leave a lawyer woefully unprepared for the future. To be successful lawyers must think about marketing and business development from day one of their career. In fact, an increasing number of law schools are adding practical "business of law" classes to their traditional curricula, to better prepare lawyers for the real world.

The chart below outlines common marketing activities and considerations for each stage of a lawyer's career. This allows young lawyers to start building their network and their expertise, which will serve them well when they are ready to be a participant in bringing in new business to the firm.

## Table 1: Marketing Activities for Each Stage of a Lawyer's Career

| Years in Practice | Suggested Skills and Sample Activities |
|---|---|
| 1 to 2 | *Internal Marketing*<br>• Develop relationships with other lawyers in the firm.<br>• Build trust by being dependable and producing quality work.<br>• Ask for assignments.<br>• Begin reading and learning about practice area specialties, legal marketing and business development, and client industries.<br>• Start and maintain a list of all the cases or transactions you work on. |
| | *External Marketing*<br>• Add contacts from law school, fraternities or sororities, family connections and past jobs to contact databases and mailing lists.<br>• Volunteer to attend events with networking opportunities such as client events, charity events, alumni events, etc. Ask more senior lawyers to introduce you to clients and contacts.<br>• Join a bar association and get involved in appropriate sections.<br>• Get involved in the community through committees or volunteer opportunities. People you work with in these endeavors should be added to your mailing list. |

## Table 1: Marketing Activities for Each Stage of a Lawyer's Career

| Years in Practice | Suggested Skills and Sample Activities |
|---|---|
| 3, 4 and 5 | *Communications*<br>• Write, co-write or provide research for articles for publication.<br><br>• Make sure your professional bio or website listing includes as much information as possible and is updated as you have new accomplishments.<br><br>• Seek speaking opportunities connected to your activities.<br><br>*Internal Marketing*<br>• Develop a marketing plan that includes individual and collaborative activities.<br><br>• Help develop marketing strategies for practice groups or industry penetration.<br><br>• Seek a marketing coach or mentor. |
|  | *External Marketing*<br>• Entertain clients, prospects or referral sources at least once a month. Focus mostly on people in companies or industries that match your developing expertise.<br><br>• Continue to add contacts to mailing lists or databases.<br><br>• Participate in responding to requests for a proposal and/or client pitches.<br><br>• Develop relationships with people at a similar level of career development in client organizations. Eventually they'll be decision-makers. |

## Table 1: Marketing Activities for Each Stage of a Lawyer's Career

| Years in Practice | Suggested Skills and Sample Activities |
|---|---|
| | *Communications* <br> • Write articles or blog posts on topics of interest to professionals in specific industries. <br><br> • Learn about and leverage social media. <br><br> • Write and speak on practical topics as often as possible. |
| 6 and beyond | *Internal Marketing* <br> • Set annual business development goals, both qualitative (e.g., take a leadership role in a relevant trade association) and quantitative (e.g., generate $X in new business from new clients). <br><br> • Mentor younger lawyers about their marketing and business development. <br><br> • Bring in new business that you can assign to others in the firm. |
| | *External Marketing* <br> • Entertain clients, prospects or referral sources at least twice per month. <br><br> • Introduce clients to other lawyers in the firm for cross-selling or other professionals for cross referrals. <br><br> • Routinely assess client satisfaction and future needs. <br><br> • Conduct market research to identify prospective clients; then seek introductions to pitch services. Serve in leadership positions in groups and organizations. Be the "relationship lawyer" for clients. |

### Table 1: Marketing Activities for Each Stage of a Lawyer's Career

| Years in Practice | Suggested Skills and Sample Activities |
|---|---|
| | *Communications* <br>• Hone your speaking and writing skills by speaking and writing regularly. <br>• Routinely update your personal marketing collateral materials. <br>• Leverage technology for marketing, such as blogs, social networks, etc. |

## [17.5] VI. FACTORS CRITICAL FOR MARKETING AND BUSINESS DEVELOPMENT SUCCESS

If you study enough successful rainmakers you'll discover a fairly common set of factors that contribute to their success, despite the fact that each rainmaker may appear to have followed a unique path to success. That's because the tactics—and even strategies—differ, but the underlying *critical success factors* are somewhat standard. The following, while not exhaustive, does include many of the ingredients for marketing and business development success.

### [17.6] A. Focus

Focus on activities that provide an acceptable ROI (return on investment). For example, you could spend the bulk of your marketing time writing scholarly articles, but the ROI on that endeavor is bound to be less than if you spent the same amount of time writing more articles for trade association journals or industry publications. It would be even better if the articles contain practical advice and suggestions for prospective clients. A focused approach is powerful because it allows for

- more precise targeting of prospects;
- better accountability and rewards; and
- easier setting of goals and objectives.

## [17.7] B. Interest

Do what you like to do and what comes naturally. If you do not enjoy the marketing activities that you've chosen, you will have less of a chance of being successful. That doesn't mean that you shouldn't stretch yourself and learn new things, but you should try to match your natural likes, dislikes, and inclinations with your activities. For example, if you are someone who fears public speaking, you might want to try to overcome that fear. But if that's not possible then focus on other activities that won't put you so far out of your comfort zone.

## [17.8] C. Stretch and Learn

At the same time, learn something new and challenge yourself regularly. As mentioned above, it's sometimes good to set a stretch goal that provides professional growth and development opportunities.

## [17.9] D. Planning and Organization

Be systematic and organized in your marketing and business development. If you always take an ad hoc approach, you'll be less likely to achieve the success that you wish. It helps to have a plan and then work your plan. This not only combats the time crunch, as described above, but also gives you an opportunity to think through what you really want to do, where your real opportunities lie, and where the client needs match your expertise and experience. Don't act without planning or you'll waste your time. Planning also allows you to evaluate and weigh critical inputs into your marketing activities such as budgets, staffing and other resources needed.

## [17.10] E. Relationships

Focusing on relationships, rather than specific cases, matters or projects, also enhances your likelihood of success. Developing a long-term relationship with a client means that you will get a portfolio of work across the lifetime of that relationship. If you're only focused on a specific matter or case, you may get that work, but your mindset and attitude will be short-term and likely so will your relationship with the client. This plays out in many ways, such as how you price work, share risk and consider the client's business objectives along with the legal considerations. Likewise you should also develop ongoing relationships with other people in your firm and with referral sources.

## [17.11] F. Loyalty

Do what's needed to achieve client loyalty, and this will undoubtedly lead to greater marketing and business development success. It's a chain of action—quality work and service lead to client satisfaction. Client satisfaction leads to client loyalty. Client loyalty then has a significant impact on your future success because a loyal client will be happy to give a referral for you, will extend the work assigned to you, and will help spread your reputation through word-of-mouth. It's critical to focus on activities that build client loyalty such as excellent service, case or project management, trustworthiness, and serving as a trusted advisor with the client's best interests always foremost.

## [17.12] G. Success Breeds Success

It's important that you build off of your own successes by telling your story and extending your brand. It will serve no good purpose, in terms of your marketing and business development, if you're overly modest about your expertise and accomplishments. There are easy ways to share your successes—update your biography and your personal collateral materials often, including examples of recent successes. Look for opportunities to put yourself in a good light, such as being a spokesperson or resource for the media, consistently speaking or writing, pitching to prospective clients, and updating your partners or referral sources about your developing expertise. Likewise, you should exude confidence. People want to work with successful people, and you need to communicate that you are just such a successful person.

## [17.13] H. Expertise

Become a subject matter expert. While you may practice in a wide variety of industries or practice areas, it's always good to develop a specific expertise and be the "go to" person in a particular subject or industry. That doesn't mean that you can never practice in other areas, it just means that when someone has a specific question or need in your area you're going to be the first phone call or email. This gives you something tangible to sell and makes you more credible with clients—clients are often skeptical when a lawyer claims to be an expert in many things.

## [17.14] I. Generosity

Be generous and you will reap rewards. For example, share what you've learned with others, take younger lawyers under your wing, offer to introduce lawyers in your firm or other professionals to clients and contacts when that introduction would be mutually beneficial, and share knowledge and information. By sharing you will be seen as a generous person with whom others want to do business—just be mindful of client and firm confidentiality concerns.

### [17.15] J. Succession Planning

Think about the succession or transition of your clients before the need arises. This is important whether you're retiring, reducing your practice, need to focus on other clients, or have some other reason for transitioning a key client relationship to someone else. It will not benefit you or your client to be the only one with the knowledge and history of the client's legal issues. If something were to happen to you—whether planned or unplanned—it would be costly for your client to have to start from scratch with another lawyer.

## [17.16] VII. WRAP-UP

There are many ingredients to successful marketing and business development, as you've seen throughout this book. While many lawyers may just dive right in and respond to opportunities if and when they arise, the most successful rainmakers cause these opportunities to occur by planning and acting in a thoughtful, strategic manner and then optimizing limited resources in the pursuit of success. We hope each lawyer reading this book will keep pushing forward, armed with the strategies and tactics described herein. Don't give up. As Ross Perot once said, "Most people give up just when they're about to achieve success. They quit on the one yard line. They give up at the last minute of the game one foot from a winning touchdown."

CONTRIBUTOR BIOGRAPHIES

# EDITOR
## CAROL SCHIRO GREENWALD, PH.D.

Carol Schiro Greenwald helps professionals grow strategically and successfully by showing them how to structure their approach and practice around their best clients. Her methodology is captured in her book *Build Your Practice the Logical Way—Maximize Your Client Relationships* (American Bar Association, First Chair Press, 2012), which provides a guide to growing a practice by fully understanding key clients in their own world in order to be a proactive resource for them. She also coaches and trains individual attorneys in the personal skills needed for excellence in client service and business development.

Ms. Greenwald has worked in-house directing marketing, business development, marketing research, marketing communications and training programs for a variety of well-known professional services firms including Whitman Breed Abbott & Morgan LLP (now Winston & Strawn); Haight, Gardner, Poor & Havens (now Holland & Knight); Richard A. Eisner & Company, LLP (now EisnerAmper); KPMG Peat Marwick; BDO Seidman; and Grant Thornton. She was also a consultant with the MarketForce division of Hildebrandt International before starting her own consultancy in 2000.

Ms. Greenwald is currently a Co-Chair of the Law Practice Management Committee, Westchester County Bar Association; a member of the NYSBA Law Practice Management Committee; and an ABA active member on the Publications Board, Membership Committee and Women Rainmakers Board of the law practice division. She is Past-President of the Legal Marketing Association, Metropolitan New York Chapter. Ms. Greenwald is also a Fellow, College of Law Practice Management, Ann Arbor, MI.

Ms. Greenwald graduated *cum laude* from Smith College, Northampton, MA, and received an M.A. in international relations from Hunter College, CUNY, and a Ph.D. in comparative constitutional and legal systems from The Graduate Center, CUNY. She did post-doctoral research on the federal court system as an Eli Lilly Fellow at the Bunting Institute of Radcliffe College.

# CONTRIBUTORS

### WENDY L. BERNERO

Wendy Bernero has more than 20 years of experience serving in senior-level management roles for major law firms, including Proskauer Rose, Fried Frank, Paul Weiss, and Akin Gump. Her consulting experience includes several years as a partner in Hildebrandt International, where she assisted firms with a broad range of strategic planning, practice management and development, client team development, research, and branding projects. Beyond the legal sector, her experience includes serving as head of product development, marketing and public affairs for Washington Bancorporation and as press and legislative aide to a U.S. Congressman.

Ms. Bernero is a regular speaker at legal industry conferences and is one of the founders of the New Partner Forum, an annual conference designed to serve the professional and career development needs of newly promoted partners. She also is a regular presenter at practice management conferences and roundtable programs, and was a panelist at PLI's 2014 Project Management for Lawyers program, the leading conference on legal project management. In recognition of her contributions to the legal profession, she was named 2013 *Thought Leader of the Year* by the New York Metropolitan Area Chapter of the Legal Marketing Association (LMA). In 2012, she was inducted into the international LMA Hall of Fame.

### MICHAEL DOWNEY, ESQ.

Michael Downey is a legal ethics lawyer and litigation partner at Armstrong Teasdale LLP in St. Louis. Outside general counsel to numerous law firms on legal ethics and risk management issues, Mr. Downey defends lawyer discipline cases, prepares legal ethics opinion letters, and has provided expert testimony in Missouri, Kansas, and the District of Columbia.

Mr. Downey is the author of *Introduction to Law Firm Practice* (2010), and his ethics columns regularly appear in the *National Law Journal, Litigation, Law Practice,* and *St. Louis Lawyer.* He has taught at Washington University School of Law for more than a decade, presented on legal ethics 350 times, and been quoted in the *New York Times, National Law Journal, WSJ Law Blog,* and *ABA Journal.*

Mr. Downey graduated first in his class from Washington University School of Law in 1998, and then clerked for the Hon. Pasco M. Bowman,

Chief Judge of the U.S. Court of Appeals for the Eighth Circuit, before entering private practice.

## DONNA DRUMM, ESQ.

Donna Drumm is an attorney licensed to practice in New York. Her passion for law practice management began by searching for legal courses while attending Pace Law School that blended her skills as a businesswoman on Wall Street, working as a Federal Funds trader at J. Henry Schroder Bank & Trust, and her business degree from Marymount College with the practice of law. She became a student and research assistant for Prof. Gary Munneke and assisted with the research for his book, *Law Practice Management: Materials and Cases* (2d Edition). Prof. Munneke invited her to become a member of the New York State Bar Association's Law Practice Management Committee upon graduating from Pace Law School and she continues to be a member. As an associate at the law firm of Boies, Schiller & Flexner, she assisted top managers during its seminal years growing from four offices to eleven. Her affiliation with bar associations became professional when she joined the staff of the Westchester County Bar Association as the CLE & Publications Director and then Executive Director until 2014. Ms. Drumm is admitted to practice in New York State and the United States Supreme Court.

## SUSAN SALTONSTALL DUNCAN

Susan Saltonstall Duncan is the founder and president of RainMaking Oasis, LLC, a business development and management consulting firm that helps lawyers and law firms create, execute, and evaluate effective strategic and business development initiatives. She has been working with law firms since 1980, providing consulting services for over 27 of those years.

Ms. Duncan helps law firms and individual lawyers develop strategic plans, client service and value programs, key client team plans and practice group and industry group plans. She conducts service feedback and needs-assessment interviews with law firm clients and provides business development coaching and training to partners, counsel, senior associates, and practice group and firm leaders.

In 2011 and 2012, Ms. Duncan served as Chief Strategy and Development Officer of Squire Sanders, a global law firm with 36 offices in 17 countries. She became one of the first in-house law firm marketing directors in the country in 1984 and is a founding member of the Legal Marketing Association.

Ms. Duncan is a Fellow in the College of Law Practice Management and in the Legal Marketing Association's Hall of Fame. Her articles have been published in numerous national publications, and for eight years she was the author of "Rainmaking" and "Fresh Out," two regular columns for the ABA's *Law Practice* magazine. Her blog, InFocus: Insights on Legal Practice Strategies and Innovations, covers timely topics in the legal profession. She speaks frequently for national and regional organizations throughout the country.

### CHRISTINE FILIP, ESQ.

Christine Filip is an attorney and the president of Business Development Partners in New Jersey. Ms. Filip is an expert level business developer and corporate strategist for professional services firms and B2B companies, as well as not-for-profit organizations. She has been a media commentator and speaker for professional and business associations for over 25 years on all facets of business development, public relations, pricing, media relationships, social media and negotiations. Her firm's work devotes significant attention to the multi-stakeholder drivers of profitability, including client loyalty and employee engagement, executive leadership and corporate citizenship. Ms. Filip is the author of over 100 articles on all aspects of business development, as well as the book, *Effective Marketing for Lawyers*, 2d ed. (2006), published by the New York State Bar Association. She is the creator of *Rainmaker College*, a three-session seminar series at the New Jersey State Bar Association.

Ms. Filip was the president of The Success Group in New York City for 21 years. In 2009 she became the Director of Marketing at Greenbaum, Rowe, Smith & Davis LLP; from 2012 to February 2014 she was the Director of Business Development at Saiber LLC. She reopened her consulting practice in February 2014.

Ms. Filip has been interviewed in all media venues on competitive strategy, pricing, negotiation skills, leadership and building relationships with the media. In 2000 she was awarded the SBA Service Award by SCORE NYC for developing and delivering marketing seminars for small business owners in all five boroughs. She has a J.D. from Suffolk University Law School, an M.Ed. from Eastern New Mexico University, and a B.A., *magna cum laude*, from the University of Rhode Island.

# CONTRIBUTOR BIOGRAPHIES

## TERRI PEPPER GAVULIC

Terri Pepper Gavulic is Director of Legal Support at Fisher & Phillips LLP, a national labor and employment law firm. Her responsibilities range from oversight of the firm's 30 offices and office managers, to strategic initiatives such as legal project management and process improvement, client and customer service, firm growth issues, training and coaching, and special projects for the firm's Management Committee, as well as operational programs such as leasing and insurance. Ms. Gavulic spent more than two decades working with law firms and professional services organizations in areas such as client relationship development and management, marketing, business development, customer service and strategy. She was previously a Vice President and CMO of the former Hildebrandt International, and led that company's client assessment team.

Ms. Gavulic is a sought-after author and speaker on subjects relating to all aspects of the business side of law firms. Prior to her law firm tenure, she worked on Wall Street as a manager of IPOs; in the non-profit sector, serving as Director of Marketing and Director of Development for the National Kidney Foundation of Georgia; as Director of Marketing for a national real estate franchise organization; and in a public relations agency. She received her MBA from the Warrington College of Business of the University of Florida in April 2009 and her B.S. in Journalism and Communications from the University of Florida in 1979.

## MARCIA GOLDEN

Marcia Golden is the Managing Partner of DJD/Golden, a full-service marketing and communications firm offering clients the opportunity to select from an à la carte menu of marketing services or to fully integrate public relations, marketing, website renovation and SEO, advertising, social media, branding, collateral design and direct mail outreach cost-efficiently. An experienced marketing, advertising and public relations professional, Ms. Golden also teaches classes in public relations, advertising, social media and business development to individual law firms, accounting firms and other professional service firms, privately and publicly held companies, non-profits, and to such professional organizations as the AICAP/AAM and Legal Marketing Association communities. A former journalist and National Public Radio newscaster, she produced a syndicated series on the environment, which led to her nomination to serve on the President's Commission on the Environment. A native of Michigan, Ms. Golden is a graduate of Michigan State University.

## ALAN LEVINE

Alan Levine has spent his 30-year career marketing professional services. He has extensive experience in the full range of marketing and communications, including marketing planning and implementation, advertising and collateral material, market research, community service, marketing events, public and media relations, and customer research. He has spent most of his career in positions of marketing leadership in law, accounting and consulting firms.

Mr. Levine has served as Director of Marketing for four prominent New York/New Jersey law firms—Weil, Gotshal & Manges LLP; Fried, Frank, Harris, Shriver & Jacobson; Pitney, Hardin, Kipp & Szuch LLP; and Cole Schotz. Prior to that, he was a marketing consultant with Hildebrandt, which had been the world's leading and largest consulting firm to the legal industry, and he was responsible for Hildebrandt's own marketing efforts.

## LAURA MEHERG

Laura Meherg is a founder and partner with the Wicker Park Group, a consulting practice that focuses exclusively on integrated client feedback programs and related client-facing growth programs. She has conducted thousands of client interviews over the past 15 years. Ms. Meherg was Director of Client Services and Marketing at Burr & Forman from 1998 to 2005. At the firm, her responsibilities covered every aspect of marketing and training. After leaving, she founded Meherg Consulting, which later became part of the Wicker Park Group. She is past-president of the Southeastern Chapter of the Legal Marketing Association and has served multiple terms on the board of directors of the Legal Marketing Association as Secretary and Member at Large.

## NANCY MYRLAND

Nancy Myrland is a Legal Marketing, Content and Social Media Consultant, Strategist, and Trainer to lawyers, law firms, and legal marketers.

Ms. Myrland has more than 20 years' experience in partnering with her clients to help them grow by strengthening the relationships that exist between firms, attorneys and clients. After serving as the Director of Marketing at Baker & Daniels (now Faegre Baker Daniels), Ms. Myrland started Myrland Marketing & Social Media in 2002.

After serving on the Legal Marketing Association Midwest Board of Directors and various committees, Ms. Myrland served on the 2013 and 2014 LMA International Board of Directors. She is also a Co-Chair of the LMA Social Media SIG, and a member of the LMA Technology Committee. In her community, she has spent many years volunteering in the business and social service sectors.

Starting in 2006, Ms. Myrland immersed herself in the integration of social media into existing marketing practices, and became a Certified Social Media Consultant in 2009. She is the publisher of the Myrland Marketing Minute blog, where she frequently writes about social media, business development, strategic marketing planning, and other marketing topics. She is also the founder of LinkedIn Coach For Lawyers, and is launching a legal marketing podcast to help lawyers make sense out of marketing and social media.

## DAVID J. ROSENBAUM

David Rosenbaum is CEO, president and chief technologist at Real-Time Computer Services, Inc. (RCS). He is a 35-plus-year veteran of the information technology field and a third-generation entrepreneur.

Mr. Rosenbaum founded RCS in 1982 with the goal of bringing Fortune 500-level technical services to small and mid-sized firms, combined with an absolute commitment to the principles of professionalism, ethics and trust.

Mr. Rosenbaum has consulted to a large variety of organizations on business issues related to automation. He has provided tactical and strategic planning in the legal, banking, accounting, logistics, public relations, brokerage, travel, real estate, human resources, oil and gas exploration, and pharmaceutical industries, for both privately held and publicly traded companies. He has automated the operations of many mid-sized businesses and professional practices, and has been retained by investment bankers to perform technical reviews and due diligence analyses preceding mergers and acquisitions. Mr. Rosenbaum has particular expertise in designing and implementing technology solutions for domestic and international companies with multiple operating offices or locations.

Prior to forming RCS, Mr. Rosenbaum worked on Wall Street managing and building front- and back-office cutting-edge technology systems for a variety of prestigious clients including Merrill Lynch, Chase Manhattan Bank and First Wall Street Corporation.

Mr. Rosenbaum holds an M.B.A. in Management Theory and Organizational Behavior from New York University's Stern School of Business, and a B.A. in Mathematics and Physics from Adelphi University, Garden City, N.Y. He is President of the Westchester Business Network, on the Steering Committee of the New York Business Forum, Honorary Chair of the Westchester County Bar Association Technology Committee, a member of the Mercy College Legal Studies Advisory Board, and President of the Ardsley Estates Civic Association.

### JOHN RUMELY

John Rumely is an experienced legal marketing professional with over a dozen years' experience in legal business development. He currently consults and is located in New York City. His experience includes serving as Senior Manager, Business Development for Nixon Peabody LLP, where he focused on the business development needs of several practice areas, and the marketing needs of two of the firm's offices. Other experience includes serving as Director of Marketing for Hawkins Delafield & Wood, where he oversaw a ground-up marketing and branding initiative. These two roles included serving as an in-house coach, working with a number of attorneys at various stages of their careers. Prior to his work in legal marketing, Mr. Rumely had over 20 years' experience in the municipal finance industry. He is a graduate of Boston College and Harvard University's Kennedy School of Government.

### NANCY B. SCHESS

Nancy Schess represents businesses, both locally and nationally, in diverse industries including banking/finance, hospitality, entertainment, building services, manufacturing, and transportation. She practices in all facets of labor and employment law, including equal employment compliance and litigation, wage and hour, FMLA and employee leaves, and plant closing compliance. Ms. Schess also practices occupational safety and health law.

Working closely with clients, Ms. Schess develops and implements preventive personnel policies and strategies that foster litigation-free workplaces. She also provides advice and counsel to help her clients successfully manage their personnel assets. Her experience includes developing and presenting customized training programs on topics including "Prevention of Workplace Harassment," "How to Conduct a Defensible Internal Investigation," "Tips on Effective Performance Management," and other compliance issues.

Ms. Schess is the co-founder of Gotham City Networking, Inc., an organization based in New York City that offers networking opportunities across multiple industries. She has appeared on television and radio and as a frequent speaker for professional associations and other groups.

### DEE A. SCHIAVELLI

Dee Schiavelli is a national business development consultant, professional speaker, and LinkedIn expert. She advises and coaches clients on effective ways to develop new business and helps them use social networking to build their client and referral networks. She has successfully helped lawyers bring in clients and build loyalty.

Ms. Schiavelli has more than 25 years' experience working with law firms and served as marketing director at several top-tier firms in New York before starting Results Marketing for Lawyers. Earlier in her career, she was a senior manager of marketing at two global accounting firms. Ms. Schiavelli has worked extensively with firm leadership, practice areas and individuals in large and small firms. Her experience has enabled her to understand law firms and how to help lawyers bring in new business.

Ms. Schiavelli is a certified Social Media Strategist who works with firms and individuals to maximize their social media presence to build their business. She focuses on LinkedIn and coaches lawyers on how to maximize their presence ensuring a client-focused profile that relates to their clients' needs. She also helps lawyers expand their network and build business-generating relationships.

Ms. Schiavelli earned her Bachelor of Science, Management and Communications, *cum laude*, from Adelphi University, Garden City, NY; she is also a Certified Professional Trainer.

### STEVEN SKYLES-MULLIGAN

Steven Skyles-Mulligan is a New York City-based branding, communications and marketing consultant with over 20 years of experience. He is currently Executive Director of Evoke Strategies Ltd., a firm which provides outsourced marketing department and virtual creative agency services to professional firms. Mr. Skyles-Mulligan regularly works with attorneys, accountants and financial advisors to help them create stronger brands, craft more compelling messages, and develop steadier approaches to effective marketing. His legal clients have included exceptional boutique firms that practice in the areas of bankruptcy, corporate, elder law, health care, intellectual property, real estate, and trusts and estates. He has also worked with clients in consulting, financial services, health care, higher education and technology. Prior to founding Evoke Strategies, Mr. Skyles-Mulligan was with the strategy group of Plural, Inc. (now part of Dell Professional Services).

Mr. Skyles-Mulligan is a regular speaker on practical branding and marketing and also co-presents at CLE programs for various bar associations and providers. He is co-author, with Carol Schiro Greenwald, of *Build Your Practice the Logical Way* (ABA/First Chair Press, 2012). He holds a B.A. in the history of art from Indiana University and did graduate work at New York University's Institute of Fine Arts.